*BRASS-KNUCKLE CRUSADE*

BOOKS BY CARLETON BEALS

HOUSE IN MEXICO
TASTE OF GLORY
ADVENTURE OF THE WESTERN SEA
MEXICAN MAZE
DAWN OVER THE AMAZON
PORFIRIO DIAZ: Dictator of Mexico
THE COMING STRUGGLE FOR LATIN AMERICA
MEXICO: An Interpretation
STEPHEN F. AUSTIN: Father of Texas
CHILE: The Long Land
LANDS OF THE DAWNING MORROW
RIO GRANDE TO CAPE HORN
PANAMERICA: A Program for the Western Hemisphere
AMERICA SOUTH
FIRE ON THE ANDES
THE CRIME OF CUBA
BANANA GOLD
THE STONES AWAKE
BLACK RIVER
DESTROYING VICTOR
OUR YANKEE HERITAGE: (3 Vols.)
  New England Contributions to American Civilization
  The Making of Bristol
  The Making of New Haven
THE STORY OF HUEY LONG
AMERICAN EARTH: The Biography of a Nation
BRIMSTONE AND CHILI
THE GREAT CIRCLE
GLASS HOUSES
ROME OR DEATH: The Story of Fascism

*AMERICAN PROCESSION SERIES*
*Already Published:*

NEW GREEN WORLD
JOHN BARTRAM AND THE EARLY NATURALISTS
By Josephine Herbst

THE BUFFALO HUNTERS
THE STORY OF THE HIDE MEN
By Mari Sandoz

TINKERS AND GENIUS
THE STORY OF THE YANKEE INVENTORS
By Edmund Fuller

WILDERNESS FOR SALE
THE STORY OF THE FIRST WESTERN LAND RUSH
By Walter Havighurst

THE WILD JACKASSES
THE AMERICAN FARMER IN REVOLT
By Dale Kramer

THE CATTLEMEN
By Mari Sandoz

ESCAPE TO UTOPIA
By Everett Webber

BRASS-KNUCKLE CRUSADE
By Carleton Beals

*In Preparation:*

LOUISIANA PURCHASE
By Henry G. Alsberg

★

★

★

*AMERICAN PROCESSION SERIES*

★ HENRY G. ALSBERG

GENERAL EDITOR

★

★

★

★

# *BRASS-KNUCKLE CRUSADE*

## The Great Know-Nothing Conspiracy: 1820-1860

*By CARLETON BEALS*

*HASTINGS HOUSE PUBLISHERS*

*NEW YORK 22*

Published simultaneously in Canada
by S. J. Reginald Saunders, Publishers, Toronto 2B

Library of Congress Catalog Card Number: 60-9120

*Printed in the United States of America*

# *CONTENTS*

# *ILLUSTRATIONS*

*BRASS-KNUCKLE CRUSADE*

## CHAPTER I

# THE TRUE AMERICAN

BIG BILL POOLE, "Bill the Butcher," lay dying on New York's Christopher Street, a bullet through his heart and a bullet through his guts, but his hulk of a carcass, two hundred pounds plus, and his mad fightingness wouldn't let him die. A week, two weeks went by. At his bedside heavyweight champ Tom Hyer and other ham-fisted cronies, downing whisky and blubbering, relayed news of Bill's condition to the crowd of anxious toughs outside in the raw March weather of 1855.

For years the Butcher had been the mightiest slugger of the Bowery and Atlantic Guard thugs; then he had formed his own West Side gang. No one among the rival Five Point bruisers from Paradise Square—the Dead Rabbits or other lawless outfits—could match him. He could drive a butcher knife through an inch-thick pine plank from twenty feet and he was quick on the draw. In close-up fights, he gouged out eyes and bit off noses and ears, and the slash of his hobnailed boots into the groin was death agony. No more puissant bully ever came out of lower New York City's limbo of sewer slums, beer gardens, saloons, rat-and-dog arenas, music halls, can-can shows, whorehouses, sailor crimp joints, and gambling dives.

Above all, Butcher Bill was "a true-blooded American." In the fight waged against Tammany by the Native Americans, the spread-eagle patriots, he was the ramrod for terrorizing opponents and burning ballot boxes. The fearsome Know-Nothing dark-lantern conspiracy, which struck with brass knuckles in the name of loud patriotism, had taken over the city, had won electoral victories in a dozen states, and was reaching out to rule the nation.

In the bedrock battleground of the loafer and the bully, the pimps and crimps, the vicious and the criminal, where the will of democracy was largely decided, Tammany —the Sons of Saint Tamina—which, ever since it was started by hatchet-man Aaron Burr, had first made secret gangsterism into a political system, was sore beset. The old parties—Whig and Democratic—were disintegrating, splitting up into petty factions. In Hartford, Connecticut, twenty-three splinter groups vied for public office. In San Francisco, California, the weird list of contending tickets was longer than an ape's arm. In New York, at various times, rival tickets were Republicans, American Republicans, Free Soilers, Native Americans, Liberty party, City Reformers (a super-patriotic Know-Nothing false front), Temperance Alliance, Anti-Temperance, Know-Nothings, Know Somethings, Nativists, Anti-Catholics, Carroll Hall pro-Catholics, Adopted Citizens. The Catholic ticket was strong enough one year to chastise Tammany for dragging its feet on the educational issue. The Whigs splintered into Wooly Heads, Silver Grays, Old Liners, and Sewardites. The Silver Grays were headed by former President Millard Fillmore, who this very year of 1855 had become a high-degree member of the Know-Nothing Supreme Order of the Star-Spangled Banner, the secret-oath-taking SSSB. The Democratic party split repeatedly: Equal Righters, Rum Democrats, Free Democrats, Free Germans, Loco Focos, Soft Shells, Hard Shells, Half Shells, Hunkers, and Barn Burners. The Hunkers wanted a hunk of the spoils; the Barn Burners got their name from the Dutch farmer who burned down his barn to kill the rats.

In this grab bag of politics, plunder, and power the Know-Nothings learned to match Tammany blow for blow.

They moved through the chaos with single-purpose ambition along their own ugly riotous path, creating confusion in men's minds, filling the streets with clamor and terror.

As early as the mid-thirties "Native" American parties had appeared sporadically, waving the Stars and Stripes in the faces of seemingly less patriotic Americans and naturalized citizens and raising up mobs to burn Catholic convents, churches and homes, assault nuns, and murder Irishmen, Germans, and Negroes. After a brief period of "glory," each such party had melted back into the murk of its own bigotry. But by the 'fifties, riding a third big crest of ignorant popular emotion, the Natives—the self-important "Anglos," the Puritans—were making a real bid for national power. The American party—the Know Nothings—with their hate campaign, became the magnet for all dazed elements in the political whirlpool; they fed on pathological fears and fanned to white heat all the petty animosities that had bored into the public mind, and now—this year of 1855—various Whig and Democratic leaders were gloomily predicting that in the next national elections the upstart demagogues would take over the White House.

In the large cities, the Know-Nothings had carved their way into the vice and crime wards where elections were mostly controlled, utilizing the brutality for which they so roundly criticized "foreigners." In New York City they stormed into the Tammany citadel, taking over gangs, starting new ones. According to Herbert Asbury in his *The Gangs of New York,* a fourth of the city's adult population was booked on police-station records, and at least thirty thousand men were active members of gangs. Not only men: in crucial battles, which were often beyond police or militia to control and had to be put down by federal troops and artillery, women fought alongside. One notorious female—who carried a tomahawk, knife, and gun, and wore boots cleated with broken glass—was close to being a rival of Bill Poole. Another sheathed her nails in steel and filed her teeth to needle points: "Hell Cat Maggie," they called her.

The hoodlums—to use a word coined later in San Francisco—fought for practice or joyous deviltry, for cock-of-the-walk prestige, for territorial jurisdiction, for water-front control of ballot boxes, but rarely had tangled over race or religion, though "foreigners" predominated in the Tammany Paradise Square outfits, "Americans"—many of whom were also Tammany hirelings—along the Bowery. But the Native Americans were giving gang fights a new "moral" flavor and of late trusted Democratic henchmen had climbed on the flag-waving Know-Nothing calliope.

A few years before Big Bill Poole was shot down, gambler king Captain Isaiah Rynders, a power among Tammany's Five Point gangs, had turned renegade. Renaming his "Empire" gambling joint at 25 Park Avenue the "Americus," he joined the dark-lantern crusade.

Rynders had come with knife and deep-notched pistol from the Mississippi river boats, where he dealt dirty poker, to carve out wealth and power in New York. His great innovation was the bowie knife. Likely he had no special love for the anti-foreign, anti-Catholic Know-Nothing slogans, but merely an eye out for the main chance: the Star-Spangled Banner was flapping gloriously, the Spread Eagle was screaming victoriously; great mobs, drunk with patriotic fervor, were tearing down the palaces they were supposed to venerate. As a skilled vote boss in that murky realm of plug-uglies, idlers, whores, hot-corn girls, rats, and river pilots, he knew that the survival of his kingdom of vice, boodle, and patronage could be preserved only by picking the winning bravos. When the human herd stampedes, don't get in its path; lead it back to the trough.

What was more, the elite who had governed America the colony and America the Republic, "the pure Anglo-Saxons," had joined the hysterical stampede and were abetting Know-Nothing secrecy and blood letting. Not merely the English-derived "yeomanry"—many were Scotch Irish—but the millworkers, brickmakers, hillbillies, and Yankee clam treaders, all the so-called "mechanics"; also the rich traders, bankers, ship owners, the landed gentry, the Hudson River patroons, and New England blue bloods; and, in the

South, such fine gentlemen as plantation owners, pseudo aristocrats, slaveowners, Kentucky colonels, and Campbellite preachers. Above all, Protestant ministers had become a band of neck-swollen, hate-mongering tub thumpers, draping God and the innocent bare-skinned angels in the American flag, which they converted into a symbol of racial and religious supremacy. It was difficult by 1855 to tell whether the leaders of the Republic were making use of the gangsters, or whether gangsterism had become the stock in trade of all levels of American society.

The "pure-blooded" Americans certainly loved American institutions and freedom—they said so loudly at every breath, warning of mortal perils for the Republic and its democracy from the hordes of "mongrel" aliens streaming to our shores. "Freedom" had become as cheap and meaningless a word as it is today. When the "ignorant," "dirty" newcomers promptly demanded more freedom and democracy than America provided, the old-time rulers of the loaves and fishes branded such suggestions as "insolent," "anarchistic," "communistic," "socialistic," and "seditious"—"a defilement of the beautiful American system."

True, some newcomers were paupers, briefly filling hospitals and relief rolls, till they tasted the joys of the American system by working sixteen hours a day: starving Englishmen—deliberately dumped here, for Botany Bay was getting too crowded—victims of the new British factory system; illiterate Irishmen fleeing the potato famine, where bodies were heaped up in piles with no one to bury them, where British landlords and bayonets ruled ruthlessly; Germans escaping from the crop failures, ugly tyranny, and religious persecutions, both Catholic and Protestant. A few were criminals cynically thrust here by Old World kingdoms. The majority, however, were enticed here by labor or land contracts, or by gorgeous booklets and posters, issued by western land corporations, by rail, road, and canal builders, that depicted America as earth's paradise. These immigrants were earnest if mostly poor Christians, seeking work, opportunity, and liberty—blessings that native-born Americans were jealously trying to keep for themselves alone: Why extend these sacred American rights and rewards to "ignorant" newcomers? The "old-timers" advocated exclusion or immigration restrictions, a twenty-one-year period for obtaining citizenship, special voting privileges for themselves.

Yet many immigrants were enlightened refugees from the 'forty-eight revolutions in Europe, fleeing from oppression, men such as Louis Kossuth and Carl Schurz and Thomas Devyr, forever passionate for human rights. They believed in such "Red" doctrines (the word even then was incorrectly applied) as freedom of religion, direct voting, popular suffrage primaries, abolition of property qualifications for voting, the referendum and recall, non-sectarian education, the emancipation of women and of slaves—measures that in time were to become the blood and sinew of American democracy, but then aroused the wrath and fear of Whigs, Know-Nothings, and all simon-pure patriots and preachers.

The newcomers brought new cultural mores, strange foods, strange ways of living: Irish tam o'shanters and scapularies and mulligan stew: German *Gemütlichkeit,* sauerkraut (long before patriots renamed it "Liberty Cabbage"), and beer gardens. Such novelties seemed an affront to cherished American habits and long-faced Puritanism hating all the arts; the invaders disturbed consciousness of kind; the new fur smelled different.

Most distressingly, the newcomers brought their own religious creeds. If new Protestant splinter sects were looked upon with distaste, Roman Catholicism aroused hatred and terror. The Catholics, "under the thumb of intriguing Jesuits," looked solely to an alien authority, to Rome (usually called "bloody Babylon") and not to the noble gilded capitol in Washington. They could never become good Americans. Their church was "anti-democratic" in structure, aim, and methods and, though this was true enough, it scarcely justified the horrendous exaggerations, let alone the burning and killing. Anti-Catholicism, inbred in the bones of the settlers of the New World since *Mayflower* days, now took on the flaming intensity of the sixteenth-century religious wars all through the years 1830 to 1860.

Ironically, though, the Catholics, in the exceptional role here of being a minority group—700,000 out of 11,000,-000—and subjected to persecution, were the ones fighting hardest for universal democratic rights, civil liberties, religious freedom, non-sectarian education, and political participation—not always modestly, or even sincerely, or in approved "American" fashion, whatever that was; when provocations became too great, the menace to churches, property, and lives too alarming, the Catholics also rallied with guns and murderous glint. Mostly, however, the old-timers, fighting for the "true Americanism" they were busily destroying, were the ones who resorted to the traditional tortures, whippings, brandings, arson, and murdering, using them against the Catholics as they had earlier used them against Baptists, Methodists, Shakers, and Quakers—though those long-persecuted sects were now considered part and parcel of the Puritan hierarchy and were now biting off Catholic noses, quite forgetful of their own recent sufferings.

The old-timers were frightened now. Aliens and the Catholic Church were menaces, or imagined to be such, to their long control of politics, religion, and education. The wasps' nest of righteous patriotism had been shaken, and what a buzzing and stinging came therefrom!

To uphold their "race" and "pride of birth," their control over American life and the keys to power, in panic and hate, the native elite resorted to secret conspiracy (excusing it by reason of "Jesuit conspiracy"), drowned out opponents with shouts, fists, and guns more frequently than by reasoned arguments, and unleashed mob violence and burning up and down the land, justifying their evil conduct by the St. Bartholomew's Eve massacre, which had occurred three centuries earlier in a faraway land. Churches and homes were burned, and murder stalked the Republic. With each rise of Nativism, from the 'thirties on, and reaching a bloody peak in the Know-Nothing mid-'fifties, riots swept Boston, New York City, Philadelphia, Baltimore, Providence, Hartford, New Orleans, St. Louis, Cincinnati, Louisville, San Francisco, and villages in Massachusetts, Maine, Vermont, New York, Indiana, Mississippi, Kentucky, Tennessee, Maryland—nearly everywhere. Patriotic mobs raided into Irish and German, Creole and Chilean, Mexican and Negro sectors with whips, clubs, guns, and torches. One New York theater was smashed up three nights running, finally torn to pieces, in spite of the entire police force and many deaths, because the chief actor, a noted Shakespearean, was English, not American.

Not all the violence was provoked by anti-foreign, or anti-Catholic prejudice. It was a time of uprooting, part of the aftermath of lawless frontierism, when the big fist and the ready gun became the symbols of Americanism. A comprehension of that background of released violence is necessary for understanding how the Know-Nothings were able to redirect much of it toward a sustained drive for political power, one that came within a breath of being successful. The times were badly out of joint.

Not that more basic sinister forces that lurk in every society were not involved. Many dark fears prowled the avenues of human blood and the avenues of traffic. The nation was torn by bitter sectionalism, seething with social unrest. The 1837 panic had created much anxiety. No moorings seemed secure, and people appeared ready to use fists and firebrands over every petty issue. And the advocates of violent reform were many and varied.

Rhode Island's Dorr Rebellion (1841–45) was scarcely over. Within the decade the murderous Anti-Rent War (1839–46), the weird battle of tin horns, calico, and big Injun masquerading, which finally freed the serfs in New York State, reached the stage of arson, assassination, and martial law. In Ohio, Illinois, and Missouri, the Mormons were being robbed and murdered, their homes and crops burned. In 1844 the founder, Joseph Smith, and his brother were dragged from a Carthage, Illinois, jail by a mob and killed.

From 1848 to 1854, in California, bands of bullies with Know-Nothing slogans of white supremacy were perpetrating excruciating cruelties on Italians, Chileans, Peruvians, and Mexicans (American citizens), stealing their lands, looting and burning their homes, murdering them, raping their women. Repeatedly San Francisco was half burned down. Such brutal excesses were abetted by United States Army General Persifer F. Smith, a bungling Mexican War officer, who boasted in 1849 that only native Americans were entitled to California's riches, and that he would drive all foreigners out of the gold fields. Mexicans had their prospecting equipment seized or smashed, the fair acres of Mexican "natives" were seized at gun point, and support for this wholesale robbery was a chief Know-Nothing plank.

The Mexican War had despoiled a sister republic of half her territory and released customary postwar hates and disorders. The Nativists hailed that aggression as a righteous crusade against "a debased Catholic country," accused American Catholics of being deserters (a company did desert to the Mexican side), and raised a howl when President James K. Polk appointed Catholic chaplains. Ironically the war added an enormous number of "foreign" Catholic citizens to the Union, few of whom from that day to this have enjoyed the full benefits of American freedom.

All the reform movements were vociferous, tinged with bigotry and ready for violence: feminism, temperance, anti-Masonry, anti-gambling, anti-capital punishment, prison reform, pacifism, labor's rights.

Thus the Know-Nothings were able to profit by the general uprooting and uncertainty. The gathering momentum of industrialization was shaking up whole communities, creating new ambitious classes, blindly grasping for power. The first militant labor organizations appeared. The rapid population shifts: migration to the West, the decline of eastern rural populations, the gold rush, the swarming in of Europeans (by 1855, 300,000 a year), people herding into cities without proper sanitation, water supplies, or housing—all this dislocation, jostling, congestion, paralleled by terrible epidemics that sometimes swept away as much as a fourth of the population, contributed to the disintegration of the old parties, the crumbling of political and moral standards, and led to violent conflicts and bloody riots, some of the worst in American history, which the "Natives" generally started, though blaming them on "foreigners."

In New York City there were no garbage collections or street cleaning between December and April; the water supply came from what was practically an open sewer; the city stank all the time. Hogs ran wild in the streets. Charles Dickens, who visited the city in the 'forties, told about the herds of Broadway swine dodging the fine carriages, and he was horrified by the slums, filth, degeneracy, crime, prison conditions, and violence, and by the venal blackmailing tactics of the press.

New Orleans, romanticized for its honeysuckle, quadroon balls, and lily-pure aristocrats, was one vast whore house, mudhole and cesspool, with human excrement floating in the gutters (there were no sewers) and, in flood time, into cellars. No wonder mental and moral indecencies and brutalities penetrated every cranny. Know-Nothingism was the logical political expression for the city.

In the 'forties New Jersey, which soon embraced Know-Nothingism, branded convicted persons on the cheek and gave them public floggings. In 1844 a young girl, convicted of petty theft, was sentenced to two hundred and ten lashes on her bare back. Nearly everywhere this or similar brutality was a built-in part of the free American system.

In the growing hullabaloo, intelligent, honorable men scarcely knew where to turn. The golden age of Channing (*Remarks on American Literature,* 1830), Emerson (*The American Scholar,* 1837), and Whittier (*Moll Pitcher,* 1832), that had brought some sweetness and light to the land, was declining. There was growing mass hatred of literature, the intellect, reason, and logic. The derisive "egg-head" epithet had not yet been invented, but in the 'fifties gentlemen and scholars, such as Horace Greeley, on occasions had to duck out back doors to escape from mobs. The voice of American intelligence grew weak and weary—and frightened—and the writers who garnered big sales were the hate mongers.

The head of New York's largest publishing house, Harper Brothers, was a militant anti-foreign, anti-Catholic crusader. On May 29, 1850, the Hartford *Courant,* which had long baited Catholics though there were only a few thousand in all Connecticut when it began to do so, declared that worse than becoming "too superstitious," and more to be feared for the welfare of the Republic, were the "Free Thinkers," and worse still, "The Thinkers." It was a delicious Know-Nothing utterance.

Above all, the nation dreaded sectional strife over the apparently insoluble slavery issue, aggravated by demagogues and extremists ready to settle arguments with clubs and knives, paving the way for the Civil War by the creation of a general spirit of injustice, violence, and ignorance.

The abolitionists who, as Emerson put it, worried about hen coops far from those in their own back yards, already had numerous martyrs. Many had had their homes burned. Whole blocks of New York and Boston went up in such conflagrations. Abolitionists were dragged through the streets by ropes; some were killed, as was Elijah J. Lovejoy in 1837 in Alton, Illinois. Boston businessmen, some of whose fortunes had been originally founded by the slave trade, bravely mobbed the Female Anti-Slavery Society, and the speakers, not the mobsters, were jailed.

In 1834, during the "Flying Horses" race riot in Philadelphia, mobs beat and killed Negroes, sacking their homes, destroying more than fifty—an atrocity that was to be repeated in the City of Brotherly Love exactly a decade later, when the Know-Nothings burned homes and churches and murdered Irish and Catholics. Race riots occurred in Columbia, Trenton, Bloomfield, Rochester, Southwick, and Lancaster. In 1838, Philadelphia Hall, newly dedicated to "liberty and the rights of man," was reduced to ashes, and the mobs also burned a Negro orphanage and Negro church. In 1849, two businessmen of Meriden, Connecticut, had their factory burned down for voting for the abolitionist Liberty party.

Negroes could not attend school in Ohio, Connecticut, and some other northern states, and suffered from official and unofficial discrimination. Negro schools were burned down. In many places colored people could not testify in court and were arrested if they weren't paupers and acted like gentlemen. The 1850 federal Fugitive Slave Law denied them all recourse to the courts, whether they were free or slave, if seized by southern slave raiders. In most of New England, from 1840 on, churches boarded up their Jim Crow sections or sawed out the floors.

The American Bible Society refused to send Bibles to slaves. In Charleston, South Carolina, as in other southern communities, a mob seized the mail and destroyed it on the rumor it contained abolitionist literature. The Postmaster General supinely said that local people had a right to destroy any mail that violated their sentiments. Hurried legislation in some southern states imposed the death penalty for preaching to Negroes or teaching them to read and write. A wave of lynching arose, North and South, and hundreds of Negroes were killed. These anti-Negro mobsters became some of the most ardent Know-Nothing backers.

By 1855, "bleeding Kansas" had been plunged into Civil War, farms were burned, newspapers destroyed, whole populations massacred, all of it abetted by the New England Bible societies sending out Sharps rifles and ammunition, and by southern Ku Klux Klan types of organizations doing the same.

Know-Nothingism augmented the violence in every direction. It attracted both the mobsters and those fearing sectional violence, who preferred to hate the Irish and the Catholics instead of slaveowners. The Know-Nothings tried to sidestep the whole slavery issue. Southerners saw Know-Nothingism as a means of limiting the voting power of the North and sidetracking anti-slavery agitation.

Sectionalism was not confined to North versus South. The East feared the reckless new West, with its stark individualism, which erupted with terrifying bizarre ideas, such as cheap money, and smashed what it did not like, which drained away the best "mechanics" whose places had to be filled by "foreigners." And the West feared the financial and cultural hegemony of the East, ruled by "bankers, Shylocks, and speculating middle men," phrases used long before the bearded Populists rose up against "Wall Street."

"No West, no East, no North, no South," chanted the Know-Nothing saviors—"only America." And good Americans, appalled by the sectional strife, were drawn into the fold—or, better said, from the frying pan into the fire. It was because of this slogan that many New England businessmen became Know-Nothings, not wishing to antagonize lucrative southern or western markets. The business elements of New Haven, Connecticut, were thus drawn solidly into the Know-Nothing camp, for New Haven was the carriage and wagon capital, the clock and watch center of the world, and the biggest markets were west and south. At the same time, they badly needed "foreign" workmen to get out their product. Truly a tightrope dilemma.

Thus the Know-Nothings were States-righters, a democratic-sounding slogan that is rarely shouted except in the cause of reactionary skulduggery. Don't raise the slavery bugaboo, insisted the Know-Nothings; let the states settle it. Existing federal legislation and compromise—what a queasy crazy quilt that was!—"have solved the problem forever."

America *über alles* was the Know-Nothing solution, and to shout "Americanism" or to utter bathos over Old Glory was a push button for automatic applause—then as now. But basic evils could not be conjured away merely by waving "the Stripes and Stars"—as the phrase was inverted those days, with a certain convict flavor—or by slapping thin-plaster deceit over yawning cracks, or by national unity enforced by a smug, terrorizing minority convinced of its God-given right to kick lesser breeds in the teeth. By waving the flag overtime, the Know-Nothings substituted race, class, and religious hatreds for the bitterness between the slavocracy and the abolitionists—and provoked worse violence.

But it enabled many persons to shed inferiority feelings, to feel superior to their brethren, and flaunt their own special moral wisdom—not by reason of individual worth or ethical principles or personal achievement, but on the basis of birth—common failing of jingoistic societies. This injection of primitive tribalism and ancestor worship into a free American society, theoretically resting on individual talent and equal opportunities, in the case of the Know-Nothings became a herd reflex, a narcotic, a nationalistic hypnotism, that seduced much of the country into shameful and thoughtless cruelties.

This "disease of nationalism," with its inevitable racial and religious bitterness, spread through the country's deepest tissues—not truly a disease, remarked a wiser contemporary, merely a symptom of deeper disorder in the body politic, not due to overeating but to the failure of the organs of society to perform their proper functions.

Nothing better illustrated the prevailing mass pathology than the wildfire spread of the Millerites, a sect started by William Miller, one-time follower of Voltaire and Rousseau, but a converted Baptist. His disordered visions, or his charlatanry, enabled him to set the date for the final holocaust, the world's destruction. Whole communities rocked with fear. Men gave away their businesses and their homes. A few killed their families or committed suicide. Mass sex orgies occurred, and exalted rapings. Many Millerites put on "Ascension robes"—the elders made good money out of this—and prayed incessantly. One wealthy man in Bristol, Connecticut, spent most of his time in the top branches of an elm tree so as to be "nearer heaven" when the disaster struck. In 1842, in New Haven, the Millerites, seeing a lurid glow in the north, rushed into the streets, wailing, and dropped on their knees. Fire engines rushing to the blaze could not get through. "Not a fire," screamed the votaries. "Turn back, it's the end of the world." They forced the firemen to get out and pray, and a big manufacturing establishment burned to the ground. Emotional mobs everywhere were blocking the fire engines of reason and tolerance.

In the cities, the Know-Nothings took over existing gangs or set up new ones: in Boston, Philadelphia, Baltimore, Louisville, Cincinnati, New Orleans, St. Louis, San Francisco (where a race-track owner was a leading backer). Often these thugs were incited to mobbism by itinerant Protestant street haranguers. The boldest New York City Know-Nothing gang was the Order of the American Star, whose youthful members, under twenty-one, rallied to the shibboleth of "Wide Awake!" The Wide Awakes, ever itching for a fight, swaggered about the streets in bizarre dress (zoot suiters?) with clubs, paving stones, knives, guns, and shoe awls, especially effective for picking out eyes or nudging voters in polling booths. Other brass-knuckle brigades were the Black Snakes, Tigers, Rough Skins, Red Necks, Thunderbolts, Gladiators, Embolts, Little Fellows, Rip Raps, Rip Saws, Screw Boats, Stay Lates, Hard Timers, Dips, Plug Uglies, Blood Tubs. The Democrats, fighting in retreat, assembled other weirdly named outfits, chiefly Irish and good fighters: Dead Rabbits, Double Pumps, Peelers, Pluckers, Shad Rows, Butt Enders, etc.

In addition, the Know-Nothing "angel" millionaire, George Law, in the early 'fifties matched every Tammany precinct headquarters with his militant personal "Live Oak Clubs," scarcely centers of sweetness and light. Already in 1855 he was making a secret bid for the presidential nomination on the Know-Nothing ticket and had bought up papers in Albany, New Orleans, Pittsburgh, and elsewhere. Nobody knew the seamy side of politics better than he did.

"Live Oak George," rival of Vanderbilt in bribing aldermen, legislators, and congressmen for franchise and steamship subsidies, fighting Vanderbilt for control of railroads and the sea lanes, was an authentic "robber baron." A second-generation Irishman, he had risen big muscled from shoveling cow manure, hod carrying, and chipping stones, to become a power in the land—builder of canals and big bridges, a banker, railroad and steamship constructor and operator. He was the largest landowner in Panama Province (Colombia) and the leading promoter of the Panama Railroad. Nowhere did death take a heavier toll from sickness, poor pay, bad food, housing, and the knouts of overseers than on the stretch of the railroad he built personally. In 1851 he had been arms agent for Hungarian revolutionist Louis Kossuth, but in 1856 shipped the rifles and bayonets to a subordinate of steamship-subsidized William Walker, the Nicaragua filibuster, while Vanderbilt shipped rifles to Costa Rica, each attempting to ruin each other and lesser competitors.

Law was the respectable visage of Janus-faced Know-Nothingism; Bill the Butcher was its ugly countenance. The murder of Bill—he did die—was a dramatic triumph for Tammany and a kick in the teeth for the Know-Nothings. Tremendously outraged, Law did all he could to catch and convict the murderer.

For some time prior to Bill's demise, Tammany had been looking around for a gangland showpiece to put against the Know-Nothing cock of the walk. Tammany boss, John Kennedy (later police commissioner, who got killed in the Civil War anti-draft riots), discovered two-hundred-and-fifty-pound John Morrissey, one-time prize fighter and gambler, run out of Troy, New York, by the police. At the moment Morrissey was a Bowery derelict, and faint laughter curled about his name after one-hundred-and-twenty-pound Billy Mulligan had chased him out of a poolroom with only a billiard cue. But little Mulligan was a paranoid killer, as San Francisco was to discover in due time.

Morrissey was a bull of a man, tough-looking with his side-twisted flattened nose. His first assignment from Kennedy was to gather hoodlums and wreck Isaiah Rynders' Park Street gambling joint—the double-crossing bastard had it coming to him. The pug barged in with such notorious sluggers as Jim Turner, Lew Baker, and prize fighter Yankee Sullivan (who later slashed his wrist when nabbed by the San Francisco Vigilantes). But Rynders had been tipped off, and Poole and his plug-uglies gave Morrissey a drubbing that put him to bed for weeks.

Morrissey planned his next exploit better. Assigned to guard an uptown polling booth, he and his thugs holed in well ahead of time behind strong barricades. Poole rolled up with his wagonload of bruisers, took in the impregnable set-up, and retired in a shower of brickbats. Tammany was exultant and set Morrissey up in a small gambling joint. From this strategic base he moved on up to fine clothes, rings on his fingers, sparklers on his shirt front, whores galore, and $700,000 in the bank. He went in for horse racing, consorted with judges, senators, and merchants, and Vanderbilt backed him on the stock exchange—but that was later.

Morrissey challenged Poole to a personal fight and accepted the latter's time and place: the Christopher Street wharf, right in enemy territory. The big Troy Irishman showed up with a dozen henchmen, but Poole, who never came around himself, sent in two hundred. They dragged Morrissey back and forth across the splinters, beating and kicking him blind, and probably would have killed him had not Tammany reinforcements come to his rescue. All gangland waited for the next round.

On February 24, 1855, Morrissey was playing cards with Mack McGuire, "King of the Newsboys," in Stanwix Hall Saloon, a new Broadway place near Prince Street, when Poole swaggered in. The Tammany tough moved in for the kill and pulled his trigger three times. But his gun didn't go off. Gargling laughter, Poole leisurely pulled out his own gun. Morrissey pleaded frantically for someone to lend him another weapon. Nobody did. But McGuire plucked Poole's sleeve.

"You can't shoot an unarmed man in cold blood."

True—especially as Tammany controlled the ward courts. The Butcher mockingly threw down his gun and snatched up two butcher knives from the free-lunch counter, telling Morrissey to take one. No one could match the Butcher with a knife, but several of Morrissey's henchmen happened in, so the Irishman sailed into Poole with fists and feet. Two policemen entered just in time to stop the fray—to the relief of both bullies—and sent them home pledged to behave.

Poole came right back to Stanwix Hall. Lew Baker and other Morrissey thugs crowded him to the bar and spat in his face. Baker flung aside his Talma actor's cape and leveled his long-barreled Colt in his elbow but merely shot his own arm. He fell screaming to the floor, but managed to shoot Poole in the leg. Both men struggled to their feet and grappled. Poole was knocked down or fell, and Baker shot him close up in chest and belly.

The assassin hid out in Jersey City until March 10, the day Poole finally kicked the bucket, then escaped on the brig *Isabella Jewett.* George Law denounced the "cold-blooded murder" of a fine American and put his private clipper yacht *Grapeshot* at the disposal of the police. It beat the brig to the Canaries by ten days and stopped it two hours out of Tenerife. Baker was brought back in irons, but a Tammany jury acquitted him.

Bill the Butcher's last gasping words were "Good-by, boys. I die a true American!"

The sensation of his final joust and his dying words moved New Yorkers deeply. Half-a-dozen new plays were slapped up and rushed to the boards; current ones were revamped so the curtain went down on the hero, draped in an American flag and gasping out ere he toppled over, "Good-by, boys. I die a true American." Audiences wept and shook the rafters. Never did American patriotism have more glorious innings on the stage.

The Know-Nothings and gangsters gave "the true American" the country's first resplendent underworld funeral. More than five thousand persons rode in carriages or walked behind the flag-draped hearse, with half-a-dozen bands playing dirges and the national anthem, between sidewalks jam packed all down Broadway: past St. James Hall, the new Grace Church, and Platt's saloon in the basement of Wallach's Theater at Tenth Street (not long since the hangout of Edgar Allan Poe); past Broadway Tabernacle, a favorite Know-Nothing rendezvous; past Metropolitan Hotel, center of the city's night life; the Stanwix Saloon, draped in black; past LaFarge House at Amity Street. The cortege turned down Whitehead Street to the East River, where waiting boats took the coffin and mourners to the Brooklyn side for interment in Greenwood Cemetery.

Out in force were Poole's Christopher Street thugs, the Atlantic Guards, and the Bowery Boys, who had first congregated at their 42 Bowery clubhouse (soon to be demolished by rival Five Pointers), and at the Green Dragon hangout on Broome Street. They wore red-striped pants tucked into high boots, long frock coats, and extra-tall plug-ugly hats (which helped cushion brain clouts), but today (a truce was tacitly in force) they were not whittling on shingles with their big ever-ready fighting knives.

There, too, strode the Wide Awakes in broad white hats. Their banners showed a large star centered by the figure "67" (Washington's age at death) encircled by thirteen smaller stars. Behind in a carriage rode their founder, young, properly lantern-jawed William W. Patten and tiny-mouthed Jacob B. Bacon, this year's head of the order's Grand Temple. They now ruled over 10,000 fanatically patriotic fighters.

The heads of other patriotic secret societies—there were some sixty in the city—were also represented. There in the long line rode F. C. Wagner, Arch Grand Sachem of the Arch Chancery, the "Temple of Patriotism" of the secret Order of United Americans, the greatest outfit of all, a jingoistic "pure American" anti-foreign, anti-Catholic society, founded by James Harper, the publisher, back in December, 1844, to counter "the secret conspiracy of the followers of Loyola and Babylon." It had spread across the nation and was now growing faster than ever. With Wagner rode State Senator Thomas R. Whitney, one of the thirteen OUA charter members and the most influential manipulator of the City Reform League (the Nativist crowd using false reform slogans) which in 1844 had elected James Harper mayor. Now powerful in Know-Nothing affairs, Whitney was on the eve of being elected to the United States Congress. Other carriages toted female representatives of the Auxiliary United Daughters of America. The OUA banners showed a hand grasping the neck of a vicious coiled snake—symbolizing the crushing of Catholics and foreigners.

The shabbiest carriage, drawn by a single washtub nag, was that of Live Oak George Law. His expensive but spattered suit hung loose on his great frame, failing to suggest that here was the personage who headed the Dry Dock Bank, owned streetcar lines, the Staten Island Ferry, the Harlem and

Mohawk railroads, had sixteen vessels on the high seas, and was contending with both Vanderbilt and the powerful Pacific Mail Steamship Company for the monopoly of the Panama-California traffic. Four years ago (1851), according to Gustavus Myers, he had bribed the New York legislature for streetcar franchises on Second and Ninth avenues—for which Vanderbilt had fruitlessly bribed the city aldermen. Law's swollen, oversized head, almost too large for his powerful body and shoulders, was accentuated by a fringe beard and a great mane of wavy hair that submerged his ears. His huge predatory nose lorded it over a tight, relentless mouth. A ruthless, vindictive man, given to personal hates and revenge, he looked out at the world with hard, unyielding eyes.

Absent from the procession was Charles B. Allen, who in 1849 had founded the Supreme Order of the Star-Spangled Banner, now the political wing of the OUA and Know-Nothingism. Squeezed out by the new ruler of organized patriotism, James W. Barker, the stubby-handed former dry-goods man, Allen was scheming resentfully in other dark corners. After moving in and capturing the secret SSSB, Barker had quickly forged it into a powerful nationwide instrument of power, and he was now the key figure in this funeral procession of the dead gangster, who with his huskies had gouged out eyes in behalf of other "True Americans" at strategic polling places.

Barker, "The King of Know-Nothingism," was passionate, humorless, and stodgy, but a shouting, ranting, stomping orator who shook his clenched fists and rocked on his heels. A dogged behind-scenes manipulator and organizer, after his pirate raid on the SSSB a few years before this, he had reorganized it into a powerful personal machine. Ruthlessly he purged deviationists and ruled the blindly obedient members, manipulated by three secret degrees, using passwords, grips, and signs, with an iron hand. "Seeing Sam," as the initiation was described, was a solemn pledging. Members had to be pure-blooded native Americans of Anglo-Saxon stock, non-Catholics, with no Catholic among immediate relatives or in-laws. Members, pledged to vote for non-Catholics selected by the secret upper-tier caucuses, swore never to betray secrets, under pain of expulsion and implied penalty of death, and to deny affiliation by replying to the curious, "I know nothing," whence the label pinned on the SSSB order. By worming into old party caucuses, the order could overturn the best-laid electoral plans.

Its hard-core membership came from the powerful OUA, already nationwide, and by 1854 the SSSB also spread from sea to sea. In Texas, independence hero Sam Houston, now a United States senator, was an ardent charter member.

"Like a vast body of pent-up waters when the floodgates have been burst asunder," exulted Thomas R. Whitney, "the membership poured forth in torrents . . . in every state and territory . . . at least one and a half million of legal voters . . . amongst its adherents many of the brightest intelligence, the best statesmen and purest patriots of the land." Among such were (very briefly) Ulysses S. Grant, former President Millard Fillmore, various cabinet ministers, senators, and congressmen. The Know-Nothing *Almanacs* claimed that George Washington was the first Know-Nothing, citing his apocryphal words at Valley Forge, "Tonight let none but native-born Americans stand guard."

"It has become a giant," crowed Whitney, "destined to grind the corrupt practices of the country into powder, to appal the demagogue, and shake to pieces the political papal structure of the United States."

Though Know-Nothingism had burst on the scene in a few short years, it had deep roots. Nativism had ridden to its first crest in the convent-burning days of the 'thirties, had risen again in the 'forties, had ebbed during the Mexican War, and now in the 'fifties had become a tidal wave roaring across the land. For a few years after 1850 it still wormed along in the murk of numerous patriotic secret societies; then, as the American party, it openly challenged the old political groups. It did little campaigning except in the dark. Usually its candidates were announced a few days before election, sometimes not until the morning of election day, yet it had astounding success. By 1855 it controlled all but one New

England state, had won Maryland, Delaware, Kentucky, New Jersey, Pennsylvania, and California, and had come within a few hundred or a few thousand votes of winning in nearly every southern state. Most of the large cities of the country, and many smaller ones, had installed Know-Nothing administrations. It had a five-man bloc in the Senate and forty-three congressmen. Not only that, but at least seventy Republican congressmen, as well as numerous Whig and Democratic representatives, were Know-Nothing members. Nearly everybody believed that in the next election it would make a clean sweep everywhere and take over the White House.

Thus it was an enormous, rooting, tooting band wagon that rolled in impressive display behind Bill the Butcher Poole. If, seen here in broad daylight, some of those monopolists of patriotism valiantly saving the country's sacred liberties seemed murky fellow travelers—well, the prospect of power and its spoils always makes strange bedfellows, and the prize plums were almost ripe for the plucking by true patriots. Here behind King Barker rode Isaiah Rynders and others of his fraternity. Here rode owners of dives, dance halls, and saloons along the Bowery. Incongruous, if for no other reason than that President Barker was a fanatical temperance advocate.

And so it was that Butcher Bill, the super-duper patriot, the true-blue American, was carried to his last resting place. Know-Nothingism laid him there in reverence and glory.

## CHAPTER II

# BURNING THE CHURCHES

WEEK in, week out, year in, year out, at the Hanover Street Congregational Church in Boston, Reverend Lyman Beecher's oratorical hell fire consumed "the whoredom of Babylon," the "foul beast of Roman Catholicism," and the Papacy. In fashionable Park Street Church, his son, Reverend Edward Beecher, held forth so pungently on the same theme that his establishment became known as "Brimstone Corner." The Beechers fed the hate flames with diatribes against "the Pope, the Anti-Christ, corrupt monks, immoral nuns. . . ." Immigrants were blind agents of two great autocratic forces: the Church of Rome and the Austrian despotism, in its turn an obedient vassal of Rome. The immigrants bowed down "to a foreign power, bedizened with the trappings of royalty and tyranny." They "flouted" the blessings of American culture and freedom. Soon the Beechers were preaching to overflow audiences.

Nearly all the Boston preachers, except the Unitarians and Episcopalians, took up the hue and cry against "Papist iniquities" and "dirty, ignorant Irish and German immigrants," "guzzlers of beer and whisky," who added to the relief burden, increased the crime rate, took the bread out of the mouths of "honest Anglo-Saxon mechanics," and menaced American society and free government. As early as 1830, the year the Beechers took up the hate crusade, Bishop Edward Dominick Fenwick complained that every Protestant pulpit in Boston was given over to scurrilous attacks on Catholicism.

Street posters appeared:

"All Catholics and all persons who favor the Catholic Church are . . . vile impostors, liars, villains, and cowardly cutthroats. A TRUE AMERICAN."

Talks, in the pulpits and out, grew more lurid. Catholic convents were described as "priests' brothels," where *illegitimate* babies were strangled and clandestinely buried in underground catacombs.

Of all the local Bible thumpers, Lyman Beecher was considered the outstanding scholar and greatest orator, for his eloquence, his fine phraseology, and his slashing attacks.

A huge, magnetic individual, son of a mighty blacksmith, he had developed strong muscles as a farmer before entering Yale University, and his fine physique gave him an aura of unquenchable vitality. All his life he yearned for physical activity and slipped out of his study on the slightest pretext: to hunt or fish with his sons, pick berries or nuts, look for wild honey, smoke hams, till field and garden, or help his neighbors harvest their hay. His thundering apocalyptic voice, "with more range than a pipe organ," bent to passionate rhetoric or the most subtle nuances of thought and emotion. Ever since his first sermon in West Haven, Lyman had prided himself that his public addresses were always startlingly "pungent."

He wore his loose, fluffy hair without a part, and his commanding, luminous eyes, his deep-cleft chin, and the lines from nose to mouth gave his face a romantic sensitive quality. But he was no poseur; he was at bottom a stern Calvinist and die-hard reactionary, although he always cloaked bigotry in the most passionate defense of liberty, freedom, and democratic institutions. He had even allowed for a degree of free human will within the Calvinist strait jacket, so that in 1835 he was actually put on church trial for heresy, but it didn't stick. Lyman had great talent, perhaps a touch of genius, and wide influence in national affairs.

The first of the Beecher clan to become prominent, he sired Harriet Beecher Stowe, author of *Uncle Tom's Cabin,* which changed the thinking (or at least the emotions) of the nation (at least half of it); and the brilliant Henry Ward Beecher, fashionable preacher and promoter of noble causes, later spiderwebbed in the Tilden adultery charges.

Both Lyman's Hanover Street group and Edward's Park Street congregation were the citadels of Boston Calvinism, splinter factions appalled by Unitarianism and more liberal interpretations of the Bible and Christian doctrine. The Park Street Church was the older, set up in 1807 "as the arch-citadel of orthodoxy," by Reverend Jedidiah Morse of the Charlestown pulpit, a most ferocious soul still fanatically fighting for the narrow beliefs and ecclesiastical tyranny of John Cotton two centuries earlier. He founded the crusading anti-Catholic New England Tract Society and the American Bible Society, fought the appointment of a "liberal" to head the Harvard Divinity School of which he was a trustee, and helped found Andover College Seminary to fight the rising tide of new ideas. He was the arch-reactionary of the land, flinty against all "the insidious encroachments of innovations," all the evil "stalking to and fro in the earth seeking whom it may devour."

Thus both Lyman and Edward (even more) believed grimly in human sinfulness and predestined damnation, a gloomy doctrine making man a helpless insect under the implacable tread of a cruel God who conformed at all times to pulpit intolerance. This cruel creed had held the colonial mind bound like a Chinese woman's foot for two centuries and had blighted creative thought, literature, music, art, political and social progress. The colonial mind never reached a more primitive level than in mid-eighteenth century—while all Europe was brimming with new enlightenment.

There was a hint of petulance in Lyman's diatribes against a rival religion, a bit like a man beating his wife because his collar button has rolled under the bureau. At moments he felt a faint chill, as more liberal forces invaded the commonwealth and his own church. The American revolution and the French revolution had been severe blows to ecclesiastical ascendancy. Yet in Connecticut, not until 1818 was church-state separation achieved by a new constitution, a reform that Lyman had fought tooth and nail. Defeat was bitter: "I suffered what no tongue can tell." He compensated for it by launching a ferocious war on Unitarianism and leading in the reactionary Finney revivalist movement started that year.

But the light could not be kept out. Ezra Stile of Yale reached beyond dogma to nobler realms of knowledge, science, and the free mind and spirit. Came soon the Perfectionists, singing psalms about the hope and glory of man and a kindlier God. It was "a volcanic release from sterile conformity," from the dull sermons, "not fit food for ostriches" as Roger Williams had noted two centuries earlier. Came the Unitarians and the noble mind and spirit of William Ellery Channing, denouncing irrevocable predestination at birth, preaching that man could attain beauty of soul and mind by his own will and dedication to God, a God of love, not of hate and damnation, but loving all, rich and poor, black and white. And so the way was finally opened for the brief "flowering of New England." For all his brilliance, Lyman was not a blossom of that flowering.

The newer concepts, mostly secondhand from the German and French enlightenment, cut at the very roots of the aged, dry-rotted tree that Beecher and his fellows were still trying to water. For the new ideas threatened the continued domination of Calvinism over minds, hearts, pocketbooks; above all, over education. Long-standing privileges were at stake. In spite of church-state separation, the Protestants still ran the public schools with public tax money in most of New England, New York, and elsewhere, by means of benevolent Protestant societies. These church-state schools included in the curricula compulsory reading of the King James Bible and compulsory attendance at Protestant religious services, both anathema to Catholics and to some other Protestant sects, whose members were also taxpayers. Textbooks belittled the Catholic religion in the most offensive ways and harped on Inquisition tortures without adequate historical perspective.

The initial weapon in the campaign to destroy Perfectionism, Unitarianism, and Transcendentalism, which so menaced Calvinist supremacy, was counterrevivalism—the use of hell fire and blind fear to castigate heresy and stop the melting away of whole congregations. For some reason, hysteria is always supposed to be akin to godliness.

Reverend Charles G. Finney's movement from 1819 to 1822, in which Lyman was so active, had hypnotized vast mobs into prostrating themselves before the Calvinist God—one of those waves of religious frenzy that periodically sweep so many Americans from their moorings of common sense. Finney's movement had brought "sinful" herds reeling tear-streaked to the mourners' bench. He sought to reclaim backsliders by restoring the original horror, sublimity, and courage that once had made Calvin a terror shaking the kingdoms of the world. His "New Measures"—as old as jungle tom-toms—resurrected the dour New England creed and spread it through the raw stumps of frontier clearings. Uprooted people, ingrowing with isolation in a new, uncertain way of life, tend to be unstable, fearful, and superstitious. Finney's dogmatic fundamentalism swept frightened folk into orgiastic groveling at the feet of the Old Testament Jehovah of Vengeance. The pathological sex undertones and overtones of sadism reflected the sickness of rigid puritanical authority. But for a while longer revivalism kept many people bringing their love apples to the same old witch doctors, and it paved the way for violence and emotion in public affairs.

Another way—also a reflex of doctrinal disintegration among the Protestant brotherhood—was to sidestep the entire dialectic problem by a militant crusade against an outside menace, a dastardly rival faith, and thereby unify doubt-riddled congregations with fear of the hairy monster at the gates. Jedidiah Morse had fought the "abominations" and the schismatics within the fold, saw he was lost, and turned to rousing the bricklayers, farmers, and mechanics of the Boston area against the "iniquities of Babylon." From the start, the Beechers fought the enemy without, and emotion held their congregations better than did argument.

Both revivalism and anti-Popery represented hallucinations. When a long-standing creed goes to pot, fright and uncertainty produce personal disintegration, a bigoted clinging to the old, or a sheep-like rushing to and fro. Presently the neurosis spreads, as imitation and group conformity transform madness into apparent reason. Whole groups and communities, sometimes all society, are engulfed by such aberrations, which then seem rational and realistic. Demagogues, of course, have a field day, and even respectable political leaders, becoming bemused and belligerent, rattle the national saber incessantly. Police-state methods multiply. The leaders, unable to face the facts of life, begin flying kites or shooting at the moon. Threats, soothing syrup, meaningless phrases, stereotyped clichés are repeated *ad nauseam* to create a false sense of alternate security and fear. The most eminent personages sound like worn phonograph grooves. The real world is lost in set prejudices and distorted with dark phantasms. Nobody presents facts. It is all emotional zigzag.

The entire nation then lives in a curious Alice-in-Wonderland stupefaction of self-righteousness. Only the old tried ways are valid, though useless. The doors are frantically closed against outside ideas and peoples, and the process of disintegration, self-delusion, and self-destruction moves forward. Such were the sinews of Calvinism running about in its own shroud of anti-Catholicism, of anti-foreignism, of Know-Nothingism that came within an ace of engulfing the land. Those who get in the way of such a turbulent emotional tide are ground under remorselessly. Hate objects become a prime necessity, since our enlightened society has been unable to evolve safety valves as effective as the bullfight or Roman lions in the arena. Hate and bloodshed become as habit-forming as narcotics. And so in the early 'thirties the rising moon of Catholicism and the arrival of foreigners in the American haven provided the current hate target. Lyman Beecher was pre-eminent in this ugly crusade that swept on through the 'forties and 'fifties and doomed the nation finally to civil war.

In an early polemic over dueling, he exulted over his opponents, "Oh, I declare, if I did not switch 'em and scorch 'em and stamp on 'em." This I-am-the-right-hand-of-God conviction meant now that Catholic "sinners" could not be "saved," only switched, scorched, and stamped on—extirpated.

Yet he was by no means as bereft as his listeners, and was able to cloak his worst intolerances in honied words about civil rights. He soon appreciated that to fill his church to overflowing, to raise money for western missions and churches, theological disputation was worthless, but attacks on the "beast of Rome" brought both people and dollars to his feet. Before long rabid anti-Catholic, anti-foreign sermons became the vogue in nearly all the Protestant churches in the land.

As the jungle drums beat louder, bands of glib-tongued free-lance ministers began barnstorming up and down. Some were renegade Catholic priests; others had been unable to hold regular pulpits or had been cast forth for sundry unsavory reasons. These greedy, self-seeking Jeremiahs rushed over the landscape, collecting subscriptions for hate magazines, leading mobs against Catholic churches, sometimes to throw the priest out and seize the pulpit, often provoking arson and murder. More and more of these self-appointed knights rode about hammering on the tomtoms of ignorance and fear, falsehood and provocation, arousing the whole country to unchristian malevolence. Virulent magazines, such as *The Protestant,* the *Protestant Vindicator, Priesthood Exposed, Priesthood Unmasked,* the *Downfall of Babylon,* and the *Anti-Romanist* threw kindness and truth to the winds. Rarely has sensational journalism reached a more debased level. The poison spread. It corroded the veins and hearts and softened the minds of the most responsible ministers, too easily convinced, perhaps too frightened, to stand out against the prevailing hysteria and brutality. Their tongues loosened in loud denunciations.

There were many things for which the Catholics—both hierarchy and laity—could be criticized, and vice versa. There were rational ways to do it other than stirring up mob hate.

Neither were Catholic spokesmen always temperate—nor humble. But as a persecuted minority fighting for equal rights, the Catholics advanced the liberties of all Americans —for no right is valid or secure as long as it is enjoyed merely by a privileged segment of the population, even if it be the righteous and patriotic segment. At bottom, of course, neither side was basically concerned with truth or justice or human rights—merely in power and its emoluments. It was a deadly battle without pity—native-born Protestant Americans, considering themselves sacred cows, trying to hold on to entrenched privileges, public tax monies, and sectarian control over the hearts and minds of children. The Protestant leaders had no desire to share their monopolies with Catholics or newcomers.

In Boston, the Beechers and others railed particularly against the Ursuline school, housed in a beautiful edifice atop Charlestown's Mount Benedict, probably the best school in the area. The Ursuline nuns (an order founded in 1536) had purchased the land in 1820 and started building in 1826. Owing to the school's popularity, two large wings were added in 1829. Its reputation soon attracted the children of wealthier Episcopalians and Unitarians, unable to stomach the current bigotry of public and private Congregationalist schools. Students came from as far away as the southern states and Canada. The Protestant ministers claimed that its sole purpose was to proselytize for the Catholic Church and wean the children away from the faith of their fathers. Although this was denied by pupils and parents, the good men of the cloth and other irate citizens brought pressure on the heads of families to withdraw their children from such sinister influences. The parents were told how priests used the confession to abuse innocent girls, and fervid barroom cerebration conjured up other obscenities.

In the ignorant mind, convents had become invested with mystery and horror equal to that of the creepiest Edgar Allan Poe thriller. All the slimy monsters rampaged there on the Charlestown hill: sex orgies, rape, illegitimacy, bastardy, infanticide. To foster such cesspool delusions, the preachers frequently referred to two best-selling books republished in the early 'thirties: Anthony Gavin's *The Master Key of Popery* and Scippio di Ricci's *Female Convents, Secrets of Nunneries Discovered.* In 1834, *Lorette, the History of Louise, Daughter of a Canadian Nun: Exhibiting the Interior of Female Convents* appeared and conditioned gullible minds to believe the most disgusting immoralities. Mary Sherwood's novel *The Nun,* in similar vein, also became a best seller.

Many such infamous convent tales were printed in the anti-Papist magazines that flourished everywhere. The Baptists and Presbyterians of Boston had both set up such publications, the *Christian Watchman* (1819) and the *Boston Record* (1816). In 1823 Jedidiah Morse and two of his sons had started *The Observer* in Manhattan, which became the leading Protestant journal of the country and was virulently anti-Catholic. By 1827 at least thirty additional anti-Papist magazines had been launched, all sending up a chorus about the "blasphemy, cruelty, and anti-Christ" nature of the rival church and demanding its extirpation in the United States. The Hartford *Observer* (Congregationalist) of Connecticut warned that to admit the religious error of Catholicism to the land was as wise as to allow "an invasion of savages on our western borders" on the grounds that "we are as a nation so much stronger than they." Convents everywhere became prime targets of abuse.

By the early 'thirties, besides these publications, a rash of books and pamphlets appeared, many bearing the imprint of respectable religious houses and carrying illustrations of sex perversions in convents, near-naked women being tortured by hot irons, holy women struggling in the arms of priestly and monkish rapists. This early version of today's cheap paperback torture, sadism, violence, and sex, given approval by many leaders of the church, was lapped up with smacking lips as gospel truth by the *hoi polloi* and even more educated people.

This sewage was enriched by the "exposures" and "confessions" of renegade priests and "escaped nuns." Few of these greedy or pathological creatures had ever been nuns, but their horrendous disclosures were received with full credence. In the decade or so that followed, particularly with each culminating crest of Know-Nothingism, scores of these rape dreamers, psychotics, nymphomaniacs, penis enviers, adventuresses, notoriety seekers, whores, and egomaniacs "escaped" and strutted in the public eye, inflaming weak minds and arousing pruriency by their tales of sexual abuse by priests. The childhood pattern of most of these glamorized delinquents turned out to be surprisingly similar. A large proportion of these "raped" girls had suicidal tendencies; some actually did resort to poison, drowning, self-starvation, even self-cremation. To modern psychiatrists such symptoms are obvious; they have technical names. All this foetid ignorance washed closer to the Ursuline convent on the peaceful Charlestown hill.

The lurid barrages from the pulpits soon aroused mob action. In 1829, a terrible anti-Irish, anti-Catholic riot roared through Boston streets for three days. Homes were stoned and burned. Persistent holy tub thumping soon resulted in more outbreaks, and in December, 1833, the militia was called out but stood passively by while 500 rioters burned homes and killed people. These unchristian manifestations in the supposed lighthouse of American culture, instead of giving the men of God pause, merely spurred them to more frenzied incendiary outbursts.

Soon Boston had its own "escaped nun"—and from this same Ursuline school. Actually, Rebecca Theresa Reed was not a nun. She was a Charlestown tramp, unbalanced by fancied slights, who had begged the nuns to let her do menial work for six months to prove she had qualifications to become a nun. She turned out to be intractable, flighty, and slovenly, and after four months the mother superior turned her out. In revenge, Rebecca concocted florid tales of cruelty and misconduct: how one nun suffering from brain fever was confined in an underground cell, and how she herself had "escaped" just in time to avoid being carried off forcibly by monks to some other city so as to hush her up. This same "kidnap-rape" wish was a motif prevalent in nearly all tales by these types.

Rebecca's anguished outburst was timed exactly right for trouble. In July, 1834, a music teacher, the nun Elizabeth Harrison, neurotic from overwork (such was the official explanation) began acting queerly. One night she fled to the home of a neighboring brickmaker who escorted her to her brother's home in Boston. By morning she had calmed down and was horrified. "Oh, my God, where were my senses? How can I repair the injury I have done?" In the company of her brother and Bishop Fenwick, she returned to the convent and was allowed to resume teaching.

Garbled versions got into the Boston papers, and the rumor spread that she had been returned to the convent by force and was being held in an underground dungeon. Denials did no good. Impartial persons, non-Catholics, including the Charlestown selectmen, inspected the edifice from cellar to garret and reported that Sister Elizabeth was working and cheerful. They were branded as liars, and troops had to be stationed to protect one investigator's home.

Street placards appeared:

*To Arms! To Arms!*
*Ye brave and free, the Avenging Sword uphold!*
*Leave no stone upon another of that Accursed Nunnery*
*That prostitutes female virtue and liberty under the garb of holy religion.*
*When Bonaparte opened the nunneries of Europe, he found cords of Infant Skulls! ! ! ! ! !*

The Boston pulpiteers seized upon these incidents to preach more virulent sermons against the institution, and flames rose higher. On August 9, a big demonstration shouted, "Down with the convent! Away with the nuns." In the midst of this hysteria, Lyman Beecher (who had been absent as head of a Midwestern seminary) popped back into the city and provided the final impetus to a shameful crime that can never be cleansed from the records of city or country.

On August 10, he delivered firebrand anti-Papist lectures to overflow audiences in four churches. The Catholic Church, he roared, "holds now in darkness and bondage nearly half the civilized world. . . . It is the most skillful, powerful, dreadful system of corruption to those who wield it and of debasement and slavery to those who live under it, who [*sic*] ever spread darkness and desolation over the earth. . . . Foreign influence and American demagogues in lurid alliance" were riding "the whirlwind" of "ignorance and prejudice, passion and irreligion and crime" that threatened to destroy all American liberties. He denounced the convent, and the next day the convent was attacked.

Catholics claimed, probably falsely, that some rioters went directly from Beecher's church; certainly, the attitude of the most famous preacher in Boston sanctioned the violence. He might as well have rushed to the convent torch in hand.

Monday night a gang of fifty men appeared on the school grounds, carrying banners and shouting, "Down with Popery! Down with the Cross!" The mother superior denied them admittance because the girls were asleep, but invited the crowd to inspect the building the next day. The mobsters milled about for several hours and at eleven o'clock set fire to tar barrels, and the fire bells were rung all over Boston and Charlestown, apparently a prearranged signal, for crowds streamed toward the hill. The authorities, although warned beforehand, provided only one constable.

As the mob smashed in the doors and began demolishing, the twelve sisters managed to get their fifty-seven pupils dressed and out the back way. The mob set fire to the edifice and a nearby farmhouse used as an auxiliary dormitory and screamed and danced around the blazing buildings. The fire engines that had raced to the scene did nothing to extinguish the flames.

The following night another mob destroyed fences and orchard trees and burned what little was left. They also tried to destroy nearby Saint Mary's Church, but were held off by troops still guarding the adjacent home of one of the investigators. On succeeding nights mobs roared through Boston and Charlestown streets. They threatened the cathedral and churches and burned Catholic homes and a boarding-house where thirty-five Irish workers lived.

A Faneuil Hall mass meeting of indignant citizens demanded punishment of the rioters. Harrison Gray Otis passionately denounced the lawlessness. Even as he spoke a vast mob was milling about the cathedral, but it was under guard, so they took their arson and murder elsewhere.

The prominent Protestant journals called the meeting "Jesuit-controlled." The *Protestant Vindicator* accused the Catholics of having themselves burned down the convent to ruin Beecher's reputation and gain sympathy. Both the press and the preachers continued their incendiary tirades, advocating that all convents, including the Ursuline school, be abolished "to prevent . . . the spread of immorality throughout the nation." To justify the mob attack, they reminded readers of Saint Bartholomew's Day and the Spanish Inquisition.

In his sermon the following Sunday, Lyman Beecher deplored mob violence, but for years he went up and down the land telling how Boston, to ward off an assault by Irish Catholics, had had to remain "five nights under arms—her military upon the alert—her citizens enrolled, and a body of 500 men constantly patrolling the streets." He described the Faneuil Hall meeting: "Citizens at the sound of the bell were convened at midday . . . to hear Catholics eulogized and thanksgivings offered to his reverence the bishop, for his merciful protection of the children of the pilgrims." Men "turned pale and whispered and looked over their shoulders and around to ascertain whether it was safe to speak aloud, or to meet to worship God. Has it come to this?—that the capital of New England has been thrown into consternation by the threats of a Catholic mob, and that her temples and mansions stand only through the forbearance of a Catholic bishop? . . . dependent on the Catholic powers of Europe and the bayonets of Austria?" Lyman was there; he knew better, but his zeal had made a liar out of him, and he aroused passions everywhere with his false accounts. He also boasted he had helped "turn the tide" of New England Catholicism. Increasingly "obstructed by public sentiment," henceforth it would have "to row upstream."

The Boston *Advocate* hastened to publish Rebecca Reed's story, *Six Months in a Convent.* Its palpable falsity was no worse than Beecher's "eyewitness" distortions. Published as a book and lavishly praised by the Protestant press everywhere, her tale sold 20,000 copies in a month and was reissued in numerous editions, breaking all previous best-seller records, and it kept on selling for years.

The Ursuline nuns, who had taken refuge in Roxbury, were threatened with death, and local citizens had to mount a Vigilante guard night and day. Eventually the sisters fled to Canada.

The Massachusetts attorney general called for the arrest and conviction of the riot ringleaders. He was showered with scurrilous letters and was burned in effigy by a stamping, howling mob. A dozen arrests were made, and eight men were finally arraigned for arson (carrying the death penalty) on October 10, 1834. The trial of ringleader John R. Buzzell began on December 2.

All witnesses for the prosecution were threatened with violence, and the courtroom was jammed with shouting fanatics who converted the trial into an anti-Catholic rally. Outside, incendiary handbills were distributed:

> *Liberty or Death!*
> *Suppression of Evidence!*
> *Sons of Freedom! Can you live in a free country and bear the Yoke of the Priesthood, veiled in the habit of a profligate court!*

This was unfair to the judge, who, flagrantly biased in favor of the accused, refused to permit the prosecution to ask prospective jurors if they were prejudiced against Catholics and at every step hemmed in the attorney general with hostile rulings while allowing the defense attorneys every leeway.

The defense charged that the convent was a profit-making institution and shouted that the mother superior and the nuns in court to testify were pretending to have colds contracted on the night of the burning in order to arouse false sympathy—four months after the event! The constant denunciation of Catholics and all convents and the court's admission of non-relevant evidence constituted a flagrant perversion of justice. It was a witch trial in reverse.

Rebecca Reed told of the convent indecencies and horrors. Other witnesses told of convent immoralities far and wide, although apparently none, certainly not the Protestant ministers who took the stand, had ever been inside the Ursuline convent or any other. Contrary witnesses, pupils and parents, though few were Catholics, were shouted down; Bishop Edward D. Fenwick and the mother superior gave "foreign imported testimony," and were savagely badgered about convent immoralities. Everything was managed so as to justify mob action.

Naturally Buzzell was acquitted. The verdict was greeted with thunderous applause, and he was carried from the courtroom in shouting triumph. He received a flood of laudatory letters and so many gifts that he had to run ads in the Boston papers to thank people. Six more defendants were automatically acquitted. But revulsion in some quarters was so strong that finally a half-witted boy—the least guilty, if guilty at all—was sentenced to life imprisonment. After repeated entreaties over a long period by the bishop and mother superior, he was pardoned.

When compensation was asked from the state legislature, few representatives who recognized the justice of reparation dared speak up; others reviled the convent school, the nuns, and the church. "Any man," wrote the *Protestant Vindicator* "who . . . would rob the treasury of the descendants of the Puritans to build Ursuline convents, must be a raving lunatic."

A year after the burning, the Charlestown authorities were obliged to stop a commemorative demonstration, which was to be climaxed by riddling the effigy of the mother superior with bullets. But a Boston militia company did destroy an effigy of Bishop Fenwick in the presence of an obscenely riotous crowd that threatened to wipe out all Catholic property and churches. Lyman Beecher and his kind had done their work well, but worse was to follow.

The brave Christian attack on defenseless women and children was imitated nearly everywhere. Violence swept all New England, then spread south and west. Catholic convents and churches were wrecked and burned, Catholics and immigrants mobbed, sometimes killed; it was a bath of blood and terror. In New York 1834 became known as "the year of riots."

Not all aggressiveness was on the side of the Nativists. When too provoked, the Irish struck back. In one melee they put the mayor, sheriff, and a posse to flight. On July 4, 1835, according to the *Observer* and *Downfall of Babylon* (scarcely unbiased reporters) Detroit Irishmen, rendered over-patriotic with too much whisky, attacked citizens on the streets and had to be put out of action by armed "natives." Nativists and foreigners tangled in bad riots in Philadelphia.

Negroes and Abolitionists, too, were mobbed, beaten, or killed all through the North. In New York City, during 1833, 1834, and 1835, ugly riots against them and Catholics brought death and burnings. Negro and Abolitionist preachers were driven out of their pulpits and a number of churches burned. In 1833, during such a riot, the Merchant's Exchange was dynamited and looted. In 1834, Abolitionist Lewis Tappan's house was sacked and his furniture set on fire in the street. A few days later twelve buildings were wrecked, a Negro seaman was tortured and mutilated, an Englishman had his eyes torn out, and the girls in five whore houses were stripped and parceled out. In 1835, punitive fires started by rioters burned down 693 homes and businesses, some thirteen acres.

The preachers seemed oblivious that much of this was owing to their incessant teaching. "The brands from the burning [of the Ursuline convent]," wrote one Catholic, "have set fires throughout the country that seem to have consumed all Christian virtues and threaten . . . religion itself." But according to Beecher, it was "the liberty of Protestants" and America's "democratic institutions" that were menaced.

John B. McMaster, the historian, wrote in the *Forum* in 1894: "The decade covered by the 'thirties is unique in our history. Fifty years of life at high pressure brought the people to a state of excitement, of lawlessness, and mob rule. . . . Intolerance, turbulence, riots became the order of the day. . . . Appeals were made not to reason but to force; reforms, ideals, institutions . . . not liked were attacked and put down by violence, and one of the least liked and first to be assaulted was the Church of Rome."

In two weeks in 1834, the editor of *Niles' Weekly Register* (September 5) clipped more than five hundred press items "relating to various excitements [violence] going on among the people of the United States. . . . Society seems everywhere unhinged, and the demon of 'blood and slaughter' has been let down upon us."

Actually the unreason and violence of the 'thirties were tame compared to those of the 'forties, and both were a mild prelude to the bitter hates of the 'fifties.

Such was part of the polluted stream that flowed into numerous Protestant and "Anglo-Saxon" patriotic secret societies that eventually swept the Know-Nothings on a powerful current toward national power and the nation toward the cataclysm of the Civil War.

*CHAPTER III*

# *A WHORE BECOMES A SAINT*

FAR from showing repentance for the Ursuline school burning, the hate mongers peddled their wares more ardently. Public meetings multiplied; more preachers harangued on street corners; all the ground-roaring words, as Ruskin called them, roared louder. Propaganda rolled off the religious presses. Rebecca Reed's puerile slander was followed by *Testimony of More than 100 Witnesses,* in which members of the mob related false tales about the convent they had never seen and rumors of immoralities and Nun Harrison's maltreatment in a dungeon.

The Ursuline convent provided a profitable literary topic for decades. An immediate literary success was Mrs. S. Sherwood's children's book: *Edwin and Alicia; or the Infant Martyrs.* In 1845, Harry Hazel's *The Nun of St. Ursuline; or the Burning of the Convent; a Romance of Mt. Benedict* went into eight editions in two years. As late as 1854, novelist Charles W. Frothingham found pay dirt in the convent disaster. Three of his novels told of Protestant girls spirited away by lecherous priests and held at the Ursuline school in gloomy cells until rescued by their lovers.

More than ever anti-Catholic literature—particularly that put out by Protestant Bible societies and religious presses—gave free rein to stories of secret orgies, the rape of young girls by priests and monks, the killing of bastard babies, the 6,000 babies' heads found in a nunnery fish pond, the antics of female Pope Joan—often with suggestive illustrations. Reverend Samuel B. Smith started his magazine, the *Downfall of Babylon,* a few weeks after the convent burning. Soon he brought out his *The Wonderful Adventures of a Lady of the French Nobility and the Intrigue of a Romish Priest, Her Confessor, to Seduce and Murder Her.*

A novel, *The Conversion and Edifying Death of Andrew Dunn,* described the prolonged anguish of a Protestant lured into the Catholic faith, alleviated only by his reconversion and death. In similar vein was *Father Clement,* reprinted from an English edition, in great demand for a decade. The worst rabble rousers of the 'fifties, Reverend Robert J. Breckinridge and L. Guistiniani, claimed this novel won them over to militant anti-Papacy.

No other book of the period had more influence for two decades than William Nevins' *Thoughts on Popery,* prepublished in the New York *Observer* and presented in book form in 1836 by the American Tract Society. "Nothing," the Society announced, ". . . so lays open the deformities of Popery in Common Minds or is so admirably adapted to save our country from its wiles." "Judas," the author declared, attacking Catholic ritual, "was the only person in the Bible who confessed his sins to another." The money-making features of Catholic rites, their alleged immorality, were extensively probed in Richard Baxter's *Jesuit Juggling, Forty Popish Frauds,* a long-term best seller.

A widely read melodrama was *Rosamond: or a Narrative of the Captivity and Sufferings of an American Female Under the Popish Priests in Cuba* (1846), run serially in Smith's *Downfall of Babylon.* Within two weeks of book publication, a second edition had to be issued. In it, Rosamond Culbertson told of her sex life as a mistress of a Cuban priest and disclosed a clerical practice of capturing and killing Negro boys and grinding them up into sausage. "Those who bought and eat [*sic*] these sausages say they are the best sausages they ever eat [*sic*]." The Protestant Reformation Society, nobly inspired, offered a fifty-dollar reward for the best essay on *The Happiness and Horrors of a Roman Catholic Priest on Never Being Allowed to Marry a Beautiful Young and Virtuous Wife.*

Abuse of Catholics, remarked the *Western Monthly Review* (June, 1835), had become "a regular trade," and the writing and publishing of anti-Catholic books "a part of the regular industry of the country, as much as the making of nutmegs or the construction of clocks."

The climax came with the "disclosures" of Maria Monk, an alleged nun who claimed to have escaped from the Hôtel Dieu convent in Montreal. She stated that she and other nuns were obliged to submit to carnal intercourse with priests, who gained entrance via a secret tunnel, and that she had become pregnant. Nuns who resisted were killed. Illegitimate babies were baptized, strangled, and thrown into a basement hole. "This," the mother superior explained to her, "secured their everlasting happiness, for the baptism cured them of all sinfulness." Maria, claiming to have been made pregnant by a Father Phelan, escaped to save her unborn child.

More likely she was frantically seeking to account for it. She had never been in the Hôtel Dieu nunnery, but had "escaped" in the simple fashion of walking out the front gate of the Catholic Magdalene Asylum, a charity reform school for wayward girls. Maria had been sleeping around since the age of fourteen. According to her mother, she had been raised a Protestant, but in an infant fall a slate pencil had been driven into her brain, and her conduct had always been bad. The charges, even if true, indicated maternal resentment and instability, a relationship that must have aggravated Maria's neurotic condition.

The girl falsely related how she had entered Hôtel Dieu as a novice, had recanted and married, then had returned to take the veil. On a first attempt to escape, she had been brought back forcibly by priests to keep her from disclosing the truth about immoralities and infanticide. She then tried to drown herself, but was saved by two workmen. This miraculous salvation convinced her she had been divinely chosen to expose "the horrors of Popery." Her husband, she claimed (according to her mother, he was Maria's lover and the father of her unborn child), gave her enough money to get to New York. He may have been the renegade priest, Reverend William K. Hoyt, long dedicated to anti-Catholic propaganda and closely associated with the worst New York rabble rousers. In any event, it was publicly charged later that she became Hoyt's mistress.

Arriving penniless in New York, again she tried to commit suicide, this time by starving herself to death in a secluded spot on the outskirts of the city, but four hunters found her and took her to a charity hospital. There, about to give birth to her child, she asked for a Protestant clergyman to whom she could tell her woes.

Whatever truth her yarns may have had, they indicated advanced paranoia, a hate complex against her own mother and against the good and kind sisters of her school, emotions complicated by the inevitable pettiness of prolonged intimacy with those of her own sex, combined with enforced celibacy. Also involved was a loathing for religious discipline. Maria's mythical "escapes" represented fantasy fleeing from reality, a reality made more confusing by unwanted pregnancy.

Her paranoid hallucinations were readily credible to gullible witch doctors. For self-seeking demagogues she was a marvelous tool, a gold mine. From her could be extracted poison for injection into weaker minds. For her, this was therapeutic, provided her with the feeling of being wanted, a superior being, an agent of God. The acceptance of her deranged fancies as truth gave her the satisfaction of imagined sanity and normalcy.

Hoyt also came to New York. Evidence indicates that he actually brought her to the hospital himself; certainly he was the one who led the anti-Papist crusaders to her bedside. Soon she was surrounded by a fever-eyed crew of religious demagogues and unbalanced fanatics: Reverend J. J. Slocum; Reverend Arthur Tappan (brother of the Abolitionist); Theodore Dwight (a Connecticut lawyer and banker, a grandson of Jonathan Edwards, and a brother of Reverend Timothy Dwight, one of the original sour "Hartford Wits," at this time the ultra-reactionary president of Yale University); Reverend George Bourne (long-time demagogue and vice-president of Hoyt's anti-Catholic Canadian society); Reverend William C. Brownlee (editor of the vicious *Protestant Vindicator*).

This publication had been started by Bourne on January 2, 1830, as the weekly *Protestant,* the official organ of the Protestant Association, to fight "Roman corruption . . . monkish traditions . . . Popish persecutors . . . the Mystical Babylon." It promised a special exposé by Hoyt "of moral and religious conditions of Lower Canada, as debased by the prevalence of Roman Supremacy." It was warmly endorsed by leading ministers and by the synods of the Reformed Presbyterians in New York and Philadelphia and by the Philadelphia Baptists.

At its inception, the magazine was discredited by a series of letters from one "Cramer," which set forth the sinister designs of the Catholic Church in America in lurid fashion to the point of absurdity. This hoax was perpetrated by the Philadelphia priest, Reverend John Hughes. The *Protestant,* deeply wounded by being made a laughingstock, sputtered about the "abominations" and "craft" of the Jesuits.

Brownlee, cleverer, less blunt, took over, revamped the Protestant Association, and altered the magazine's name. He put on a strong subscription drive by staging lectures on such subjects as "Is Popery that Babylon the Great, which John the Baptist denounced in the Apocrypha?" These meetings produced bad riots. Then the Maria Monk plot was hatched to lash public vindictiveness to a hotter pitch.

The scene in the hospital was a touching one. Maria, close to her time, her large breasts half showing under her bed jacket, her deep little black eyes imbedded in her plump, pouting chinless face, watched these so-called men of God clustered about to hear her sensational story: Hoyt, bulky and dark, with long, smooth white hands and sallow hothouse skin; Slocum, plain-faced with mousy hair and remote ice-green eyes, a clever vitriolic writer; Tappan, eager, insinuating, passionate with patriotic determination to keep the country unsullied by foreigners and "Jesuit plotters"; Bourne, big, shaggy, shrewd eyes ablaze, sharp for whatever profitable use could be made of Maria; Brownlee, with thick eyeglasses on a thin sanctimonious face and a thin, shrill voice.

Of them all, white-haired Dwight looked at her most intently, his tongue moving over the tight lips in his steel-trap Yankee face. He seemed the one most genuinely horrified by her story, though it showed in his icy eyes more than in his stiff, unchanging face. It helped her to embroider her long story, made it seem true even to herself. When she told how she had wandered toward death, his eyes glazed, his bloodless lips moved, perhaps with compassion.

Seventy years old that day when he stood beside Maria's bed, Theodore Dwight may have felt some anxiety over the passing of time and life's lost opportunities, although likely he would never have admitted this; his self-righteous confidence was too strong. Long active in Nativist and anti-Catholic affairs, in 1814 he had been secretary of the notorious Hartford Convention of New England statesmen, later described as America's first "Know-Nothing Assemblage," which in its bitterly reactionary, overtly seditious attitude, its anti-war threat of secession, had dug the grave of the Federalist party. Harshly the Convention had denounced the Democratic administration for excluding Federalists from government employment and appointing naturalized citizens to high office. It demanded restriction of immigration and changes in the citizenship laws. "Blind sailors navigating a dead sea," but they would still be floating around after twenty years, and even longer. In 1833, Dwight wrote a long apologia of this earlier excursion into Nativist bigotry.

A Connecticut blue blood and anti-foreign to the core, he denounced "the outlaws of Europe, the fugitives from the pillory and the gallows," who "have undertaken to assist our abandoned citizens, in the pleasing work of destroying Connecticut [there were several thousand foreigners in the whole state]. . . . Can imagination paint anything more dreadful on this side of hell!" This pathological bigot actually believed every word Maria uttered.

Shortly after his bedside visit, he published a rehash of her story and her accusations: *Open Covenants; or Nunneries and Popish Seminaries Dangerous to the Morals and Degrading to the Character of a Republican Community.* It was incredible how any sane man could sincerely believe the balderdash of old wives' gossip he spewed forth; it reeked with the acid of his long years of sterile self-suppression. Yet it carried a laudatory preface by Samuel F. B. Morse (son of Jedidiah), the artist and inventor who was also up to his ears in the Nativist hate crusade.

Soon Dwight returned to Hartford to edit the Hartford *Courant,* with which he had long been closely associated. He converted it into an even more virulent Know-Nothing paper and stirred up no end of falsehood and intolerance in his last-ditch effort "to roll back the wheels of revolution." While editor, he burst into verse:

*His Holiness, from his prolific nests,*
*Sends us Jesuits and bishops and priests—and priests,*
*Monks, friars, and nuns all in solemn array—*
*Sweet charity's sisters come out in a drove*
*And Sacred Hearts proffer their labors to love!*
*What a display*
*The rare show offers*
*To fill his coffers!*
*Huzzah!*

*Then let us rouse up ere the danger has past*
*Unawed by its thunders, and blast—and blast. . . .*

(There were only two Catholic churches in all Connecticut.)

The Democrats accused him of organizing a vicious whispering campaign to brand Van Buren, who was a member of the Reformed Dutch Church, a Catholic. Dwight sent daily emissaries, it was said, to factories, urging workers to defeat "the Magicians and the Pope—Van Buren, the Pope."

For Maria in the hospital, confession to the friendly souls ringing her bedside was a catharsis, a shrugging off of her burdens onto broader shoulders. Confession is often a relief for even less troubled souls, an easing away of subterranean guilt complexes, and she probably felt a pleasing ego involvement with these persons apparently anxious to help her. She was cleansed by this recapitulation of her hallucinations as truth—for, quite likely, they were supreme truth to her.

How about the male harpies crowded about her bedside? Strong personalities, seemingly, but they were obviously angry, unhappy men, whether slyly self-seeking or deeply conscientious. The greater the aggressive hate they displayed, the surer they were of leadership. The figures of speech used by Know-Nothing or Nativist leaders such as Bourne and Brownlee in their harangues have a typical dream-fantasy quality that betrays their inner perversion. They constantly talked about burning down the evil edifice of Roman Catholicism and they suggested many sadistic punishments. They wanted to whip and frighten Catholics and foreigners, but "only as a good, loving father would do," in order to awaken them and lead them out of the brimstone flames to safety. The Know-Nothing hate orators constantly revealed their inner psychotic dilemmas: fire, arson, sadism, the father complex. Theodore Dwight betrayed gnawing resentment at the greater talents, fame, and success of his older brother.

Slocum was to be the amanuensis of Maria's *Awful Disclosures,* although Dwight had a hand in it also, and Hoyt and Bourne made suggestions. For pre-publication publicity, Hoyt took Maria, after her daughter was born, back to Montreal, to sue the priest she claimed had seduced her. Apparently he was an imaginary person, for no suit was brought, but, according to *L'Ami du Peuple,* they used their jaunt to "indulge in an intimate liaison." Place, time, and hotel were cited.

Bourne took her manuscript to Harpers' publishing house, headed by James Harper, the fervent xenophobic nationalist, hater of Catholics and foreigners, later to become New York City's first Know-Nothing mayor. The manuscript was too scandalous for the Harper imprint, his brothers decided, though they printed many anti-Catholic books; but obviously it was a sure-fire money-maker, so a false-front firm was set up by two Harper employees, Howe and Bates. The book appeared in 1836, and became a best seller overnight.

Although Maria was obviously psychopathic, her avid public, spurred on by the firebrands, was whipped to white-hot emotion. In this furor nearly all rational religious disputations regarding the mind and soul of man disappeared. As the tide of ugly emotion rose, Protestant ministers took the little nymphomaniac to their bosoms, rallied behind her in outraged chorus over her tragedy, and propagated her "awful disclosures" as truth. They brought her to their pulpits to tell of her ordeals and expose the "filth" of the convent life.

She was not overly pretty, though presentable in her new elegant clothes, and in her nun's costume, sometimes with her bastard baby in her arms, she was appealingly sweet and innocent-looking. She was short and plump, with alluring buxom curves; her face was round and full, but her deep-set little black eyes lay on either side of a heavy, blunt nose. Her sensuous pouting mouth had little forelip and little chin. A deeper look into those dark eyes revealed malevolence, slyness, and greed: the eyes of a cunning gourmandizer and sensualist.

A born exhibitionist, enjoying public adoration, she now was provided with a feeling of respectability and self-value, and had a perfect outlet for her aggressive instincts that pulled her deranged faculties into a more normal pattern. Aggressive psychopaths have frequently been saved from inner disintegration by a righteous crusade. Primitive societies, anthropologists tell us, worship the mentally abnormal person as sacred messenger of the divine spirit, thus providing tolerance via superstition. Even in modern societies such unbalanced types often come to exercise hypnotic power over vast multitudes. In some uncanny way, they strike down through normal reason to powerful subconscious forces. Such inspired characters found religions; they smash saloons; they raid Harpers Ferry; they may even come to rule over whole nations, as Hitler did. The hysterical absorption of great crowds in hate crusades of this type can be explained only by the fact that hate mongers break down normal restraints on such proclivities by providing an apparently harmless and "noble" outlet for desperate submerged forces. Maria was now in the happy state of having her paranoia accepted as normal and praised by the respectable and the elite.

The Catholics issued prompt rebuttals of her *Awful Disclosures,* pinpointing falsehoods, presenting affidavits. Slocum came out with *A Reply to the Priests' Book,* with affidavits obviously *non sequitur* or fraudulent and excerpts from early exposés by writers such as Scippio di Ricci. A book of synthetic illustrations, entitled *Dreadful Scenes in the Awful Disclosures of Maria Monk,* revealed the artist's lascivious imagining of what went on between priests and nuns and how bastard babies were murdered.

A few Protestant ministers remained discreet, a few were even outraged by the fraud. An offer by Brownlee's Protestant Association to send a committee, including Maria Monk, to Montreal to conduct an on-the-spot investigation, was indignantly rejected, but two impartial Protestant ministers of high repute were allowed to look over the Hôtel Dieu establishment. They nosed through it from cellar to garret and announced that it bore no resemblance whatever to the place described by Maria Monk. Slocum retorted hotly that masons and carpenters had altered its appearance. At a public meeting he demanded that he and the rabid anti-Catholic nationalist, Samuel F. B. Morse, be permitted to make an "honest" inspection.

A few people, formerly gullible, were now shaken by doubts. But the great public had taken Maria to their hearts, this pathetic abused child with her poor little baby, and refused to be disillusioned. Other "escaped" nuns began climbing convent fences and regaling the public with spicy tales, at considerable profit to themselves or their ministerial backers. One such imitator of Maria Monk was Millie McPherson, reported to have fled from a Kentucky convent in 1836 to escape the attentions of a priest. Like Maria, she mentioned the name of her would-be seducer; this one was real, and when the *Western Protestant* printed his name, he brought suit for libel and won, although he was awarded only one cent in damages. Millie, seeing she was likely to be in serious trouble, vanished. The *Observer* and *Downfall of Babylon* and other Protestant papers published stories that she had been murdered by priests to prevent her from telling the truth. This was firmly believed by horrified multitudes.

Soon another nun "escaped" from Hôtel Dieu, Saint Frances Patrick, as she called herself. She appeared in New York under the auspices of Samuel B. Smith, editor of the *Downfall of Babylon.* She claimed to have known Maria Monk in the convent and that Maria's account was absolutely authentic, that the convent had since been hurriedly altered. If the Protestant ministers looking it over had opened a certain closet door, they would have discovered two strangled babies.

Smith was trying to shore up his reputation as the leading hate monger. In his *Downfall of Babylon,* started in Philadelphia on the heels of the Ursuline convent burning, he had stated that his publication would "shake the mighty Babylon to her center" with revelations that would make "the darkest night . . . blush, and nature shrink with horror." He had long specialized on bawdy accounts of orgies between priests and nuns. So tremendous was the demand for his sleazy product that he moved the paper to New York. But Brownlee, while not disdaining such salacious material, was more judicious and clever, and his handling of the Maria Monk materials had boosted the *Protestant Vindicator*'s circulation far beyond that of the *Downfall of Babylon.* With Saint Frances, Smith had a chance to regain his share of the limelight. He announced that her "confessions" would run serially in his publication, and he rushed into print a preliminary pamphlet telling of her escape, with an amazing introductory poem about "hotbeds of vice . . . horrible shrieks . . . captives driven from their homes." He told of "immoral convents" with secret tunnels; ergo, Hôtel Dieu had secret tunnels.

Frances' story was called *A Decisive Confirmation of the Awful Disclosures* [of Maria Monk] . . . *and of the Existence of Subterranean Passages.* Saint Frances, a more seductive little trollop than Maria, strutted on lecture platforms and in pulpits, showing her wares and titillating congregations with spicy revelations. So well did she go over that Smith was able to make a deal with Brownlee to have Saint Frances and Maria appear together on platforms.

Saint Frances had never been in the Hôtel Dieu; she had never met Maria before. Both girls knew this, Brownlee and Smith could hardly have been unaware of it, but on the platform the two little exhibitionists would fall into each other's arms, sobbing and gushing as though it were the first time they had seen each other since their convent days, then proceed to tell their open-mouthed audiences of their life together at Hôtel Dieu, the immoralities and rapings to which they and other nuns had been subjected by priests, and the murder of infants. The dual emotions of pity and prurience, with horror piled on thick and heavy, of lust and repulsion and moral indignation, more than satisfied the flushed, lip-licking listeners in God's tabernacles.

When Saint Frances was exposed as a complete phony, Brownlee immediately covered up by saying she had been a paid agent of the Jesuits in order to discredit Maria. Although we now know (from Communist party turncoats) that most renegades are congenital liars and emotionally unstable, often with suicidal tendencies, an aura of authenticity and mysterious know-how clings to such figures. Even after the exposure, Saint Frances and Maria were invited to share the platform. People more or less conceded that the pert Saint Frances was a faker, but not Maria, although the act put on by the two girls was proof that Maria was perfectly willing to be a party to lying and extortion. This made but little dent on the more fanatic ministers and their followers. Gradually Saint Frances was dropped, but Maria continued to be invited to churches up and down the land to recite her shameful tales.

Late in 1836 Colonel William L. Stone, Protestant editor of the New York *Commercial Advertiser,* happened to be in Canada and, though he was a fervent Nationalist and pronounced anti-Catholic, obtained permission to go through Hôtel Dieu. With Maria Monk's book in hand, he went over every inch of the establishment, even inspected a row of basement jars that might possibly contain lime for disposing of infant bodies. He came forth into the sunlight rubbing his brow. Being an honest man, he branded Maria's story false from start to finish.

The rabble rousers subjected him to a ferocious smear campaign. He was "Stone blind," an agent in the pay of the Jesuits. A play was presented ridiculing him. A book-length satiric poem, illustrated with lithographs ("done on Stone"), made fun of his inspection tour with his "magic wand" and his "eagle-eyed efforts" to "find those little bones." The wool had been deftly pulled over his eyes.

*Ladies; the charm has worked; the trials o'er*
*Virgins ye are, as pure as ever before.*

More anti-Stone pamphlets poured out. Brownlee's crowning argument was that Stone could not possibly have done a thorough job of inspection in only three hours.

But Stone's high reputation and his forthright conclusions raised doubts in new quarters, and Protestant ministers began drawing back from the filthy mess. A few even denounced Maria as a rank impostor.

Other sordid details came out when Hoyt, an innate blackmailer, sued Slocum and Maria for a share in the profits from her *Awful Disclosures,* still bringing in big money. Maria and Slocum thereupon brought suit against Harpers' *et al.* However, Bourne held the copyright and contract, and it was so drawn that only he and Harpers' benefited. The court refused to award Maria and Slocum a penny, nor did Bourne offer to split.

Maria cracked under the strain of controversy and from being so much in the public eye, subjected to constant discipline and false posing—or, perhaps, her nymphomaniacal proclivities could no longer be held in leash—and in the midsummer of 1837 she disappeared. After considerable time, she popped up in the home of Dr. W. E. Sleigh in Philadelphia, claiming she had been abducted by six priests and held incommunicado in a Catholic asylum to prevent further disclosures. (Another book by her was in preparation.) She was on the brink again.

William Hogan, an excommunicated priest and rabble rouser, rushed to Sleigh's home and, over the physician's protests, hurried Maria back to New York. Sleigh issued a pamphlet declaring that in her deranged mental condition she was not fit to be at large. At once he was slandered by the hate mongers as a notoriety seeker. Brownlee, who had the most stature of the fanatic band, hotly denounced Sleigh as a greedy, contemptible man out to make money from Maria's misfortune.

Maria's new book *Further Disclosures* was rushed through the presses. It elaborated on her previous experiences and described Nun's Island in the St. Lawrence River, where she claimed nuns from the United States and Canada went to give birth to their illegitimate children, which were then baptized, killed, and buried. Brownlee dressed her up as a nun again, and took her on another round of lectures.

The scandal grew larger in 1838 when Frances and Maria both gave birth to illegitimate children. No one dared claim that Maria's second father was a priest: it had been revealed that the previous year she had run off with another man and had lived with him in a Philadelphia boardinghouse under the name of Jane Howard. Brownlee declared that her immoral conduct and pregnancy were deliberately arranged by the Jesuits in order to discredit her exposures. Her original story was true, he insisted. But she was fast becoming a liability, and even Brownlee was obliged to recognize that Sleigh was right, that Maria was not in a fit mental state to be exhibited at lectures.

Reverend R. J. Breckinridge, a Presbyterian, who poisoned the minds of the people of Baltimore, among other places, for a generation and laid the foundations for some of the most shameful Know-Nothing violence in that city, tried to get into the profitable "escaped nun" act by sponsoring Olivia Neal, who hopped the fence of the Carmelite convent in Baltimore. But it soon became obvious that Olivia was slightly fey. The authorities took charge of her, and competent doctors found her wholly insane. The Nativists, however, propagated the lie—repeated over and over for years—that she had been kidnaped by priests. Great mobs menaced the convent.

But Breckinridge had his established rackets and his hate organ *The Baltimore Literary and Religious Magazine.* Also he gained some reputation for his book *Papism in the United States in the Nineteenth Century.* Above all, he was one of the most tremendous orators of his times.

When the Olivia business blew up in his face, he flitted down to Richmond to give a series of anti-Papal sermons, and all the ministers in that city joined in a vote of heartfelt thanks that, through his sole efforts, their city had been "saved from Popery." Although knowing this meant war with the Catholics, he steamed up the American Bible Society to put Bibles into every school in America. His oratory was in such demand that he was invariably asked to give an anti-Popery sermon at each meeting of the National Presbyterian Assembly. Some years after this he persuaded the Assembly to denounce the validity of Catholic baptism by an overwhelming vote. Soon after the Olivia debacle, he got into another jam when he accused an almshouse keeper of conducting a "Papal prison" and was put under arrest when the latter sued. He escaped only because of a hung jury. But for years he was closely affiliated with Brownlee's Protestant Reformation Society, the *Protestant Vindicator,* and the whole Bourne-Brownlee clique of rabble rousers.

Brownlee had finally given up all hope of reconditioning Maria. In 1840 he tried to publish the memoirs of a third escaped nun from Hôtel Dieu but by then the sands of credulity had run out. Some years would have to slip by before a new crop of escaped-nun hoaxes could be foisted on the public.

Maria married; either she was committing bigamy or she had lied about her previous marriage. By this time she was a complete alcoholic, and this and her freakish hallucinations caused her husband to desert her. Some years later she came into the limelight again when arrested for picking the pocket of her companion in a Five Points whore house. She died in prison.

Her whole life was a pathetic confusion, although not without its brief days of distorted glory. The real prostitutes, beyond the reach of the law, were the ministers of the gospel who exploited her physical and mental abnormalities so unscrupulously.

Such was the pitiful end of the angel of the Protestant churches. Such is the story of the "Uncle Tom's Cabin of Know-Nothingism." It had stirred the whole country to hate and violence. *Awful Disclosures,* product of the disordered brain of a whore and the schemes of unprincipled religious demagogues, sold more than three hundred thousand copies prior to the Civil War. Even in 1874, when another edition appeared, Maria's name was still a rallying cry among the ignorant, and her daughter (who ironically became a Catholic) capitalized on it by writing her autobiography.

In 1916, the volatile Georgia Populist, hate monger, Jew and Negro baiter, Tom Watson, in *Watson's Magazine* took up the cudgels once more to prove that Maria had told the truth. He published affidavits by old men who declared that secret passages really had existed at Hôtel Dieu. Tom Watson was the man who the year before had stirred up a great wave of anti-Semitism, which had led mobs against the governor of the state and had brought about the lynching of an innocent Jew, framed for rape, Leo Frank.

*The Menace,* the notorious anti-Catholic sheet of Girard, Kansas, which during the same period reached a 2,000,000 circulation, also found gold in Maria Monk's stale tale. For half a century and more her falsehoods poisoned the minds of millions; even today her ghost has not been wholly laid.

But although the Protestant clergy, who had swallowed the baited hoax hook, line, and sinker, were at long last glad to drop Maria Monk—indeed, they disliked to hear her name mentioned—the demagogues soon found new ways to wheedle money for the great crusade. By then the politicians were beginning to perceive there was gold in them thar hills. The Know-Nothing movement was well on its way.

CHAPTER IV

# THE FLAG JOINS THE CRUSADE

ANXIETY over possible Catholic control of the new West was stirred up by Lyman Beecher and Samuel F. B. Morse. This political twist, added to the rumpus over convent immoralities, gave the crusade a flag-waving character. Politicians were quick to see that religious prejudice was a strong lever for gaining office and preferment.

Here was the beginning of a long period of ugly intolerance. It was a culmination, in similar virulent form, of the religious struggle in England centuries before and of New England's ecclesiastical totalitarianism that had ruled for more than a century, at times with sadistic cruelty.

United States culture was largely of British origin, colonial settlement a process in the imperialistic, religious, and trade rivalry of England and Spain—a cold war that had endured two hundred years. Early New World beliefs, distorted by war propaganda, were tinged with deep fears of Roman Catholicism. Few New Englanders had ever laid eyes on a flesh-and-blood Catholic, but this distortion echoed in colonial writings for a hundred years and more. Now, actually seeing priests, churches, and worshipers, Protestant Americans were preconditioned to hate and to persecute to a degree beyond what the intrusion of different ideas and customs would normally have provoked. Anti-foreignism, too, was deeply rooted in colonial life and legislation: exclusion and non-residence laws, alien laws, vagrancy laws, religious and property restrictions on suffrage.

Thus Know-Nothingism represented the latest despairing upsurge of religious, racist, anti-foreign bigotry, feelings now intensified by the tide of immigration so disturbing to the ignorant provincialism that long had held sway. The struggle took on aspects of tribal Mohammedan fanaticism—death to the foreigner and the Catholic "infidel." This linking of religious bigotry with anti-foreignism proved a gold mine of profit and power for propagandists and unscrupulous politicians. It was distressing that men of the stature of Beecher and Morse were among the prime instigators of such ignoble passions.

This, of course, was merely one phase of Nativism—a deep-rooted aversion for everything that did not fit into the pattern of American life as conceived by men of rigid provincial concepts, who, lacking in historical, scientific, or social knowledge, considered everything different to be both inferior and a menace. A blind patriotism of frightening emotional power went lumbering and glowering across the fair American land. The underlying principle of Nativism was exclusiveness and hatred of everything non-conformist, within, without. It stood for the *status quo,* considering every change dangerous and diabolical. It represented futile security seeking—the belief that safety lies in rigidity and changelessness. Actually, the oxygen of all social life is evolutionary adjustment.

America was settled by insular-minded people, and it took more than a century for their thinking to acquire continental dimensions, just as today it will probably take that much time or longer for us to adjust to world dimensions. Terrified by the open spaces at their doorsteps, the early settlers tried to re-create the snug elbow-rubbing conditions of the tight little isle they had left by shutting out the darkness of the wilderness, like fearful children drawing the curtains at night. For a time all new settlements westward were sternly prohibited partly because of this fear, partly to maintain ecclesiastical despotism and prevent the escape of dissidents and non-conformists. It took some years of cautious, clever two-faced negotiations by Reverend Thomas Hooker before he could gain permission to leave Cambridge and settle his flock in the Connecticut Valley. In England the New World originally was pictured alternately as a paradise and as a horrible realm of murkiness, filled with monsters and menace. This distorted concept of the wilderness to the west was long perpetuated by the seaboard colonists. It was still easy, therefore, for demagogues to instill in easterners credence in the newly added horror of hoofs-and-horns Catholicism out West.

The fears had been mushrooming for some time. As early as 1830, "Philathes" of Hartford, Connecticut, in *An Exposition of the Roman Catholic Religion,* had warned that Rome had chosen not New England but the Mississippi Valley as the grand theater of her operations and future power. In its fourth issue, January 23, 1830, the starkly anti-Papist magazine, *The Protestant,* spoke of two European seminaries set up "to train up, multiply, and support Jesuit Priests and Teachers to enter the valley of the Mississippi." The King of Bavaria, a Papist, had become "the head of an association to diffuse the religion of Rome in this country." Vienna, the metropolis of a Popish imperialism, and Papist France "were united in the project." July 23, 1832, a western minister sounded the same alarm in the Cincinnati *Journal.* The whole Mississippi Valley had been "mapped out as well as surveyed by the emissaries of the Vatican; and Cardinals were exulting in the hope of enriching the Papal States by accessions in the United States."

Returning from Europe, Samuel Morse, Jedidiah's oldest son, took up anti-Catholic propaganda in conjunction with his younger brothers, who had been successfully publishing the New York *Observer* since 1823. Sensitive, a badly adjusted soul with extraordinary imagination, several times Morse had run away from school back to Father Jedidiah because of homesickness. A student at Andover, a rock of religious reaction, and a graduate of Yale (1810), he was fond of Chaucer, Spencer, Dante, and Tasso, but his great interest was painting. After clerking for a year in a Charlestown bookstore, he studied art in Europe from 1811–13, where he won attention and honors, particularly for a painting of Hercules, a choice of subject that may have indicated some hidden yearning. He brought back to the United States French daguerreotype photography and set up the first studio. He also founded and became the first president of the National Academy of Design. A truly fine artist—forgotten now because of his invention of the telegraph and Morse code—he painted remarkably good portraits of prominent people, including Lafayette, President James Monroe, and Eli Whitney. He experimented with new ways of mixing pigments, even using milk and beer, and developed a method of printing maps by letter press without engraving, but he became badly soured by a failure to win a commission to paint murals in Washington and increasingly despondent over American indifference to art—even as are artists today.

On a second tour of Europe, during the Rome Holy Year celebrations of 1830, he enjoyed the elaborate pageantry, but when the Papal procession went by and he failed to remove his hat, a soldier rushed at him with angry contorted face and knocked it off with his bayonet. Already deeply prejudiced against Catholicism by his father, Morse's last shred of tolerance was knocked out of him by this personal indignity. In the *Protestant Banner,* with vast resentment, he told about the soldier's "curses and taunts . . . the expression of a demon in his countenance."

In 1834, in twelve letters in the *Observer,* entitled "A Foreign Conspiracy Against the Liberties of the United States" and signed "Brutus," Morse "exposed" European Catholic missionary societies—particularly the Austrian Leopoldine Society—as masking plots by Old World tyrannies, the Holy Alliance crowd, to overthrow American republican government by planting "Jesuit-controlled" immigrants at strategic points in the West to be ready for *Der Tag* when they would rise up and seize the entire Mississippi Valley, then march on Washington and spread the faith by fire, sword, and a new inquisition.

Actually the Leopoldine Society (named in honor of Archduchess Leopoldine, Empress of Brazil) had been started by Frederick Rese, vicar general of Cincinnati Diocese, during a brief trip to Europe in the hope of getting aid for struggling churches and missions on the frontier. Another American prelate had set up the Society for the Propagation of the Faith in Lyons, France. These organizations were no different, except for denomination, from Protestant societies set up in England to aid frontier religion and the conversion of Indians. The first of these, inspired in the sixteenth century by Reverend John Eliot, the Massachusetts "Apostle to the Indians," still operates. The earliest New England missionary society to turn "the wilderness into the Garden of God" was started in 1802.

At the time of Morse's bitter attack, it had been some years since the Leopoldine Society had sent over anything—meager amounts at best. All told, the Lyons society over the years had contributed a total of merely $17,000, only part of which had gone to the West, a sum scarcely sufficient to menace the foundations of the republic.

Morse suppressed these facts and blew the bubble of fear up to bursting point. He pleaded for Protestants to lay aside their sectarian feuds and awake to the dreadful menace, unite against Catholic schools, throw out all Catholic office holders, and put an end to lenient immigration and naturalization laws. "Stop the leak in the ship through which muddy waters from without threaten to sink us." His letters were issued in book form and went into five editions.

In 1835 he published a new series, "Immigrant Dangers to the Free Institutions of the United States through Foreign Immigration," this time in the *Journal of Commerce.* These, too, had a wide sale in book form. He enlarged on the "Catholic plot" to seize the West, in still more lurid colors. The Jesuits were rapidly fastening "their chains" on "a sleeping victim"—America. "Will you longer be deceived by the pensioned Jesuits who have surrounded your press, are now using it all over the country to stifle cries of danger and lull your fears . . . ? Up! Up! I beseech you, Awake! To your posts! Fly to protect the vulnerable places of our Constitution and laws. Place your guards! You will need them, and quickly, too. And first shut the gates."

A student, Lewis Clausing, showed up at Morse's home with a manuscript telling of the Jesuit plot to conquer America. Plagued by a guilt complex from having killed an opponent in a duel, Clausing had become a paranoid suffering from delusions of persecution. Shaking like a leaf, he told Morse that the Jesuits were trying to kill him. He saw Jesuit spies under every bed, just as Cotton Mather saw black cats and devils in that same old-maid horror den. Morse hid Clausing in his house, but the terrified student took his own life. Morse published his manuscript as *The Proscribed German Student; Being a Sketch of Some Interesting Incidents in the Life and Death of Lewis Clausing; to Which Is Added, a Treatise on the Jesuits, a Posthumous Work of Lewis Clausing* (1836). Morse admitted that Clausing had become unbalanced, but claimed it was wholly due to treatment he had received in his youth at the hands of the Jesuits and did not detract from the truth of his revelations.

The following year, Morse made green hay out of current tawdry sensationalism, the craving for "confession books," by bringing out *The Confessions of a French Priest* as a "warning to the people of the United States." Jesuit-plot books, emphasizing Catholic schemes for western conquest, now appeared like a rash on the Protestant press publication lists.

Morse's chief coworker in the anti-Jesuit attack was Lyman Beecher, who had gone to Ohio to head up Lane Seminary, with the sole purpose—he claimed—of combating the designs of Rome in that area. There, the father of Harriet Beecher Stowe had suppressed all discussion of the slavery issue, which so incensed the students that most of them walked out and formed a new college—Oberlin.

Beecher's *Plea for the West* (1835), though less sensational than Morse's books, had a big vogue. It was a compilation of his lectures up and down the Atlantic seaboard sounding the alarm and collecting money for Protestant missions and schools "to save the West from the Jesuits and immigrants." Nearly all immigrants were "agents of Rome" and of "despotic Old World nations" trying "to stamp out American republicanism." The greatest danger lay in Catholic schools, designed primarily to win Protestant converts and thereby gain control of the country.

"It is plain that the political destiny of our nation is to be decided in the West." There would be "decided the fate of the free institutions and liberties" of the entire world. In any case, the newcomers were "unacquainted with our institutions, unaccustomed to self-government, irrecessible [*sic*] to education, and easily acceptable to prepossession and inveterate credulity and intrigue and easily embodied and wielded by Jesuit design."

The truth was that a majority of the German immigrants were Lutherans or Free Thinkers, more hostile to the Catholic Church than the Nativists, a matter of grievous complaint on the part of many Catholic spokesmen. Actually less than a fifth of all immigrants were Catholics, and most of them were trying to escape from poverty and tyranny: the Irish from feudal alien landlord rule and British bayonets, the Germans from serfdom and religious persecutions and petty wars. Nor did Beecher's thesis—generally held by Know-Nothings, then and later—that all immigrants were dumb driven cattle and tools of alien designs hold water. The Germans had a high percentage of literacy. By 1851 there were one hundred and fifty German-language newspapers in the country, nearly all of them Abolitionist and favoring political and social reform. Both Germans and Irish were more politically minded, more insistent on exercising their electoral rights, and more vociferous about all human rights, than were many native Americans. The newcomers were seeking freedom. As *Chambers Edinburgh Journal* put it a few years after this hullabaloo over Jesuit plots, "The one great cause" of emigration "is the desire for political and religious freedom . . . the young, the restless, and the imaginative thirst for the ideal freedom, and many seek for the realization of utopia in America."

But for Beecher and Morse and the growing crowd of Nativists, all foreigners came as secret emissaries "of a religion which has always sustained thrones and been sustained by them . . . in all ages found in the ranks of despotism." Morse raked up bloody tales about the Inquisition, but did not mention that English Protestants had set up the brutal Cromwell despotism (which the Irish remembered more bitterly than anybody) or that the British were currently supporting reactionary monarchy; that England, and no Catholic power, had tried to destroy the United States in 1812 and had burned the national capitol. He insisted that the vast majority of new immigrants "were under the direction of the feudal potentates of Europe, associated to put down at home and abroad the liberal institutions of the world." He called upon his readers not to shut their eyes and stop their ears "and cry Peace, while destruction is coming."

Not everybody saw it this way, then or later. One Virginia clergyman, perhaps an apologist for slavery (quoted by James P. Hambleton in his *Political Campaign in Virginia*), viewed the whole anti-foreign anti-Catholic propaganda as "a piece of cold cautious Yankee cunning" to blind southern eyes. The real traitors were "not foreigners but men born and living where Hull and Arnold were born and resided. Their treason is deep, diabolical, and meditated for a long time."

In every age and clime the assimilation and adjustment of new peoples in an alien land have created problems, often not resolved for centuries. Acceptance, toleration, fair play are long delayed. The many centuries of European ghettos, of Jim Crowism in the South, attest to the sad fact that integration, although eventually inevitable, is an even more disturbing process, especially for the ignorant. When nationality, religion, race, folkways differ, all the herd instincts and fears are aroused, and peoples become the prey of facile-tongued racists and chauvinists who easily stir them to stamp out by violence what they do not understand. As the Irish poet Yeats once remarked, "Tie a red rag to a gull's leg, and the other gulls of the flock will tear him to pieces." Actually most "American-born" westerners did not share the anti-foreign alarm of eastern-seaboard demagogues—although later it was stirred up—but were clamoring for more, not less, immigration, since there were an abundance of land and serious labor shortages everywhere. Workers were needed for public improvements, building railroads, canals, roads, homes, and churches on a far-reaching scale.

There were as yet few Catholics in the new West. Congregationalist, Presbyterian, Methodist, and Baptist preachers, subsidized by New England, rampaged up and down the rivers, forests, and lakes, barging into gambling joints and saloons, and fighting each other with almost blasphemous language, even raising mobs to attack and burn each other's establishments. But nearly all the busy western divines echoed the line against the Papist menace, especially the militant Campbellites, a new faction strong everywhere in the West. Carry Nation's grandfather and father were Campbellites. Stories were spread that Catholics were storing arms and powder in the churches. The Protestants certainly were, for protection against Indians and marauders, but the Catholics were accused of preparing to overthrow the government.

Morse and Beecher soon had a host of imitators. Respectable newspapers such as the Cincinnati *Gazette* and the Detroit *Journal* took up the cudgels against local Catholics and their schools.

In Hartford, Connecticut, Reverend Horace Bushnell of North Church ranted against "slavery, infidelity, and Popery," charging that "Catholic emigrants are pouring into the country. . . . Every one of them and their descendants are meant to be our enemies, and most of them probably will be." Reverend W. W. Turner warned the American Education Society, meeting in Enfield, Connecticut, of the strenuous efforts in the West to convert the country to the Roman Catholic faith. The "beast" was pushing across the prairies. "Foreign missionaries annually sent across the ocean were well trained in schools of European learning and unsurpassed by any individuals on earth for wily and deceitful policy." Samuel B. Smith popped into this arena also: his *Downfall of*

*Babylon* sheet and his book, *Flight of Popery from Rome to the West,* spine-tingled with the menace.

The South, too, was in danger! When Bishop John England set up a school in Charleston for Negro slaves, the fanatics raised a hue and cry that it was part of a vast secret plot between Catholics and Negroes to murder all white Protestants, and it had to be closed.

Soon Protestant missionary societies, whose organs bristled with sensational anti-Catholic items, began collecting more money; preachers and teachers were rushed West to disseminate anti-Papist propaganda. Nothing was more effective for stimulating contributions than keeping a fire built under every Catholic barn dance. The *Home Missionary* editorialized about the great battle "between truth and error" being fought out in the West—the battle between "law and anarchy, between Christianity and her Sabbaths, her ministry and schools on the one hand, and the combined forces of Infidelity and Popery on the other." The *Western Messenger* gloomily reported that the West was "fast becoming the Pope's heritage" and would "soon be all under his thumb."

The spores of hate and suspicion cast abroad by Beecher, Morse, *et al.,* bore fruit in 1834 in the formation of the New York Protestant Association to show how "the knowledge of Gospel truth" was "inconsistent with the tenets and dogma of Popery." A March 13, 1835, meeting in Broadway Hall—"Is Popery Compatible with Civil Liberty?"—broke up in a free-for-all when a group of Catholics forced their way in. The clergy on the platform fled amid the crash of breaking lights and benches. Although the Catholic clergy condemned this, the Association triumphantly hailed it as proof of dangerous Romish aggressiveness.

By this time the new over-all Protestant Reformation Society, a united front against the menace, headed by Maria Monk profiteer George Bourne, was sending out a swarm of ministerial agents on barnstorming tours, who won large audiences, even at Harvard and Princeton, and secured subscriptions for the rabid *Protestant Vindicator.* Collections in churches paid all expenses and provided funds to print millions of pamphlets and books denouncing Catholics and the foreign menace. In 1835 Robert J. Breckinridge aroused the General Presbyterian Assemblies, meeting in Philadelphia, to put him in charge of a special committee to deal with the "prevalence of Popery in the West." His first report denounced the Pope as "Anti-Christ, a man of sin and son of Pestilence," an "apostate from God" corrupted by "profane exorcisms, idolatrous incantations, and unauthorized additions, mutilations, and ceremonies."

This new success in Pope baiting was partly owing to the stress on political dangers. But in order to convince wealthier church members, from whom the largest contributions could be obtained, the argument now ran that the purpose was to "save" not "exterminate" Catholics. Morse, of course, wished them exterminated, but Beecher graciously declared they had a right to exist and enjoy equal rights. Brownlee himself, though so rabid, drew in his horns, especially after his Maria Monk swindle collapsed, and followed the "new line" of saving Catholic souls. To his surprise, he found it more profitable. Using one of his pathological arson metaphors, he stated, "I do not persecute them . . . [except] as I would persecute my neighbor . . . fast asleep in the bed . . . his house on fire . . . by rushing through the flames and dragging him, his wife and little ones . . . to a place of safety."

Yet even this type of preaching was still virulent enough to cause violence, riots, and church burning, and plenty of wilder dervishes were still abroad. Posters on churches and halls continued to flaunt the old sensationalism:

CELIBACY OF PRIESTS AND NUNS EXPOSED

THE GHOSTLY TYRANNY

MONASTERIES, NUNNERIES, AND NATIONS
CONVERTED INTO ONE VAST BROTHEL

PROOFS! HISTORICAL FACTS!

But the nobler slogan of "Snatch sinful souls from the burning" paid off well. By 1840 all important Protestant churches had been won over to the anti-Papal crusade, Presbyterians, Congregationalists, Methodists, Lutherans, Dutch Reformists, Episcopalians, and Baptists. Only among Presbyterians did the stand create a crisis—100,000 members had to be purged—but otherwise, by the end of the decade, a solid Protestant church front was presented to "the menace." The "New Reformation" was roaring on its way.

Political action became organized as early as 1835. On March 27, perhaps as a result of the Broadway Hall riot (plus "Whig trickery"), a caucus of "American-born citizens" met in New York City's Fourteenth Ward to name independent candidates. Another ward followed suit. The nominees were endorsed by the Whigs also. They denounced foreign interference at the polls.

In June, James Watson Webb, editor of the New York *Courier and Inquirer,* a fervent Nativist, called a city-wide caucus of "strictly American citizens." The Revolutionary War veterans were eulogized and their replacement in appointed office by the "clannish Irish" was bitterly condemned. Since most Revolutionary War veterans by then were well over seventy, the number of replacements could not have been large. But it was "*Resolved,* that we as Americans will never consent to allow the government established by our Revolutionary Forefathers to pass into the hands of foreigners."

At a meeting the following month, the Native American Democratic Association was organized, headed by James O. Pond, and the *Spirit of '76* started as its official organ to oppose foreigners and Catholics in office, push for laws to halt "pauper and criminal" immigration, and extend the naturalization period to twenty-one years. Organizations were set up in most wards, and a 5,000-name petition was rushed to Congress. Similar associations were formed in New Jersey, Cincinnati, Philadelphia, and smaller communities.

The upper South boiled with new Nativist groups. In New Orleans, a Native American Association was set up in

1835, but as in subsequent organizations of this type in Louisiana—except for minor factions—the anti-Catholic bias was omitted. "There are too many around here to fight them," remarked one leader years later, defending himself against recrimination by the national Know-Nothing order. By 1837 a national organization—the North American Association, was effected in Washington, D. C., and various Native American publications were started.

In the New York City 1835 fall elections, the Whigs lay low, putting up no candidates, and a full Nativist slate, headed by James Monroe (nephew of the former president) for Congress, was presented. A leading backer was probably Alexander Hamilton, Jr., although his name does not figure as an officer until 1838. Novelist James Fenimore Cooper called foreigners excessive drunkards who controlled American seaports and influenced diplomatic appointments.

The Democrats won, but the Nativist vote was impressive, and one Brooklyn assemblyman was elected. Other Nativist tickets were presented elsewhere in the state and in the country with scattered successes.

Many prominent papers, viz., the reactionary Hartford *Courant,* supported the new movement, hewing to deep-rooted American prejudices, above all fear of foreigners. Yet the 1790 United States census showed that 98 per cent of Connecticut's population was of English stock, with a few Scots. There were not enough Irish, Dutch, and French in the state to make a good-sized village, and by mid-1835 there were still few foreigners. For three generations Connecticut, extremist defender of a dying order—specifically "the Standing Order"—bitterly hated all manifestations of Jeffersonianism and democracy and loathed the foreigners in their midst. It was governed by a Congregational-commercial aristocracy more British than British and, according to John Adams, was rigidly ruled by not more than twelve families; as Aaron Burr said, "We might as soon attempt to revolutionize the kingdom of heaven" as to hope for political liberation in such a state—not that Connecticut was heaven.

However, dissent was not lacking. The Democratic

Hartford *Times* (June 13, 27, 1835), stated: "The idea of an American party, exclusive of foreigners who have been naturalized, may suit the contracted understandings and narrow prejudices of the supporters of the Alien Laws but no true friend of the country." The paper denounced "the invidious line" that set up the native-born American as "ruler and superior." "Welcome, thrice welcome to our land the children of every clime—and as for the politicians who . . . dead to the spirit of freedom, refuse the blessings of liberty to those who ask it—indignation and wrath, tribulation and anguish be their portion. . . . For any native . . . at this date . . . to attempt to deprive an *adopted* citizen of the rights he has acquired on our terms, without having committed any crime is horrible, is unholy and unjust, and whoever or whatever party does this, will in the end reap bitter fruits of repentance."

The early 1836 New York City Native American ticket was headed by Samuel F. B. Morse for mayor. His rabid views were beyond question, but he was a Van Buren Democrat, and the Whigs, unable to swallow him, put up their own candidate, so he received only 2,000 votes, and the Democratic candidate was elected by a huge majority; but the Native American-Whig coalition gained control of the city council and so was able to cut off all patronage to naturalized citizens and Catholics.

This toehold, the chance to put followers on the pay roll, gave Nativism an impetus, especially as the 1837 depression filled the cities with hungry unemployed, and the foreigner could be pictured as a hairy monster taking the bread out of the mouths of honest "Anglo-Saxon mechanics" and their families. In February occurred the terrible flour riots, led by John Windt of the Working Man's party. Nativist publications, the *Native American,* the *Crisis,* etc., tried to rouse native American workmen against foreign elements. For labor—politically conscious since the organization of the Working Man's party in Philadelphia in 1828—this was sadly divisive. The party had made its entree into New York City in 1829 with the help of such utopians as Robert Dale Owen,

Thomas Skidmore, Fanny Wright, and George H. Evans. But now, under the lash of depression, the Nativists made considerable inroads into labor ranks.

Depression jimjams appeared everywhere, and the Nativist fervor hit Boston again. On June 11, 1837, a fire engine ran into an Irish funeral procession. The resulting "Broad Street riot" involved 15,000 bawling, brawling so-called humans. The Irish quarter was sacked, with many casualties.

In New York the Democratic party, under the stress of hard times, split badly. Five thousand seceders, many former members of the Working Man's party, gathered to protest boss rule. Tammany thugs cut the hall lights, but the audience, prepared for this, produced new long-burning locofoco (phosphorous head) matches. Thereby the Locofoco (Equal Rights) party was born, with fighting support from the New York *Evening Post*. As a result of the Democratic schism, the Nativist ticket (actually a Nativist-Whig coalition), headed by Aaron Clark for mayor, was swept into office. Nativist victories were chalked up in other communities, particularly in Pennsylvania, and a few Nativists were sent to Congress.

More pressure was put on Congress to pass anti-immigration and anti-Catholic laws. A special Congressional committee, stacked with pro-Nativists, reported favorably on an immigration-restriction bill, warning of efforts of European despots to stamp out American Republicans by means of immigrant agents, but it was laid aside on the pretext of more urgent business.

For several years thereafter, the New York Nativists accepted Whig leadership and were relatively quiescent, except for petitions to Congress about "ignorant and lawless aliens." However, the movement grew in the back counties and spread south and west. By 1839 many Native American associations had been set up. The New Orleans Association, particularly active, issued an "Address" to the public in 1839 about "the hordes and hecatombs of beings in human form, but destitute of an intellectual apparatus—the outcast and offal of society, the pauper, the vagrant, and the convict—transported in myriads to our shores, reeking with the accumulated crimes of a whole civilized and savage world." How could these vile creatures be given "equal rights, immunities, and privileges with the noble native inhabitants of the United States?" Smugness had become a disease.

By 1841, New Orleans' mental hooligans organized the American Republican party, which had considerable influence in the elections and was able to get the state legislature to petition Congress to extend the naturalization period to twenty-one years. This party spread to St. Louis, Lexington, Philadelphia, and finally completed the circle back to New York.

In all instances restrictions on immigration and citizenship were stressed, as were the exclusion of all but native Protestant Americans from office, the preventing of the union of church and state, and the preservation of the Bible as a school textbook. "No alien spiritual power" should be allowed to "encroach on the institutions of our country."

The Bible in New York City schools and elsewhere flamed into a hot issue in 1840, although it had been simmering for ten years. In 1831 the New York Common Council had granted money to a Protestant orphan society out of educational funds. Fiery Bishop Hughes demanded a proportionate share for Catholic institutions, was ignored, and widened his attack to the Public School Society, denouncing its use of public monies for sectarian education that forced Catholic students to submit to compulsory Protestant Bible reading, services, and textbooks.

The Public School Society, controlled by Protestants, particularly Methodists, maintained more than one hundred schools, mostly with state and municipal tax money, over which it had a monopoly. The Catholics counted this as discrimination. The King James Bible was an obligatory textbook; Protestant prayers and services were also obligatory, and the textbooks blatantly anti-Catholic. When a teacher whipped a Catholic child for refusing to read the King James

Bible and the child was expelled, the cup of bitterness for both sides ran over.

*Samuel Putnam's Reader* spoke of John Huss, "zealous reformer from Popery," burned at the stake after "trusting himself to deceitful Catholics." This was true enough, but not historically poised. New York City *Reader No. 3* contained an imaginary conversation between Hernando Cortez and William Penn, who reproached the Spanish conquistador for broiling the feet of Emperor Cuatemotzin. It was no bed of roses, as Cuatemotzin himself reportedly told Cortez. That Puritans had also tortured, scalped, and treacherously murdered Indians and stolen their lands did not get into the texts. Actually the Spaniards, for all their cruelties, had tried to convert the Indians; the northerners, with exceptions, had displayed their superior Christianity by exterminating them. The *School Ecclesiastical History* by C. A. Goodrich was largely devoted to the crimes of Catholicism; of course nothing was said of the lashing, branding, and eye gouging used by Bishop Laud of England and early American Puritans. The book denounced "Romish missions" and presented biblical prophecy to establish that the Catholic was "a man of sin . . . of Iniquity," that this "son of perdition" would be overthrown. Thus, the textbooks echoed the myths and falsehoods concocted by the English as anti-Spanish propaganda centuries earlier. American patriots had reverted to the proscriptive policies, cruelties, and coercions of Dictator Cromwell, the catch-poll constables and Star Chamber attitudes of Bishop Laud.

The conflict came to the boiling point when Whig Governor William H. Seward took a hand. Young Seward was a strange choice for the reactionary Whig party, for he was a thoroughgoing Jeffersonian, but his casual manner, twinkling eyes, and unruly hair had great appeal for the voters. He was demanding that the Whigs cut loose from the great landed patroons, the Livingstons and Van Rensselaers and their lawyers, and become the party of the people. He believed that democracy included all people, all races, Negroes and whites, all creeds. Unlike most men in his party, he welcomed immigrants, insisted that they share political and religious freedom, that non-sectarian schools be established for all children.

In his January, 1840, message he deplored the enormous number of children, especially in New York City, who were deprived of an education because of the sectarian schools and racial prejudices. How could foreign-born children become good citizens if left without schooling? New York City's Catholic population numbered 70,000, and he advocated using public funds so as to include "teachers speaking the same language . . . and professing the same faith" as the children.

On the strength of his proposals, Catholic churches operating parochial schools petitioned the Common Council for a fair share of the state school funds administered by that body. No mention was made of local funds. The battle was joined.

"Save the Bible! Save the schools! Save the children!" became the cry. The New York Methodists launched a bitter counterattack, charging that the Catholic Bible called for submission to Papal authority and sanctioned murdering heretics. Reverend Hiram Ketchum, head of the American Bible Society—which Jedidiah Morse had helped found and which had been bedeviling the Catholics for a decade or more—flew to the barricades. He had been making a concerted drive throughout the country to oblige all schools to adopt the King James Bible as a textbook but had refused to accept contributions to send Bibles to Negroes. At this juncture he declared that the Protestant Bible was "peculiarly appropriate for the common schools," and to exclude it would be "a hazard to our civil and religious liberties."

Thus the Protestant press confused the issue, which was not one of exclusion of the Bible—the Catholics never demanded that; they merely opposed compulsory acceptance, with lay interpretation, of the Protestant Bible by *all* pupils and specifically by Catholic pupils. The Protestant press declared that the Catholics were "trying to shut out the light of divine revelation."

The Catholics certainly had reason to argue that the Bible was not a proper public-school text; parts were of questionable taste; some of it immoral, at least by standards then actually or assertedly prevalent; and much of it unintelligible to smaller children. The Protestants declared that the Roman Catholic Church wanted people kept "ignorant and illiterate," berating the Catholics for failing to educate children while denying them the means to do so. With considerable justification, the Protestants considered Catholic education to be suspect—that chiefly it was designed to control rather than enlighten the minds of followers. That the Protestants were also sinning in this same direction did not occur to them. "Give them [the Catholics] funds now controlled by Republicans [read Protestants]?" For what purpose? To train the children to worship "a ghostly monarchy of vicars, bishops, archbishops, cardinals, and Popes! . . . Take away our children's funds and bestow them on the . . . creatures of a foreign hierarchy!" New anti-Catholic publications mushroomed from Texas to Maine.

After acrimonious debate, the Catholic petition was voted down by the Common Council. Bishop Hughes drafted a revised version, with pointed attacks on the falsehoods of Protestant teachings in the pseudo-public schools that were "poisoning" the minds of Catholic children. He cited the texts by name and page and contended that only by obtaining an equitable share of tax money—the Catholics were also taxpayers—could the Catholics also put up independent schools and protect their children from such lies. He held protest meetings, and the uneasy Common Council called for public hearings on October 29.

All the bigots of educational monopoly were present. Hughes, the sole Catholic representative, spoke for three hours to a packed antagonistic audience. Lucidly, if overheatedly, he presented the Catholic position. He tongue-lashed the Methodists for their misrepresentations and offered to bet a thousand dollars they could not prove their charge that the Catholic Bible sanctioned the killing of heretics. The *Observer* and other Protestant publications sternly reminded the bishop that there was a New York law against betting.

In rebuttal, the Protestant emissaries, spearheaded by lawyer Theodore Sedgewick and Hiram Ketchum, used up two day-long sessions attacking Hughes' position. Leading Methodist, Presbyterian, and Reformed Dutch divines spoke their pieces at great length. All were loudly applauded. One preacher declared that rather than become a member of the Roman Catholic Church, with its "entire system of Popery . . . its idolatry, superstition, and violent opposition to the Holy Bible," he would prefer to remain an infidel.

Violence ensued, and this time the Catholics were clearly the chief sinners. They broke up meetings held by the Public School Society and by Brownlee, intemperate acts that outraged many neutral and reasonable persons. The New York *Herald,* the ultra Whig paper edited by the arch-reactionary James Gordon Bennett, but hitherto rather impartial, came out against the Catholic school demands, as did the *Commercial Advertiser* (Stone) and the *Journal of Commerce,* both strongly Nativist anyhow. Once more the Council turned down the Catholic petition.

Protestant animosity flared anew when Governor Seward's 1841 message again backed the Catholic position. Twenty thousand children, he pointed out, were being deprived of school by the intolerance of the Public School Society's teaching. "I seek the education of [these children] . . . not to perpetuate any prejudices or distinctions which deprive them of instruction, but in disregard of all such distinctions and prejudices. I solicit their education less from sympathy than because the welfare of the state demands it and cannot dispense with it."

At once Hughes petitioned again, this time the state legislature, for an equitable apportionment of educational funds. The matter was referred to Secretary of State and Superintendent of Common Schools John C. S. Spencer. His report advocated abolition of the Public School Society and the establishment of a bona-fide public-school system under elected commissioners in each ward to administer the school funds. This, he claimed, would protect minority elements against undesired sectarian instruction. How it would protect Protestant children in overwhelmingly Catholic wards, or vice versa, he did not elucidate. But at any rate it would end a city-wide monopoly by a single prejudiced body.

In the fight to block the secretary's proposal for a new school law, the *Observer* printed a frightful Bill of Excommunication allegedly directed against Reverend William Hogan of Philadelphia (prelate of the Philadelphia cathedral during a controversy over trustee versus bishop ownership—that was before he turned renegade and "rescued" Maria Monk). Copies were placed on the desk of every legislator. It frightened the lawmakers—Democrats and Whigs—into postponing decision. Not for years was it discovered that the entire excommunication text was fictional, copied verbatim out of Sterne's *Tristram Shandy*. Failure to recognize its source suggested that the legislators themselves could do with more and better education. Senator Joe McCarthy couldn't have done a neater job of falsification.

The furor spread across the country. New Protestant defense and propaganda societies, similar to those started by Morse, sprang up everywhere. In Philadelphia they were numbered by scores, but finally merged into the Union of Protestant Associations.

In New York City, Morse was again launched by the Nativists—the Democratic American Association—as candidate for mayor. But on election morning the papers published a fraudulent letter saying he was withdrawing from the race, so he polled only 77 votes, his fellow candidates only a few hundred.

Morse hastened to organize the American Protestant Union as a "national defense society" to oppose "the subjugation of our country to the control of the Pope and Rome" and preserve "our civil and religious liberties." He also helped merge the anti-Catholic Philo-Italian Society into an over-all Christian Alliance, of which Lyman Beecher became president and he himself a vice-president.

"Our great object is the protection of religious freedom. . . . Our prayer should be, and our hope, that the great Babylon may fall, and the banner of primitive Christian truth and freedom may float over the Vatican itself."

The most active worker in Morse's new vineyard was Reverend Horace Bushnell, of Hartford, Connecticut, who called upon his Holiness Gregory XVI to abdicate and forswear Catholicism. His letter was given wide, sensational circulation. Bushnell admitted to a Hartford Catholic priest that perhaps he had been "a little hard on the old gentleman." Presently he wrote *Barbarism Is the First Danger,* which ended with the charge that the influx of foreigners meant national decline, an unavoidable "relapse toward barbarism," and he closed in caps: "OUR FIRST DANGER IS BARBARISM–ROMANISM NEXT."

Morse's group was instrumental in both Democratic and Whig caucuses in arousing anti-Catholic elements and gaining friendly nominees. It was strong enough to force the Democrats to throw naturalized citizens and Catholics off their ticket and denounce school reform.

Bishop Hughes called a mass meeting at Carroll Hall October 30 and told his audience that they had been betrayed by both major parties; they had no alternative but to launch their own ticket for state senators and assemblymen. This aroused verbal pyrotechnics that charged the Catholics were really bent on ruling the country. Hughes denied any desire to meddle beyond protecting Catholic rights. Tactically it was a clever move. Although the New York City Whigs were anti-Catholic and closely allied with the Nativists, the upstate organization was controlled by Seward and Thurlow Weed, one of the ablest party bosses of all time. Both hated all Nativists, and when New York City Whigs got into the state legislature, they usually jumped through Seward's hoop.

The Catholic move stimulated the Democratic American Association, fully backed by the American Protestant Union, to put out anti-Catholic candidates, the "Union Ticket," in the hopes of matching the votes for the Carroll Hall slate. However, the Know-Nothings polled less than five hundred votes, whereas the Catholic ticket sheared 2,000 votes off the normal Democratic vote, permitting the Whig candidates to squeak through by a slim 300-vote margin. In a pinch the Catholics, it was now clear, could exercise a balance of power. It was a lesson the Democrats would not soon forget.

Although substance was given to charges that Catholics were being manipulated politically by their ecclesiastics, actually far less than half the Catholic votes of the city had followed Bishop Hughes' injunctions, and had supported other candidates, chiefly Democrats. This was the one and only example in one hundred and fifty years of American politics where a strictly Catholic ticket has ever appeared at the polls. The Nativists themselves were responsible for this brief effort by Hughes.

The controversy brought a new batch of street-corner rabble rousers out of the cracks. In February, 1841, Reverend Charles Sparry, agent for Smith's *Downfall of Babylon,* was mobbed in Philadelphia for the filthiness of his attacks and subsequently was arrested for peddling obscene literature. He had printed extracts from a Catholic book, Den's *Moral Theology,* without indicating they were examples of evil Den had condemned.

A few years later Sparry launched the *National Protestant* to rehash the old tales about priests and nuns, so that his second issue had 3,000 subscribers and it was a growing success. He scoffed at the idea of "saving" Catholics. "Most couldn't read, the rest weren't worth saving." Soon he had sixty-one agents, mostly clergymen, touring as lecturers, chiefly in churches, to disseminate "the truth" and gather subscriptions.

Involved in financial difficulties, he had to sell out, with the stipulation he would refrain from publishing a similar magazine. But he stole the plates of the last issue, so it came out under two different imprints. The name was then changed to *National Protestant Magazine or the Anti-Jesuit,* whereupon Sparry, violating sales terms, started *North American Protestant Magazine or the Anti-Jesuit.*

In Baltimore, anti-Catholic *Pilot and Transcript* and

*The Saturday Visitor* were launched. Other "anti-Roman" magazines appeared in Albany, Cincinnati, and elsewhere. In Tennessee, Reverend A. A. Campbell founded the *Jackson Protestant.* A few years later the *Protestant* of New Orleans, where anti-Catholicism had never made much headway, proved successful. The Philadelphia *Protestant Banner,* started early in 1842 by Reverend Joseph E. Berg, "the no-Popery writer," took for its motto "Light and Love," and laid down its aims: "We bear testimony against the delusions of Popery . . . that God may snatch our mistaken brethren from the toils of priestcraft and save their souls from death." These guano-peddling publications sharpened anti-Catholic attacks, particularly on the Bible issue, even in more staid publications such as *Christian Intelligencer, Christian Watchman,* the *New England Magazine,* etc. The tide of hate was rising again.

"All" the Protestant press, wrote the Catholic *Freeman's Journal* (New York), carry "violent attacks [on Popery], bitter denunciations, malicious misrepresentations, mendacious sketches and stories, false perversions of fact, or uncharitable inferences and constructions." Regardless of "creed or profession, whether orthodox or heterodox, Calvinist or Lutheran, high and low church," all "unite in indiscriminate attack." The national Assembly of the Old School Presbyterians (who had previously purged the "New School") passed strong anti-Catholic resolutions, stressing the peril to the schools, and instructed its 1,100 preachers to use their pulpits for Nativist propaganda.

The Bible issue, woefully misrepresented, aroused the most extreme fears and emotions. The entire country was rocked when a Catholic priest in Carbeau, New York, outraged by the distribution of Protestant Bibles to his parishioners, angrily burned several copies publicly. Nor did it help the Catholics when Bishop Hughes boldly defended the act: "To destroy a spurious corrupt copy of the Bible" was "justifiable and praiseworthy." Book burning had long been charged against the Catholic Church and, in other lands and places and epochs, had certainly occurred.

Now in the 'forties false stories of Catholics burning Bibles everywhere in the country were reported in Protestant papers, particularly by the Philadelphia *Banner*. The *Observer* remarked, "The late Bible conflagration may yet kindle a flame that will consume the last vestiges of Popery in this land of ours."

In January, Governor Seward again aroused Protestant wrath by demanding even more strongly that public schools be taken out of sectarian hands—a stand that more than anything else eventually blocked his path to the presidency. This time a bill was rushed through both houses—even though Seward, beaten for re-election, had handed over his office to a Democratic successor. The bill ended the use of school taxes by the Public School Society and set up a non-sectarian public system, a notable step forward in free education and the freedom of the mind—at a time when such a step was patently unpopular. "Triumph of the Roman Catholics!" grieved Morse's *Observer*. "The dark hour is at hand! People must only trust in God to be saved from the beast!"

The night the governor signed the bill, all over New York City mobs chased lone Irishmen and beat them up, stoned Bishop Hughes' home, and Catholic churches were saved only by prompt militia action.

It was about this time that Charles Dickens visited New York City. Except for the slavery issue—and he described the miseries, tortures, and mutilations of Negroes, brandings, ear cropping, welted backs, iron-scarred legs and arms, by "a miserable aristocracy spawned by a false republic"—and his attacks on the venal blackmailing press, he avoided controversial issues. He must have been aware of the religious controversy and its violences, for the chairman of the committee for the monster Astor House ball honoring him was none other than the Know-Nothing editor, James Watson Webb. Twenty-five hundred people attended, and society folk dressed as characters from his writings enacted scenes from his novels. Perhaps this homage influenced him to keep silent. He did mention religious aberrations and insane revivalism, but said both were inherited from England. He took time nearly everywhere he went to visit Catholic schools and institutions and praised them highly, perhaps a subtle suggestion that current bigotry was not in order.

New York tended to depress him. He spoke of the pigs rampaging along Broadway among the fine carriages—"a solitary swine. . . . He is in every respect a republican pig, going everywhere he pleases and mingling with the best society."

Here where "Liberty . . . hews and hacks her slaves" and indulges in "smart-alec" dialogue, New York's Tombs Prison had "such indecent and disgusting dungeons . . . [as] would bring disgrace to the most despotic empire in the world." He deplored the city's narrow ways, reeking with dirt and filth, "knee deep" with mud and declared that "Debauchery has made the very houses prematurely old . . . underground chambers where they dance and game . . . through the wide gaps [of ruined edifices] other ruins loom . . . hideous tenements which take their names from robbery and murder; all that is loathsome, drooping, and degrading is here."

But Bible reading in the schools was more important that year of 1842 than the physical shame of a city. The setting up of free public education for the first time failed for the moment to produce a non-sectarian education, for the Protestant Union party, in which Morse was active, gained complete control over the new school board. Newspaperman William L. Stone (of Maria Monk fame) was named superintendent and enforced use of the Protestant Bible as a school text more rigidly than before.

Bishop Hughes announced sadly, "There is no alternative left for us but to build our own schools. It is a sacrifice we must make." And it *was* a sacrifice, for his parishioners were mostly poverty-stricken people.

But as controversy died down, ward superintendents quietly dropped compulsory Bible reading out of thirty-one schools. Thus the idea and practice of free non-sectarian education gained ground. Actually the basic principle was completely beclouded by both sides, Protestant and Catholic. At least, the framework had been established for such free education for future generations. Even so, endless election fights and court battles had to be fought for half a century in nearly every state for that ideal to become a reality.

In the 'forties, Philadelphia had the worst trouble of all. A polite request by Bishop Francis Patrick Kenrick that Catholic children be allowed to use their own Bible and be excused from non-Catholic religious instruction was quietly granted. Then a hundred ministers banded together in the American Protestant Association to "awaken . . . the community to the dangers which . . . threaten the United States from the assaults of Romanism." It spread quickly to other large cities.

This body, the American Protestant Reform Society, and Nativists raised a hullabaloo about "the interference of foreign prelates in our schools." There was a quick upsurge of Nativism, and a Native American Republican mayor was elected in April, 1844.

Anti-Catholic rallies were held in Independence Square and Kensington in the heart of Philadelphia's large Irish quarter—an insulting provocation—to protest against the "banishment" of the Bible from "public institutions." But the Irish showed restraint and no trouble resulted.

But in May, 1844, electioneering Native American Republicans called another rally in this same Kensington. The Irish, alarmed by rumors that the Know-Nothings intended to attack homes and churches, drove them away. A new and larger meeting was called: "Be punctual and resolve to sustain your rights."

Several thousand Nativists plodded through rain to the Market House across from the Hibernian firehouse. Shots rang out—stories differ as to which side fired first—and Irishman Patrick Fisher and Nativist George Shiffler were killed. A gray-haired Nativist shouted, "On, on, Americans! liberty or death!" and the melee was on. Irish laborers and firemen repulsed the attack on the firehouse, stormed the Market House, and broke up the meeting.

That night a Nativist mob retaliated by wrecking

several homes before being dispersed by militia. But two captured Irishmen were taken to the mayor's house, with shouts of "Kill 'em! Blood for blood!"

The editor of *Native American* draped his front page in black, labeled the riot as "another St. Bartholomew's Day," and called upon all "loyal Americans" to fight for their liberties against "the bloody hand of the church."

All next morning excited crowds congregated on street corners. In the afternoon shouting "Save the Bible!" and inflamed by bloodthirsty orators, the Christian soldiers hurled themselves roaring into Kensington, where they demolished the firehouse and burned thirty Irish homes before the militia could disperse them.

On the third day law and order broke down further. A mob of thousands looted and burned whole blocks of Catholic homes, then roared on to burn Saint Michael's Church, where the priest barely escaped with his life, and headed for Saint Augustine. The mayor, hastily summoned from his daughter's birthday party, got there in time to harangue the rioters from the steps, but he was knocked down and trampled, and the church was set on fire.

The next day the militia and specially sworn police blocked further destruction, but there were deaths on both sides, and for days roving bands continued to burn—a convent and other Catholic property and homes—in the city of brotherly love. On command of the bishop, all Catholic services were suspended indefinitely, pending proper guarantee of constitutional rights. Catholics fled from the city. Nativist societies were set up in every ward.

On July 4, 70,000 people (according to estimates, perhaps exaggerated, in several Protestant organs) escorted the widows and orphans of the fallen Native Americans, a massive demonstration, and the militia was powerless to stop the ensuing rioting and destruction.

The next day a mob raided Saint Philip de Neri Church. A small cache of guns and ammunition stored there for defense after the first two churches were destroyed was discovered, but the militia scattered the vandals before the edifice was set on fire. The next day, the mob came back stronger than before but dispersed in panic when they heard orders to the Hibernian Greens—the all-Irish militia on guard—to shoot to kill. One rioter—former Congressman Charles Naylor—was seized and held.

From here on the various eyewitness accounts vary slightly, but not in any essential way. Those by Nativists tend to minimize the mob's violence and stress the wanton brutality of the soldiery against citizens with only peaceful intentions.

On the seventh—Sunday—the mob returned in force with two ship cannon to blow in the doors, and the Hibernian Greens retreated inside. The rioters' powder was wet, but they battered their way in with a big log. The attackers vastly outnumbered the Hibernians, but they faced rifles at point-blank range, men determined to kill and die. The mob leaders promised that if yesterday's prisoners were delivered to them and the militia would leave the premises, they would withdraw peaceably without burning the church. But when the Hibernians again took up posts in the street outside, they were attacked, and one was killed.

Later, rioters again broke into the church but were dissuaded by a private guard of citizens, which had taken over, from setting it on fire. But all afternoon the mob kept growing and a call for military help was sent out. By nightfall an army company appeared, threw up barricades about the church, and mounted cannon to dominate every avenue. Another company en route, led by General Cadwalladar, marching with drums and fife, was attacked on Queen Street and fired on rioters, killing three and wounding many.

News of this brought fresh crowds toward the church. Rioters showed up again with their two cannon, which they fired point blank at the militiamen guarding the portals. A battle was joined that lasted for several hours, with rifle and cannon fire. Still another company had to be called out to help capture the cannon and restore peace. In all that riotous day two soldiers and twelve civilians were killed, and scores wounded.

The church was saved, but all next day angry mobs boiled through the streets, and thousands of Catholics again fled from the city. The governor hurried down from Harrisburg to plead for order. Things finally quieted down.

The Protestant and Nativist press all over the country told how the Irish and Catholics had attacked American citizens carrying on their political campaign in free American fashion, had killed patriots, and trampled on the American flag. An official investigation, with no Catholics or Irish represented, placed the entire blame on the Irish and whitewashed the rioters. A grand jury, obviously packed, blamed the whole trouble on Catholic efforts "to exclude the Bible from our public schools." The meetings in Kensington were "a peaceful exercise of sacred rights guaranteed to every citizen by the constitution and laws of our state and country." By implication it condoned mob violence and defiance of law and order, mob attacks on the police and militia, the burning of churches and homes. A second grand jury blamed the destruction of the churches not on the mob, but wholly on the Catholics.

Third-term Native American Congressman Lewis G. Levin (by birth a South Carolinian and the man who ramrodded the Philadelphia fanaticism) rose in the House, a stout gentleman with a florid tongue: "Drilled bands of armed foreigners rushed with impetuous fury upon Native Americans who carried no weapons but, in the majesty of freemen, stood armed only with moral power. The element opposing them was physical force . . . an European weapon . . . peculiar only to feudal institutions of the Old World."

So it was solely moral force that had burned a firehouse, churches, and homes, had sent cannon balls hurtling against a house of worship, had killed militiamen and Irish citizens. The results were singularly physical—and "American." Lithographs of "martyr" George Shiffler were widely sold and hung in Nativist homes.

Rioting spread to other cities. In St. Louis a mob attacked a Jesuit college when rumors spread that anatomical remains carelessly left by medical students were the relics of Protestant martyrs. Armed Irishmen drove the rioters off.

Real trouble was brewing in New York, where inflammatory mass meetings were called to display the flag that allegedly had been trampled upon by the Philadelphia Irish. A blood bath seemed inevitable, especially as the city was in the hands of a newly elected Know-Nothing mayor, James Harper, the publisher, and had a Know-Nothing council. But Harper informed his followers that no violence would be tolerated. The *American Republican* shouted back, "Blood will have blood. It cannot sink into the earth and be forgotten."

Bishop Hughes, who had already criticized the Philadelphia Catholics for not properly defending their homes and their churches, ordered every Catholic church and school in the city surrounded by a thousand to two thousand armed Irish guards and warned the public that if a single church were burned, all New York could be converted into a "a second Moscow."

The inflammatory mass meetings were called off, and the city suffered only a minor fracas at a Catholic church in Brooklyn.

But the anti-Catholic anti-foreign elements had tasted blood, and the American Republican party, with its new organ, the *American Citizen,* was on the march against the enemies of "pure Anglo-Saxon culture." Waving the flag lustily, they proposed "to redeem America from all foreign influence."

The automatic cheers did not hide the real fear. Between the 'twenties and 'thirties "foreigners" had taken over abandoned farms in New England, western New York, Pennsylvania, and Ohio; by the 'forties they were swarming into Missouri, Illinois, and southern Wisconsin. By 1850, more than a third of the residents of Boston and New York were foreign born. The Nativists started from the premise that their own customs, speech, religion, morals, and politics were superior, that anything "foreign" was inimical to the life and government of and by the existing dominant group.

This fear of newcomers, coupled with false patriotism,

produced ever-mounting mob violence, and Nativists won control in many states, by provoking racial, religious, and nationalistic bigotry. At this moment of rapid change and national growth the Nativists simply could not see that to "redeem" the country from all foreign influence was a way of degeneracy and death, not progress. Even less did they comprehend that this process could not be halted. Nor could they foresee that America's greatness, its wealth and power, would be built up so rapidly and stupendously precisely by the hard work, inventiveness, talents, and love of democracy and freedom of millions of newcomers from Europe. What unreasoning, ignorant fear did do, was to produce America's first fascist movement, using standard fascist weapons of emotion, violence, and terrorism, blindly attacking and destroying on every hand the institutions and the principles it claimed to be trying to save.

CHAPTER V

# THE BLOODY RED MENACE OF REVOLUTION

JAMES HARPER, son of a Long Island minister, was apprenticed in 1817 to a Methodist family to learn printing. Seven years later he and his brother John started a print shop in a dingy little room on Dover Street, Manhattan, under the name J. and J. Harper. They printed 2,000 copies of Seneca's *Morals* and the year after put out Locke's *Essay on Human Understanding*. According to the New York *Times*, they did more reliable work than any other printers. James ran the press; John tended to the business end.

As business grew and quarters were enlarged, two more brothers, Joseph Wesley and Fletcher, were brought in, and in 1833 it became Harper Brothers. Wesley was the literary genius who decided most editorial matters. Fletcher handled sales, and in 1839, thanks to close relations with the ministerial politicians of the Public School Society, secured a lucrative textbook order.

The concern finally took over a big iron building, painted to look like marble, on Franklin Square. The lower floor housed seven stores; the rest of the edifice accommodated the steam presses (Harpers were among the first to use them), stitchers, folders, and other printing and packaging equipment, salesrooms and editorial offices, which were reached by an outside circular iron stairway.

James was tall and well built, with dark hair and heavy eyebrows. He had a genial smile, always a kind word, and throughout life was a devout Methodist. He was involved in Nativist and anti-Catholic, anti-foreign activities from the early 'thirties on. Moderately active in the 1840–42 school fight, James grew increasingly concerned over vice and corruption. A Whig, he blamed much of the dishonesty and graft in municipal government on the giving of jobs to foreigners by the Democratic machine. Soon he was to have organized political backing.

Early summer, 1843, a "Native American" meeting proclaimed modestly in the name of "our revolutionary forefathers"—always a telling bit—that, while offering the United States as an asylum for the oppressed, "we reserve to ourselves the right of administering the government in conformity with the principles laid down by those who have committed it to our care."

Three days later, June 13, "Native American" butchers and meat sellers grew incensed at the Democratic administration for licensing "foreigners" as meat sellers, inspectors, clerks, weighers, and watchmen, and a group, happening to meet in an Eleventh Ward blacksmith shop, then and there formed an organization to fight the Irish and Catholics—such is the account given by Anna E. Carroll, a contemporary rabid anti-Papist close to the Know-Nothing crusade.

Other wards followed suit and joined forces to launch the *American Citizen* (July 15) to voice their grievances and ideas. The following year a second paper, *The American Republican,* was started, and its virulent sensationalism soon gave it a circulation that rivaled that of the leading daily, the New York *Sun.*

In August a city-wide rally launched the American Republican party, to save the Bible, keep foreigners out of office, and require twenty-one years for naturalization. Reverend Hiram Ketchum was most active. Resolutions attacked the "Papal power" as being opposed to "republican government." The common school system had been "bartered away to gain votes."

This fresh upthrust of Nativism had appeared even earlier in Philadelphia, where a Nativist mayor was installed and the *Native American* launched in April, 1844, a publication that did much to stir up the bloody riots. Later in the year, the *National American* was started under the editorship of arch-Nativist Hector Orr, and the following year a third party organ, the *Native Eagle and American Advocate,* was added to attract workingmen by playing on prejudices about immigrant wage and job competition. The secret Order of United American Mechanics (still in existence) was formed, with an official organ of the same name. It spread to a few other cities. From Brooklyn it moved upstate along the Hudson, playing an obscure and dubious role in the bloody anti-rent fight against the patroons. A New York state council was set up.

A rash of American Republican and Nativist publications broke forth all over the country, three more in Philadelphia, three more in New York City, and several upstate; in Massachusetts, New Orleans, Indiana, Ohio, Michigan, Baltimore, Missouri. Leading papers, such as the New Haven *Courier* and Hartford *Courant,* long arch-reactionary Whig publications, and others in Baltimore, Vermont, Maine, North Carolina, New Jersey, Kentucky, Tennessee, Pennsylvania, Virginia, and elsewhere, became organs for the new movement. Magazines were launched: *The Metropolitan* and the *American Republican Magazine.* The latter's first lead article was: "The Insolence of Foreigners."

Protestant societies resumed militant anti-Catholic, anti-foreign propaganda. Fresh lecturers were sent out by the new party and by these groups to spread the doctrine. On all sides once more the dark spiral of ugly Nativism and supernationalism rose up into a tornado of destructive nastiness. Above all nationalism was the slogan of the day—no modern Egyptian or Cuban ever beat the drums harder. The "Manifest Destiny" patriots, among them the future Populist leader, Congressman Ignatius Donnelly of Minnesota, made the most extraordinary and war-like claims for expansion: Canada, Texas, Cuba, the Virgin Islands, Santo Domingo. In Congress

Robert C. Winthrop spoke of "the right of our manifest destiny to spread over this whole continent." The Star-Spangled Banner should rule all North America. Such phrases as "from sea to sea, and the pole to Panama," even "pole to pole" were heard.

In the 1843 fall campaign in New York City, ably managed by Daniel F. Tiemann, the new party, to prevent absorption by the Whigs such as had occurred in the middle thirties, refused to endorse any but its own candidates, who were pledged to accept no other nomination. The November campaign document stressed Bible use in the schools, attacked Papism and Bishop Hughes and naturalized citizens.

Although they put up untried men, they were helped by a Democratic split and rolled up 8,690 votes, 27 per cent of the total. According to Hammond's *Political History of New York,* "the wealth, talent, and respectability of the community" went into the Know-Nothing ranks. That was typical *status-quo* action by menaced powers-that-be. Of course plenty of riffraff were attracted too.

In the 1844 spring elections, managed by Alexander Copeland, the party put up James Harper for mayor. He promised bipartisan patronage, and the Whigs put up only a straw candidate. He stressed municipal reform, honest government, and lower taxes—the customary politician's baggage —and strong appeals were made for workers' votes. "Our laboring men," the Nativist orators declaimed, "are met at every turn and every avenue of employment with recently imported workmen from the low-wage countries of the Old World. Our public improvements, railroads, and canals are thronged with foreigners. They fill our large cities, reduce the wages of labor, and increase the hazards of the old settlers." Orator Matthew L. Davis shouted, "If I had the power, I would erect a gallows at every landing place in the city of New York and suspend every cursed Irishman as soon as he steps on our shores." One Irishman, an anecdote relates, groaned, "Would to God every Irishman and every son of an Irishman were an infidel so we could all live together like good Christians."

Later, in his *American Commonwealth,* James Bryce pointed out that more often foreigners, especially the Irish, were scapegoats, "much as the cat is used in the kitchen to account for broken plates and food which disappears. New York was not an Eden before the Irish came."

The party executive committee issued a distortion of Samuel F. B. Morse's charges of ten years earlier: "There exists in the continent of Europe, in the heart of its most despotic government, a society protected by the Crown of Austria, patronized by the most unflinching supporters of civil and religious despotism . . . for the express purpose of exporting to this . . . free America the abject slaves of the country who, found in fetters of civil and religious serfdom, would be incapable in thrice twenty-one years of understanding the principles of civil and religious freedom which alone fit a man to become an American citizen." Statements put out in Philadelphia, Louisiana, and Boston, where the new party got off to a flying start after two months of intensive anti-Catholic church sermons, were couched in similar redundant gibberish and bad grammar.

A flood of new anti-Catholic books and periodicals poured forth. Bitter anti-foreign provocations peppered the pages of General Duff Green's Baltimore *Pilot.* In 1840, the Whigs repudiated the Louisville *Tribune* for similar "native American" diatribes. Much of the new crop of sensation mongering was on the child level. Between 1841 and 1845 Charlotte Elizabeth Tonna published nine super-pious, atrociously written, but big-selling books for adolescents "to infuse into tender minds the sentiments" that should be entertained "respecting Jesuitical craftiness and deception." All had the same plot: a daughter or son lured to Popery by an insidious priest. After long, painful biblical arguments between parent and child, sometimes the priest, too, the child (often the priest likewise) was finally saved for Protestantism. The long-winded theological passages were trite, boring beyond belief, a shocking insult to minimal intelligence, but people had been fed on this unappetizing drivel for centuries and could not do without their hasheesh. The more drawn out and inane the disputations, the better the book sold. A prolific crop of such idiot tomes greatly aided the revival of Nativism.

Outright sensationalism also had its innings once more, as in Bishop A. McMurray's *Awful Disclosures! Murders Exposed! Downfall of Popery! Death Bed Confusion! Death-bed Confession!* . . . (1845).

The New York 1844 campaign was marred by threats and bitterness, but election day passed without ballot burning or fighting at the polls. The Democrats themselves realized that graft and corruption had reached such vast proportions that nothing could divert public wrath; Harper could not be defeated. Also, they preferred to lose to a new group rather than to the Whigs. Harper's plurality was 4,000, and both branches of the Common Council became Nativist. The infant in the cradle had strangled the father, the Whig party, and was in undisputed control of the city.

That was in April. In May and again in July occurred the frightful Philadelphia riots: Americans killed, Irish and Catholics hunted down and murdered in the glare of burning homes and churches. Although New York escaped a similar spectacle, this did not deter Harper from purging foreign-born citizens and Catholics from the pay rolls, along with a swarm of corrupt politicians.

Other Nativist party organizations sprouted upstate. On June 21, a call was sent out for a state-wide get together, and organizers were rushed north and west to build up other units. But the September 10 meeting in Utica was not promising, and a second one, held September 21 in New York City, abandoned the idea of entering the wider state arena.

Continuously Seward denounced Nativism and religious bigotry, but the Whigs' New York City machine defied him and made a deal with the American Republicans, now managed by John Lloyd, to support their local candidates for the state legislature and Congress in return for Know-Nothing support of Henry Clay against Polk. Clay had frequently made anti-foreign remarks, and his running mate, Theodore Frelinghuysen, was prominent in New Jersey anti-Catholic evangelical and Bible societies. A similar Whig-Nativist deal was made in Philadelphia.

Enthusiasm was whipped up at giant mass meetings. Firebrand orators denounced foreigners and Catholics. Posters called upon the Protestant churches to line up against Popery by supporting Clay and Nativist candidates. The American Republican campaign song rolled sonorously under the gaslights:

*Then strike up "Hail Columbia," boys, our free and happy land;*
*We'll strangle the knavish politicians and break the hellish band,*
*We'll snap the reins, spurn party chains and priestly politics,*
*We'll swear it by our fathers' graves—our Sires of Seventy-six.*

Even Horace Greeley, distinguished editor of the *Tribune,* although he hated Know-Nothing bigotry, out of Whig loyalty voted for the American Republican candidate. Oddly enough, out of similar party loyalty, Bishop Hughes did the same—his first vote as an American citizen. The Nativists elected a state senator, fifteen assemblymen, four congressmen. Three congressmen were elected in Philadelphia. But in upper New York State the Nativists, also abolitionist elements (the new Liberty party), bitter over Clay's equivocal position on slavery, failed to vote for him, so he lost the state and thereby the election. Polk became president. Millard Fillmore in a letter to Henry Clay (November 14, 1844) ascribed the defeat not to Nativists but chiefly to "Abolitionists and Foreign Catholics," who feared Frelinghuysen and the Native Americans.

This Whig disaster permitted Seward to capture control of the city machine. Strong measures were called for, since many discouraged upstate Whigs and Whig newspapers were going over to the Know-Nothings. Seward saw clearly that alienating naturalized citizens and Catholic votes would mean eventual party suicide. The avalanche of Whig voters into the American Republican party had to be stopped regardless of the immediate Whig fate at the polls, and he demanded an out-and-out party war on Nativism. No more deals. No more coalition tickets. Both city and state Whig committees issued strong statements that the party recognize no distinction among citizens on the score of religious faith or place of birth—American traditions which the raucous monopolizers of "Americanism" were defiling.

It was a sane position although actually too late to prevent the steady deterioration of Whigism. But for stuffy leadership and over-dependence on the Protestant clergy, the reactionary Whig party, rather than the Democratic party, logically should have been the true haven for conservative Catholics and also for foreign voters, since after a brief period of adjustment, the émigré (as history has demonstrated) usually becomes more patriotic and status seeking than the native.

In Connecticut, although the foreign population was still small, the Whig party was so Nativist that no American Republican organization appeared. There was, however, some threat of starting one by the Whig editors of the New Haven *Palladium* and the New Haven *Courier,* who demanded that the foreign vote be "strangled."

Although Clay had carried the state by a squeak, the Hartford *Courant* was bitter. It charged the Democrats with using every effort "to band together the foreign Catholics and secure their votes, *as a religious sect.*" It denounced the "bigotry, ignorance, and fanaticism" of this "Locofocoism," which prompted one observer to remark, "it was merely grimacing at its own ugly face in the mirror." The *Times* asked why the *Courant* had published pro-Whig propaganda from Protestant ministers. This really was "sectarianism in politics."

But rabid Theodore Dwight retorted (November 16, 1844) that the fact that so many foreigners had voted against Clay and for the Democratic candidate proved that the five years required for naturalization was "too short a time to obliterate the impressions made under despotic governments and to acquire the degree of intelligence and the interest in free institutions which entitle them to be placed on a par with those who have always lived under them. They know nothing of the past history of the country or the glories of its great men." He did not explain how or why true Americans, born citizens, so showed their lack of love for America as to vote Democratic—much less how a true American with a family going back ten generations could believe that a Whig autocracy could represent American freedom. It was the old "frother's" last gasp; he died the following year at the age of eighty-one.

But more practical politically minded Whig leaders (influenced by Seward) saw, if but dimly, the handwriting on the wall, and the administration, contrary to prior pronouncements, proceeded to abolish the law prohibiting aliens to own property, also property qualifications for voting (although many local qualifications of this sort plague the state even today), and as a result many desirable foreigners and worthy future citizens were attracted.

Considerable Nativist effort was made in Boston. Their language was that of Joseph T. Brickingham: "In the plenitude of the generosity which has induced us to feed the hungry, clothe the naked . . . we have warmed into life the torpid viper and the fanged adder [to] . . . spit their venom upon our dear and blood-bought privileges, our sacred most cherished institutions." Irishmen "fresh from the bogs of Ireland . . . [are] led up to vote like dumb brutes . . . to vote down intelligent, honest native Americans." The foreign haters failed in 1844, but took over the city in 1845.

In the 1845 New York municipal elections, the American Republicans, thanks to Seward—although he had a hard fight to prevent the Whigs from nominating Harper—had to go it alone. Although Harper's original vote had been more than half Whig, he had—despite anti-foreign, anti-Catholic proscriptions—made a favorable impression by actually cleaning up corruption and hence had a strong personal following, so that the American Republicans were hopeful that this, plus control of patronage, plus the vote of Whigs with strong Nativist leanings, would bring victory, especially as several Whig papers bolted to Harper's side. Only Greeley at the *Tribune* stanchly adhered to the Seward line, pointing out that unless the Nativists were roundly beaten the New York Whig party was doomed.

The result was that both Nativist and Whig tickets were snowed under, and the Democrats piled up the biggest plurality in city history, although Harper—in spite of the bone-crusher attack from both old parties—topped the Whig vote by 10,000. The Nativists, yesterday in full control of the city, elected only a Brooklyn ward constable.

Even so the Know-Nothings were not discouraged, for they still believed they would be the heirs of a dying Whig Party, now relegated to third place. Also the American Republican party was spreading across the land, south and west, taking on a national contour. It continued to win victories in Philadelphia, and Know-Nothing Aspinwall Davis was elected mayor of Boston. Six American Republican candidates were elected to Congress, and the leaders estimated that the party now controlled well over 100,000 votes in the country. Not ordinary voters, either. Except for weather-eye politicians, nearly all were fanatic crusaders; that their bigotry was vicious made them that much more political dynamite, for only rarely is truth an asset to a politician.

A national convention was called for Philadelphia, July 4, 1845, and 141 delegates representing fourteen states, including Kentucky, Mississippi, Georgia and North Carolina, showed up. This, only two years after a little group of malcontents had blown off steam in a New York blacksmith shop. Much of the session was given over to rabid anti-Catholic denunciations. A super-patriotic platform demanded the usual immigration and citizenship restrictions to protect the country against foreigners "steeped in ignorance and the traditions of despotism." None but natives and non-Catholics were to be allowed to hold office.

Ever since colonial times, such denial of rights to Catholics had been written into the constitutions or the laws of New Hampshire and the Carolinas, and the oath required of office holders in New York State by the constitution adopted in 1789 (though there was not a single Catholic congregation or church in the state) still made it impossible for any conscientious Catholic to hold office. The Bible—said the national gathering—was to be continued as a school text everywhere, and the right guaranteed "to worship the God of our Fathers according to the dictates of our consciences, without the restraints of a Romish priest or the threats of a Hellish Inquisition."

Seemingly, they were asking for a right they already wholly possessed! What they were really demanding was the denial of American rights to citizens differing from them in customs, ideas, politics and religion. They were promoting the evils of non-adjustment and non-assimilation they professed to abhor—forcing newcomers to act defensively as clannish groups and protect themselves as aliens, not as naturalized Americans. What other reaction could be expected from organized criticism, abuse, ridicule and violence?

Yet the Nativists, for all their misdirected zeal, did not achieve much success. In the next New York election they polled only 9,000 votes. In a subsequent election of delegates to a state constitutional convention (made necessary by the prolonged rent strike on up-Hudson patroon estates) the Nativists polled only a little more than four thousand.

Nevertheless, handsome Nativist showings were made in Philadelphia and elsewhere, and six congressmen were sent to Washington, so another effort was made to set up a New York state ticket. But the entire Nativist state vote totaled only 6,170, and in 1847 their municipal vote was only about two thousand. The Whigs, having purged themselves of Nativism, won the election, a triumph for Seward's foresight, and the Nativist party folded, not even naming a new municipal committee. Only one congressman (from Pennsylvania) was elected this year.

But thirty-odd New York delegates attended the May 4, 1847, national convention in Pittsburgh, then one in Philadelphia, September 11. Eleven states were represented. "Let the Bible and American education be the only passport to the American ballot box." No one should be permitted to vote "unless born on our soil." Zachary Taylor and Henry Dearborn the Whig candidates were endorsed, but no separate Nativist campaign for them was mounted.

In New England, where the American Republicans had made only nominal headway, the Whigs continued to maintain a strong Nativist slant. In Boston, June, 1847, anti-Catholics marched on the Fort Hill district to provoke the Irish and raised no-popery banners on Bunker Hill. Priests dared not visit their sick on Deer Island. Repeated difficulties arose—as they had for twenty years—over attempts to prevent Catholic burials in the cemeteries, and legal action had been taken repeatedly since 1833 to prevent Catholics from establishing their own cemeteries.

As more immigrants flooded in, anti-foreignism grew stronger, influenced by, among other writings, Chickering's *Immigration into the United States.* He warned that since the two major parties were so evenly balanced, the newcomers could decide the next presidential election. Although many such had prospered, it was "difficult to see in them qualifications equal to those of our own citizens." The New Haven *Journal* waxed hysterical over the prospect of "paupers" coming in. "One thousand one hundred and twenty-four Democrats just imported! England and other European Powers are landing in hordes upon our shores, all the refuse and off-scourings of their population."

The Hartford *Times* still stanchly maintained a contrary view: Let these "paupers" come in, the more the merrier. "There is room enough for them all, and to spare. There is land enough for all and employment enough for all. Without the aid of these . . . despised paupers, not half our existing railroads and canals would have been constructed."

The Nativists were spitting against the wind, playing King Canute. By 1847, 200,000 newcomers were arriving each year and the numbers would increase. The fact was, the country needed every bit of man power it could get. More and more transportation was needed; manufacturing had taken a big spurt; waste spaces cried out for settlers. Without immigration, the country's maturity in an explosive world would have been dangerously delayed. All this, the standpatters, the

Whigs, the traditional Puritans, the slaveholders, and the Nativists could not comprehend. Their patriotism consisted of fighting the country's true greatness and its future.

It was a great population movement, one of the greatest in all history, and it changed the face of the world, not merely that of America. The new cheaper mid-American crops ruined Old World agriculture, no longer able to compete, and the rise of new American industry and the shifting balances of trade were so tremendous that wars and revolutions blossomed all around the globe.

By 1900, 10,000,000 foreign-born persons would be residents of the United States, and more than twenty-six million of the 66,000,000 Americans were of foreign parentage. More than half the people of the country were descendants of those who had come well after the days of Washington and Jefferson; of these newcomers more than half were of non-English-speaking stock, races neither Teutonic nor Anglo-Saxon.

In the 'forties, this influx and the rapidity and force of growth and expansion again briefly overwhelmed the provincial super patriots, who had to bide their time until another wave of fear would dash over the rocks. The 1846–48 Mexican War stopped them, too. Political experiments and controversies, other than those having to do with the immediate conflict, never prosper in wartime, for war absorbs and redirects all lurking hate-fear complexes into nationalistic fetichism, concentrating emotion on patriotic symbols. Wartime patriotism means *all* the nation, not a creed or class. The acme of all political revivalism, war is a passionate if not intelligent unifying force. The Nativism of the 'forties had stressed national unity in theory but not in practice, for it sought merely the unity of the dwindling band of Puritan Anglo-Saxons, not the entire nation. It sought to maintain domination by a religious and social elite, by the middle class and by workers, threatened by immigration. On its side the slavocracy feared northern predominance unless immigrant citizens, like their own slaves, could be stripped of suffrage. For the time being, broader wartime patriotism, channeled into victory propaganda, dulled the edge of this race-religious white supremacy doctrine.

Another world-shaking event, on the heels of the Mexican War, also dampened eastern political feuding: California's gold rush. Why bother about political rights or beating up the Irish, if you could get to the pot at the foot of the rainbow? But not all could escape.

As Nativism dwindled on the political vine with the approach of war, it went underground; it hid under the stones. The hard core of bigotry went into subterranean secret organizations—an example already set by the Temperance movement and the earlier Masonic movement (also political and anti-Catholic), against which Seward and Fillmore had first sharpened their political spurs. Of late, also, various secret benevolent societies had been formed on this or that exclusivist principle, usually close to the Know-Nothing memtality.

These multiple secret organizations afforded channels through which false patriotism, racist ideas, and religious bigotry were to flow on unabated until the great Know-Nothing torrent of the 'fifties burst forth.

In June, 1844, editor James Webb started the Native Sons of America, but the inner clique of Nativists preferred to set up their own outfit. On December 21, New York's Mayor Harper helped start the Order of United Americans (briefly called the American Brotherhood) generally known as the OUA. Thirteen Nativist ramrods—thirteen was the magical patriotic number—met at the home of Russell C. Root on Forsyth Street. Present and prominent among others were Simeon Baldwin, Charles A. and Thomas R. Whitney, David Talmadge, George W. Parson, and Will Atkinson. The first chapter, headed by John Harper, called with some redundancy Alpha Chapter No. 1, constituted the Arch Chancery, the provisional governing body for a projected state-and-nationwide apparatus. It made its headquarters in an "elegant hall, a beautiful temple of patriotism" at 203 Prince Street. A secret ritual, elaborate handclasps, passwords, and other awe-inspiring mysteries were adopted.

Later, each state was to have its own Arch Chancery of three delegates from each chapter, to be headed by a Grand Sachem, these to be federated under a Grand Arch Chancery, headed by *an* Arch Grand Sachem to exercise national jurisdiction. The "Brotherhood," disclaiming "all association with party politics," was for "mutual aid and assistance and to oppose foreign influence in our institutions of government in any shape in which it may be presented to us." Only native-born white Americans over eighteen could join. "Americans ought to be governed by Americans." The order promised to protect "every man's civil and religious rights," but not, of course, those of naturalized citizens, Negroes, or Catholics. At all costs, the Bible was to be retained in the public schools. The organization proposed to alert everybody to the dangers of "the thraldom of foreign domination."

As Thomas R. Whitney put it, this "subterranean streamlet" was planned gradually to "undermine the foundations of the corrupt political structure, or, like quicksand," swallow "the ground plans for Papal encroachment! . . . The fangs of the Papacy are even now in our vitals." Only "cowards" would "shut themselves up as the periwinkle in his shell."

By 1845 a second group, the Washington Chapter, was set up. The third, Washington Chapter No. 2, was to become the most wealthy and influential, and from it came most of the top schemers in the later Know-Nothing conspiracy. By September, five chapters were in existence. The later Franklin Chapter No. 9 made Samuel F. B. Morse, "born on Bunker Hill," an honorary member because he had "risen superior to the influence of immigration and treacherous priestcraft." In November, a woman's auxiliary, the United Daughters of America, was organized and soon had ten chapters.

During 1846, after preliminary anti-Catholic agitation, the Order was brought into Massachusetts by Congregationalist Reverend Alfred Brewster Eli, the Nativist mayor of Springfield. In 1848, the OUA was launched in New Jersey and Pennsylvania; in Connecticut, 1849; California, 1850; Maryland, 1851. By 1854 it had spread to Vermont, Maine,

New Hampshire, and Michigan, and a true national Grand Arch Chancery was set up. By 1855 state organizations had been established in Ohio, Indiana, Illinois, Rhode Island, the District of Columbia, Alabama, Louisiana, Missouri, and Wyoming Territory. By then 92 New York chapters and 16 state organizations were flourishing, with a membership, according to Whitney, of 1,500,000.

Similar secret groups, some active and strong, some political, some non-political, were soon at work in New York and elsewhere, maintaining the OUA or Know-Nothing phraseology. Among the oldest, an offshoot of the secret Revolutionary Sons of Liberty and the Sons of Saint Tamina (a Delaware Indian chieftain), was Tammany Hall (Columbia Order) started by William Mooney and Aaron Burr in 1789. This became the Democratic party machine. But another offshoot was the Society of Redmen, definitely Nativist. It was reorganized in Baltimore in 1835, again in 1847 as the Improved Order of Red Men. These were sublimated Indian minstrels, who poured ketchup over themselves or used rouge, put on Indian feathers, and did shuffle dances in their secret ritual and pretended to be dumping tea into the harbor. The order is still restricted to "White American citizens," under the eagle, "the noblest bird of the feathered tribe that boldly looks upon the dazzling sun"—typical Know-Nothing blather.

The Patriotic Order, Sons of America, was started in Philadelphia in 1847 (most authorities say incorrectly 1845), with a National Camp, State and Subordinate camps, and had three degrees: Camp or Red Degree, Council or White Degree, Commanding or Blue Degree—the flag itself, no less. Members had to be white native-born anti-Catholics. Several efforts at merger with the OUA, with which it cooperated closely, were made. The order languished during the Civil War, but revived strongly immediately after. It dropped anti-Catholicism, but remained bitterly anti-foreign, talked of cheap and "Red" foreign labor, paupers, and criminals, and otherwise echoed the spread-eagle verbiage. By 1900 its campfires were "burning brightly and its standards . . . waving in nearly every State and Territory," preserving "from utter annihilation those cherished ideas that have made us a distinctly separate and prosperous race." White supremacy talk for small brains! Its headquarters are now in Chicago.

The Benevolent Order of Bereans (New York, 1844), chiefly made up of Orangemen—Irish Protestants—was militantly anti-Catholic and super-patriotic; and the OUA, in spite of its foreign membership, sometimes joined hands with it in political and anti-Catholic matters.

Most important, besides the OUA for mass support of the Know-Nothingism of the 'fifties, was the semi-secret American Protestant Society, started in Philadelphia in January, 1844, and deeply involved in the riots. Successor to the earlier intolerant Bourne-Brownlee Protestant Reformation Society and the American Protestant Association of ministers, it was viciously anti-foreign and anti-Catholic. Strongly supported by churchmen, it was soon put on a nationwide footing. By 1855 it had thirty active New York units—Valley Forge, Washington, Bunker Hill, etc. Although only one of scores of secret Protestant anti-Catholic groups started about this time, as early as 1849 it had an annual $30,000 budget to distribute more than two million pages of anti-Catholic diatribes, such as "Awful Effects of the Confessional," telling of priestly seductions of innocent girls. Its organ, the *American Protestant Magazine,* had an enormous circulation. A children's department seasoned young minds against "the wiles and dangers of Popery."

In 1848, the Foreign Evangelical Society (1839) and the Christian Alliance (1842) both engaged in sending missionaries to Catholic countries, "wherever a corrupted Christianity" existed, merged with the American Protestant Society (which retained the American field for attempted conversion of Catholics) as the American and Foreign Christian Union, pledged to combat "the blasphemy against God," the monster "dripping with the cruelties of millions of murders, haggard with the debaucheries of a thousand years." The most complete anti-Catholic library in the world, according to the Fourth Annual Report (1853), was set up in New York.

Many non-secret missionary and Bible societies and

churches were pounding the anti-Papal anvil with might and main: the powerful American Tract Society, American Bible Society, and American Education Society resumed the duty of "defeating Rome and saving Catholic souls" and once more stirred up indecent scandals, riots, and bloodshed. Even colleges began bringing in salty anti-Popery speakers.

The American Education Society, basing its work on "Light and Love," strove to enlighten Protestants about "the evils of Romanism" and persuaded nearly all churches to inaugurate monthly prayers for "the salvation of Papists." By 1848 (Fifth Annual Report) it was spending $20,000 annually for agents to convert Catholics. It brought "persecuted Protestants" from abroad (and most *were* persecuted, though a few were frauds) and exhibited them in pulpits and on lecture platforms. Illinois Protestants were so moved they bought farms for all members of one group.

Another rash of convent immoralities, appeared. Sauce was added by French settings, France being a wicked country where any perversion was credible. Rachel McCrindell came out with a number of novels, *The English Governess* (1844), *School Girl in France* (1846), *The Convent* (1853), piquant with sexual episodes. Middle-class society is always shocked by elderly gentlemen titillating young girls—but a priest! That made the flesh creep! In 1853, she published *Snares of Poetry*. Reverend Sparry hurried back to the central limelight (he'd never been far from the golden circle) with another horrendous exposé. In 1843, the virulent anti-Catholic novel *Father Clement* was republished in Baltimore. Historical novels about the Inquisition and other sadistic horrors became popular.

Another busy speaker and writer was excommunicated Father William Hogan of Maria Monk fame. In lectures and books he kept up an incessant barrage on Catholic ritual, confession, and other ceremonies, which he called "pickpocket devices." Transubstantiation was a circus sideshow trick. "It would be easier to swallow a rapier ten feet long or a ball of fire as big as Mount Orizaba, than to transfer flour and water into the *great and holy God* who created the heavens and the earth and all that is therein." Brownlee, who published at least six such books between 1841 and 1844, one of them the *Apocalyptic Beasts,* called the doctrine of purgatory the most "unscrupulous pickpocket" of them all.

A play by T. S. Whitley, *The Jesuit, a National Melodrama in Three Acts,* written for the New York stage in 1850, was based on the Mexican War and the rivalry of a naval officer and a cunning, unscrupulous Jesuit for a beautiful Mexican girl.

The muddy literature oozed forth, a turgid, sticky flood. Joseph Turnley's *Priestcraft* and *Popery in Power* were best sellers. Travel books stressed the backwardness of Italy and Ireland under Papal domination. Histories depicted all Popes as dissolute rascals (there were, it seemed, a few) and the Church as the "mother of abominations." Much of this murky literature was inspired by the Protestant Society and OUA. Both were sending out many organizers and propagandists. Papal plots were traced back to the Puritan colonial days, even though the few Catholics who strayed into the Puritan totalitarian domain were flogged, branded, or had their ears cropped off.

Amusingly, several pro-Catholic histories showed that Catholics were solely responsible for the discovery and settlement of America (nobody could argue about Columbus or Ponce de León, that was certain), for all Indian missionary work, for national independence and national growth. The Catholics claimed they were the first to establish religious tolerance (the Maryland law, although the punishment for non-Christian heretics in that code, branding, cropping, eye gouging and flogging, somewhat marred their claim). Since, by mid-century, little tolerance had survived in the entire country, there seemed little point in taking credit for it.

The Mexican War was well over. The postwar period, besides bringing the usual terrible epidemics, particularly Asiatic cholera—5,000 died in Boston—was disturbed by typical postwar coercion and brutality, and saw the augmenting of juvenile delinquency (which always seems to surprise people), crime, cruelty, and suppression. What with twenty years of active intolerant anti-Catholic, anti-foreign propaganda, plus experience in both open and secret political organization (with brief tastes of success and patronage), the Nativists were in a good position to take advantage of prevailing antagonism, fears, and confusion and to resume mob violence.

Typical of revived bigotry was an incident that occurred soon after the capture of Montezuma's halls. It struck at the higher culture. In New York British actor Charles McCready, reputed to be superb, was playing *Macbeth* in rivalry with an American actor (reputedly equally superb) at another theater. McCready, being English (perhaps Irish?), was driven off the stage two nights running by rotten eggs and smashing of seats. On the third night, the mob overpowered 300 policemen with torn-out doors, windows, and paving stones, and wrecked the interior completely. The Seventh Horse Regiment had to be called out. Several were wounded, and they fired into the crowd, leaving 149 rioters writhing in their blood on the stones. More than thirty of them died. McCready was rushed out of the city in disguise and driven to Boston.

Not that Know-Nothingism revived in political form immediately. For, after the war, the Manifest Destiny boys again overshadowed the political scene: the dispute over Oregon, the use to be made of the territory seized from Mexico, the struggle for canal and railroad rights in Panama and Nicaragua, in which George Law played such an important part. Schemes to take over Cuba. Schemes to grab the Dominican Republic. Schemes to buy or steal more of Mexico. Schemes to annex Canada. The William Walker and other filibuster expeditions roiled the peace of lower California and Central America. A bit later an American war vessel blew Graytown, Nicaragua, off the map, not a house or public building left. The "Free World" was already being created.

If war had muted political activity, the usual crop of profiteers lurked behind the advancing flag. In 1847, George Law started the government-aided United States Mail Steamship Company. He shipped arms to the filibusters, and after the war prepared to utilize the Know-Nothing movement for his own personal ambitions.

Soon issues submerged by the war reappeared and new ones took on life: abolitionism, temperance, labor organization, feminism. Bands of tight-lipped, strong-jawed women were wrecking saloons, smashing bar mirrors and bottles, rolling out barrels to be stove in and emptied into the gutters. Sectionalism became really pronounced. The Liberty party, founded in 1839 by moderate abolitionists, continued to grow and become more militant. In 1848, it merged with the Free Soil party and took on national (i. e., northern) proportions.

In the general confusion and resurgence of the spirit of violence inherited from the war, the Know-Nothings could open a wider path than before. The ugliness gave them a fresh opportunity, particularly as the old parties seemed to be breaking up. The Whig party had splintered and lost ground because of its anti-war position and was expected to disappear. The Democrats were also badly split. Even so, the Whigs staged a surprise comeback, largely by putting forward a war general, fresh from the Battle of Buena Vista. It had been one of the funniest, if quite bloody, battles of history, the public being ignorant of this, of course. Actually both sides were withdrawing from the field, although the Mexicans under Santa Anna had clearly won the engagement. Taylor woke up first to what was happening, and so he won a great victory.

The Democrats also dug up a general, Lewis Cass of Michigan, whose glories, if his bungling could be called that, went back to the War of 1812 and a number of Indian engagements. He was a big-voice exponent of expansion, pleasing to the Manifest Destiny boys. His saber rattling did him little good, and the hero of Buena Vista took over.

But it was not until the following year that the OUA was reorganized to engage in *sub rosa* political work. An Arch-Chancery executive committee was set up to handle all secret matters and take sole charge of all funds, without having to report to the membership. This all-powerful executive committee, although the order was allegedly non-political, could not resist dabbling in political matters, mostly, it is true, to oppose foreign influence at the polls and in the parties. Its activities never were carried on in the name of the Order. Thus its members were secretly ordered to attend a "Union" mass meeting staged by Henry Clay in Castle Garden, February 23, 1850.

By 1851, the OUA had 168 chapters in the country, and by then the executive committee had all four feet deep in political work. On February 17, that year, the Grand Convention mapped out fifteen rules for a new secret system of political manipulation, this to be exclusively in the hands of the executive committee, having unlimited tenure, although advised by an annually elected nine-man Grand Convention "cabinet," the make-up of which was pretty much controlled by the committee. Members were not consulted, nor were they obliged to vote according to executive-committee recommendations. To have attempted to impose such obedience by the top schemers for political power would have disrupted an organization whose members were still strongly attached to the Whig or the Democratic parties.

There were plenty of public occasions when the OUA members could strut their stuff. The Order paraded on every patriotic holiday and event, as at the Washington Monument celebration (October, 1847) and John Quincy Adams' funeral (March, 1848) and invariably on February 22 and July 4. In 1851, the Order staged an elaborate observance of Washington's birthday. Members turned out to parade in full regalia with continental hats, banners, and music, and singing "Our Fatherland."

*All hail to our sunny land of the West*
*And the bright flag that proudly floats o'er her.*

The paraders were accompanied by militia contingents, quite an eyeopener: the New Battalion of American Riflemen, the Washington Continentals and City Continentals, the Constitutional Guards of New York and of Brooklyn. Visiting units were the New Jersey Continentals, the City Continentals, the

Constitutional Guards of Sag Harbor. Vast Templar Hall—the Broadway Tabernacle—was packed to hear patriotic speeches. At least two thirds of the audience were "American ladies," chiefly members of the auxiliary UDA. At another big rally in Castle Garden, Jacob Broom of Pennsylvania aroused a "flaming hysteria of patriotism."

The OUA began lobbying actively to secure the nomination of members in both parties. Rank-and-file members were actively canvassed and pledged to vote for no one else, regardless of party affiliation. Here was the first important landmark of what soon was to become known as "dark-lantern politics." The basis for a new strong thrust of anti-foreignism and bigotry was being prepared.

The novel combination of super-patriotism and secrecy appealed to those who considered themselves superior to their newer fellow citizens. Also, secrecy, with its concurrent anonymity, by reducing the fear of personal penalties, made cowardly souls brave, especially when violence was demanded. At hand now was the highest, largest crest of Know-Nothingism. But the reefs were also bigger now, and more dangerous.

Immigrants and new citizens, growing in numbers, strength, and confidence, had become less willing to be shoved around, were better able to fight for their rights. They refused to be intimidated or to be deprived of legal safeguards or moral dignity. The Germans especially posed a problem for Nativists more than ever after the failure of the European 'forty-eight revolts brought in a superior type. Mostly anti-Catholics, a large number were Free Thinkers; they could be attacked only as atheists, anarchists, and Reds—taunts frequently used.

The Richmond *Whig* said in 1854 that political refugees in all large cities had formed "Red Republican societies that purpose to pull down the government." These clubs were advocating such diabolical innovations as universal suffrage, free courts, taxation of church property, no Bible oaths. In the more benighted South such doctrines aroused double the apprehension.

The *Frei Verein* political convention at the time of the annual San Antonio, Texas, German musical festival, denounced both organized parties, also slavery, temperance laws, capital punishment, religious oaths, Sunday blue laws, debt imprisonment. Among other sinister proposals were graduated income and inheritance taxes, internal improvements, free trade, free schoolbooks and schools, abolition of religious textbooks in public schools, equality of labor and capital, full immigration. On the other hand, some Germans in the South, chiefly out of expediency, were upholders of slavery, lest they be disenfranchised by slaveowners and Know-Nothings.

But all the German Vereins had armed marching brigades; all were zealous about defending their ideas and their voting rights, even more so than the Irish. In 1854, nearly all German political groups were drawn together at a big Cleveland convention into the strong Central Union of Free Germans to oppose slavery, despotism, and the Bible in schools. They wished, the Nativists claimed, to use the United States as a springboard for a free world society, a heinous crime of dangerous involvement, quite treasonable. How could the Nativists foresee that within a little more than half a century this would become the alleged militant position of the United States?

Texas, of course, had some 25,000 Mexicans, plus many cross-border floaters. Although the citizens among them were of more ancient vintage than any Anglos, all Mexicans were labeled "foreigners" by the conquering breed, especially as they consorted with slaves and helped them escape into Mexico where they could be free, respected human beings. An Austin planters' reunion in 1854 advocated that all Mexicans, citizens or not, be kicked out of the country. An anti-Mexican Vigilante committee was formed in Gonzalez.

The Irish, who had come to the New World mostly for freedom and bread, which the Nativists begrudged them, were an easier target, being more illiterate. The facts of history were shoved aside. Half the soldiers in the war for independence, according to James Bernard Cullen, had been

Irish, a fourth English-Scotch, the rest Americans. The Know-Nothings, who claimed George Washington as a member, conveniently forgot that, when he was commander in chief of the Continental Army besieging Boston, he angrily suppressed the frolic of "Pope's Night," November 5, when customarily the head of the Roman Catholic Church was burned in effigy, calling it a "ridiculous and childish custom, void of common sense." Such an insult to religion was "so monstrous" it could not be "suffered or excused."

But the newcomers clearly were subservient to an authoritarian religion with an alien supreme head, which did not overly encourage freedom of thought or action. Not that some embattled Protestant churches—although they might have no *Index* to stultify the spirit of man—had ever created an atmosphere of free exchange of ideas; often they imposed their doctrinal concepts as effectively as did the Catholics, and sometimes less tolerantly.

However, the Irish, if less enlightened than the Germans, had the knack of politics and were learning to use it in the American way—not a very admirable way, for the most part—and to keep religious matters out of day-to-day strategy. Not only that, the Irish had always been ready at the drop of the hat to start a glorious brawl. By mid-century many had gone into the public police forces, and they liked nothing better than cracking the pates of the Know-Nothings. Numerous militia companies in Boston, Connecticut, New York, Philadelphia, and elsewhere were 100 per cent Irish and perforce Catholic. Among the first efforts of Know-Nothing governors in Connecticut and Massachusetts was to disband such units. But Irish demands to share the freedoms of America were now backed by tangible police force. More and more Catholic workers fought Protestant workers. On one canal enterprise Yankee workers posted signs, "No Irish allowed." The Irish daubed them up to read, "No Yankees allowed."

The tide was turning. In parts of New England the Yankees, although still exercising all power, had become the minority group, and were threatened with becoming the minority group everywhere. Increasingly they were displaying the typical touchiness, aggressiveness, and extreme clannishness of minority groups—"un-American evils" previously ascribed only to the Irish and Germans.

The Catholic cause was not always helped by aggressive Bishop Hughes of New York. Whatever his lip service to American doctrines of freedom, he was interested in them only for the benefit of Catholics, rather than the community at large, and although he deserved respect and admiration for his unflinching devotion to Catholic rights—he was a real fighter, ready for polemics on the platform or in the press, if need be on the terrain of force—even so, although deprived of actual rack and screw and hot irons, he was pretty much a Torquemada in ideas and methods.

His zealous November, 1850, sermon in Saint Patrick's was indiscreet, to say the least. Pagan and Protestant nations were crumbling before the force of Rome. In time the true Church would "convert all Pagan nations, and all Protestant nations, even England, with her proud Parliament. . . . Everybody should know that we have for our mission to convert the world—including the inhabitants of the United States—the people of the cities, and the people of the country, the officers of the Navy and the Marines, commanders of the Army, the Legislatures, the Senate, the Cabinet, the President and all." This was grist for the mills of all the Protestant press, and his words aroused nationwide alarm. The worst interpretations were put on them.

How, demanded the Know-Nothings, could Hughes and his Catholics be so partisan in behalf of Papal political reaction and absolutism in all Europe—as Hughes revealed time after time—and be sincere in advocating American republicanism? Obviously he could not be. To what extent was he trying to use and impose European methods to undermine and destroy American institutions? He disclaimed all such intent, but few non-Catholics believed him. For his ultramontane feelings were strong. He denounced Louis Kossuth, the hero of the hour who was drawing cheering multitudes. Had those frenetic shouters known that Kossuth was being finaced in his American liberation crusade by arms maker Colt for the direct purpose of stirring up American intervention in Hungary and thereby selling arms, they might have been sobered. Hughes had some argument on his side, however, for Kossuth, a bitter and outspoken foe of Catholicism, had taken direct punitive action against the Church in Hungary. But all too often Bishop Hughes managed to authenticate Know-Nothing charges that the Catholic Church stood for un-American principles and he supplied enemies of the Church with plenty of gratuitous propaganda thunder.

But by now, only by dark-lantern methods could the Nativists knife "foreign" candidates and officeholders. Often Nativist candidates were instructed to avoid any anti-Catholic, anti-foreign utterances—although pledged behind closed doors that once in office they would throw all foreign-born and Catholic citizens out of jobs. Thus the Know-Nothings first developed in this country the clandestine bore-from-within tactics by false-front agents which later were to be perfected by the Communists.

In 1852, in accordance with decisions made at a national conference in Louisville, Kentucky, the OUA leaders bent every effort in the national Whig and Democratic conventions to get Millard Fillmore and General Lewis Cass named as the respective candidates. Cass, the old Indian fighter and unsuccessful 1848 Democratic candidate, was a thoroughgoing reactionary who wanted no restraints put on southern slavery. Fillmore frequently had expressed anti-Catholic and anti-foreign sentiments and was conciliatory toward slavery, an attitude that had brought a rift with his former school friend Seward and a struggle for control of the New York party.

In New York City, the OUA was behind Thomas R. Whitney, in connivance with the Whig machine, in organizing a false-front City Reform League that wholly concealed its Nativist principles and intentions. The Whigs left the top position on its ticket vacant and endorsed the "Reform" candidates. On its side the OUA endorsed eleven Whig candidates.

But the City Reform ticket polled only 1,480 votes

and an openly labeled Nativist ticket the same number. The hold of the OUA over its members—some ten thousand in the city—was not as iron-clad as believed. But the techniques of secret voting controls, of dark-lantern politics, were being worked out. The ground design was to rivet Nativism on the American people and outlaw all lesser breeds. Already in numerous places, at various times, unbeknown to its victims, it had destroyed reputations and careers.

In January, 1851, Whitney launched a thick literary magazine, *The Republic,* as the official OUA organ, and it helped him to become a powerful figure in New York and national affairs, to reach the state senate and Congress. Its front page showed a flag and spread eagle, an Indian kneeling in homage before a "patriot," and the names of the founding fathers. The stories and poetry, as well as articles, were all exaggeratedly patriotic. Above all, they glorified the Independence heroes. In the first issue, he ran a rhapsody about that "admirable institution [the OUA], with its presiding spirit of love of country" and its "high and ennobling purposes." It borc "on wings of light and intelligence the admiration of every patriotic heart." The Order intended "to check the progress of the demagogue, and to avert the jealous influence of Foreign Powers, Princes, Potentates, and Prejudices. It harbors in itself no prejudices . . . knows no sectional differences, no line of demarcation between the people and the interests of this broad and happy Union. Its sympathies are alike with the fair and sunny South; the frosty North and the golden glowing West. Wherever the banner of our country floats, that is its home." In its benevolence the Order sought to "smooth the pillow of sickness, to bury the dead, and to comfort the widow and to protect and cherish the orphans."

A wit once remarked, after listening to congressional oratory about veterans' widows, "When a politician begins rocking the cradle of orphans with one foot and wiping the tears of widows away with the other, watch out! He has both hands free to steal your watch."

Another issue of *The Republic* was devoted to a deadhorse beating of the Leopoldine Foundation "set up by Metternich . . . to convert the United States from heretical Protestantism to the parental sheepfold of the Papal Hierarchy . . . whose path is stained with blood, whose chariot is drawn fiercely onward ages after ages, amid groans and tears, and whose fiery breath, fatal always to liberty, seeks now to cast its blight on this fair land." The Order would never slumber until the American people were "*re-nationalized*—and the persecuting spirit of foreign influence . . . driven effectively and forever from among us."

From the first issue, *The Republic* gave much attention to winning over labor elements. The OUA intended to look after the interests of "our mechanics and working men and women . . . sorely pressed by the unfair competition and combinations of pauper Europeans." It would "strive to keep alive the glowing, and warm into full life, the latent fires of patriotism that dwell in their hearts and inspire them, and all, with a true sense of their dignity as free men, free women—virtuous and patriotic *Americans*."

Whitney's vast love for American workmen was set forth more specifically in his subsequent rhapsodic book on the Know-Nothing movement, *A Defense of American Policy*. He told how the native mechanic was crowded from the workshops by cheap European labor and driven to actual want, and he denounced the "horrible" demands of the newcomers: the abolition of landed monopoly, ad valorem property taxation, an eight-hour day (five hours for children) instead of the "existing ten, twelve, or sometimes sixteen hours a day," priority of wages over all other creditor claims, universal suffrage, direct election of officials, a unicameral Congress, recall, reduction of the period required for naturalization, abolition of Sunday and blue laws, abolition of prayers in Congress, of Bible oaths, education of the poor by the state, old-age homes, free schools, penal reform, abolition of slavery and of capital punishment.

These suggestions made Whitney froth. Why pass "laws to encourage and sustain them in their idleness and then build comfortable asylums [for them] to loaf in, drink lager beer, and puff the meerschaum without money and without pride?" These "fiendish" foreign workers were "deliberately" striving "to pull down the human fabric which generously protects them." By what right did "the ignorant, besotted . . . refuse of European municipalities" challenge "the suffrage rights of the old citizen"? After receiving "our kind care," the immigrant has become "strong, happy, and free! He is no longer groveling in the dust of servility—the heel of the oppressor is not upon his neck. Under the protecting aegis of the Stripes and Stars, he stands erect. . . . He is as proud as an emperor and twice as happy. But does this satisfy him?" No! "His appetite is gross with what it feeds upon. He wants *more* liberty! Our laws don't suit him. He *demands* a change. He asserts as *rights* what we have granted as privileges. . . . Son of Ingratitude . . . deliberate impertinence."

All these absurd "foreign" demands for shorter hours, decent working conditions, the abolition of slavery, rights for women, political reform—every one of which later came to pass as an integral part of the American way of life—showed to Whitney, the warm-hearted friend of "American labor" that the foreigners in our midst were planning "to mount to power on the bloody red waves of REVOLUTION."

# CHAPTER VI

## SSSB

IN December, 1853, the stocky former storekeeper, James W. Barker, conducted a "free-speech" meeting in New York's City Hall Park. Handbills were scattered, and a crowd of several thousand gathered. In hoarse drumming words he accused the authorities of arresting Reverend Daniel Parsons, an anti-Papist street haranguer, in order to please the Catholic Church. This, he shouted, was a violation of the Constitution and of sacred American freedom.

The rally had been called by the Supreme Order of the Star-Spangled Banner (SSSB), a super-patriotic secret society founded four years earlier to keep foreigners, naturalized citizens, and Catholics out of public office. As in most such secret societies, members had to be native-born Americans and, in upper echelons of the order, native-born for at least three generations. Members were required to conceal their affiliation with the mysterious organization and never disclose its secret ritual. If asked by outsiders, they were obliged to respond, "I know nothing," so newspapers began referring to them as "Know-Nothings"—the first actual use of this term in the twenty-five-year history of Nativism, a crusade now growing more militant than ever.

Reverend Daniel Parsons was one of a fresh batch of religious hate mongers barnstorming about the country, causing riots, the burning of Catholic churches, the homes and the clubhouses of foreigners. In New York and elsewhere, rioters repeatedly overwhelmed the police and sometimes the militia, too. Parsons, who had already plagued other cities, now focused on Manhattan. Every Sunday he led a gang of ruffians, aching for a fight—and often getting it—into enemy territory along East Side wharves, and harangued against the Irish and Catholics. After a bad fracas on December 11, 1853, he was arrested for inciting disorder.

An angry mob of Nativists swarmed about the mayor's home. Serious trouble would have occurred had not a magistrate hastened to sign an order for Parsons' release. The following Sunday, 10,000 people turned out to hear the preacher; the Sunday after, 20,000. The vast gatherings of fanatics opened New Yorkers' eyes to the unsuspected power of the mysterious Know-Nothings, who in the previous election had polled only 4,000 votes. Five times that many people boiled in the street those icy December Sundays.

Tribal drum beaters seemed to burst from every cranny, breathing fire and destruction, not merely in New York but across the land. One of the more picturesque was Hector Orr, "the Angel Gabriel," who wore a long white robe and assembled listeners by blowing on a trumpet. He caused violence wherever he preached—chiefly in Boston. There in May, 1854, after minor disorders, he led a mob from place to place, until inevitably a clash occurred with Irish laborers. Warmed up, the mob tried to burn a Mount Bellingham Catholic church but were prevented by prompt police action. The crowd refused to disperse unless given the cross on the roof. To avoid bloodshed the police finally let a boy climb up and throw the cross down. It was seized with delighted yells and burned. The inflamed mob then tried to burn another church in East Boston, but troops forced them to disband.

In New York, Angel Gabriel's close associate, eloquent Samuel G. Moses, brought on several full-fledged melees with the Irish. Pistols were used, heads were broken, and fighting kept on till quelled by the militia. Sensing a profitable emotional climate, Orr hurried to the green pastures beside the Hudson. On June 11, he spoke to a big crowd from city hall steps.

He came riding up in an express wagon, blowing a brass trumpet. In his left hand he carried a long tin can resembling a small ice-cream freezer. Under his large shiny patent-leather hat, with a brass eagle on it, his face was thin, his skin dark, and his black hair flowed down over his shoulders. Black eyes glowing insanely, he descended from the wagon, holding up his long white but not spotless robe with some loss of dignity though not of haughtiness.

He poured out his godly sentiments, his wrath about the "beast of Babylon," and his denunciations of slavery, with a decided accent, not quite Scotch, his alleged nationality. His clenched fists at the ends of his long arms struck hither and yon. Then he led a band of a thousand screaming followers to the Brooklyn Irish districts.

Fortunately an army of special police were able to keep order. Although 10,000 listeners gathered, no turbulence occurred except for a bad clash with Irish on the return ferry.

Orr went on through New England. At Nashua, New Hampshire, his listeners mobbed the Irish quarters, causing considerable destruction. In Bath, Maine, his hearers rushed to a Catholic church and, aroused by a flag and hot words flung out from a balcony, burned the edifice. Another church burning occurred in Palmyra, New York. But on returning to the Boston area, he found himself in hot water.

The Charlestown authorities, still smarting from the stigma of the Ursuline convent burning, arrested him during his first sermon there for distributing handbills on the Sabbath. A mob tried to break into the jail to free him but was dispersed. He was put on trial and fined. From then on he was given trouble by the police everywhere. In Washington, D. C., he defied a police order not to hold a meeting and spent two weeks in jail.

Announcing that freedom was dead in America, he departed for British Guiana, his native country. It came out then that he was a mulatto, half Scotch, half Negro. On his home soil, he stirred the blacks to arson and murder against white Catholics.

Another lightning rod for riots was "Father" Leahy, whose sermon, "The Unchristian Treatment of Females in the Confessional by Popish Priests," was announced by handbills and signs promising "Awful Disclosures." In best burlesque style, "ladies and youths" were excluded. The center of many brawls, he was repeatedly arrested, finally was given life imprisonment in Wisconsin for killing a man in a quarrel. A frame-up, the Know-Nothings said, although the evidence seemed to indicate otherwise.

Reverend L. Giustiniani developed a profitable sideshow stunt. His entourage included Germans whom he "converted" in every city with tearful scenes of dramatic repentance and glory. In Cincinnati, outraged Catholics burned the church where his meeting was being held, probably the only Protestant church so destroyed in the country, but it kept a far larger blaze burning in the breasts of the outraged Know-Nothings.

Another firebrand was Italian immigrant Alessandro Gavazzi, a former priest and teacher turned revolutionist, who fled from Italy to England, then in March, 1853, came to America under the auspices of the American and Christian Foreign Church Union, a scandal-making organization against the "corrupting" Roman Catholic Church. "Romanism," it said in its *American and Foreign Christian Union,* had replaced error for "the truth as it is in Jesus." The organization, militant in the school controversy, averred that the Bible would not be "expelled" from American classes "so long as a piece of Plymouth Rock remains big enough to make a gun-flint out of."

Although his name is rarely heard today, Gavazzi probably aroused more national fervor than Kossuth. He had sworn to devote his life to "stripping the Roman harlot of her garb," and riots and bloodshed occurred wherever he went. A great six-foot orator, he spoke "with almost savage physical energy." Although a renegade, he wore a long monk's robe, embroidered over the chest with a blazing cross. His long black hair and fiery eyes were a call to violence and incendiarism. "Popery cannot be reformed . . . nothing but annihilation . . . I am the Destroyer!"

His arrival in America coincided with the tour of Papal Nuncio Gaetano Bedini, sent over to settle inner-church property disputes. Bedini was received personally by President Pierce, the secretary of state, and other Washington dignitaries, and visited much of the United States. Gavazzi denounced him as the "Butcher of Bologna," and charged him with having personally tortured and assassinated the patriot Ugo Bassi—although Bassi was a murderer and rapist. "Lies of the Church," shouted Gavazzi, and stirred up mob violence in the prelate's path.

Huge Boston crowds burned the nuncio in effigy. It happened again in Baltimore. Bullets were fired into his room. In Wheeling, West Virginia, he was saved from assassination, after a howling mob overwhelmed the police, by armed Irishmen, who also prevented Catholic churches from being burned. He was manhandled badly in Pittsburgh. Cincinnati Germans, bitter over his role in suppressing the 'forty-eight revolution, joined with anti-German Nativists, marching 2,000 strong with his effigy swinging from a gallows and banners inscribed: "No Priests, no Kings, no Popery"—"Gallows-Bird Bedini"—"Down with the Raven Butcher." He had to abandon plans to visit New Orleans, by then stirred to frenzy by parades and placards declaring Bedini had had Bassi scalped before killing him, that he had murdered "hundreds of patriots, their wives and children." When the nuncio finally sailed from New York, the police, routed by an enormous mob, had to smuggle him aboard his vessel well down the harbor.

In city after city, angry mobs liberated street preachers from the police. In Pittsburgh, an itinerant preacher led his claque into a Catholic church, ousted the priest, seized the pulpit, and insulted the worshipers by attacking the Pope. Visiting preacher Joseph Barker stirred up so much trouble that he was sentenced to a year in jail. The city, rocked by indignation, elected him mayor by a big majority—he went from jail cell to city hall. He gave the Catholics short shrift and committed other abuses, but in the next election was defeated only by the narrowest margin.

All over the country Catholic churches were stoned, dynamited, burned, wrecked. Crosses were stolen, windows smashed, altars torn out. Only prompt police action saved New York's Saint Peter and Saint Paul Cathedral. After a Catholic church had been destroyed in Maine, a mob broke up a cornerstone ceremony for a new one. Everywhere priests were threatened, spat upon, their robes torn off. One in Ellsworth, Maine, was tarred and feathered and ridden from town on a rail. A grand jury refused to bring the culprits to trial. In Portland, Maine, school children trooped after the priest shouting vile names, sometimes stoning him. He dared not venture out after dark, and one night a rock was thrown through his bedroom window. Church windows were repeatedly broken, the doors smashed in.

Everywhere nuns, because of their reputed immorality, were propositioned grossly on the streets, and the police frequently had to rescue them from assaults. In New Orleans, Galveston, Charleston, among numerous places, mobs stormed the "Popish brothels." The Providence *Journal* (Rhode Island) so stirred up the community with false charges against the local Sisters of Mercy convent that the nuns were repeatedly insulted when they went about their good deeds. In March, 1854, the paper charged that an "American girl" was confined there against her will. The girl herself denied this, but a big mass meeting was called, and only prompt action by the police and armed Irishmen prevented the mob from destroying the place.

A new crop of "escaped nuns" made headlines and toured the country. Josephine M. Bunkley, unlike most of this tribe, really had been a novice and published her spine-tingling tale: *The Testimony of an Escaped Novice from the Sisterhood of St. Joseph, Emmesburg, Maryland* (1855). The mother superior reported that the discontented soul had been free to leave at any time, that her alleged elaborate "escape" had been unnecessary. But the public reveled in her lascivious accounts of goings on between priests and nuns.

In many places Protestants began bringing court actions to secure the "release" of captive nuns. The enforced appearance of the nuns and the heads of such convents in court was very painful to them, and there is no record of anyone's testifying she was being held under duress. Bills were introduced in many legislatures and in Congress to abolish convents.

Anti-Catholicism in Louisiana, never pronounced even among early Nativists, after haranguers such as Gavazzi, assumed large proportions. In May, 1854, a handbill was circulated in New Orleans attacking a Catholic candidate for district attorney as "a bigot . . . All Ireland and Germany would rejoice in his election." He would convict "no Irish or German Creoles . . . Father Mulligan and the Jesuits" would "rule this city."

Hysteria grew everywhere. People in Bangor, Maine, became panic-stricken when mysterious markings on houses caused them to believe that the families had been marked for death by Catholics. An itinerant German hairdresser had used this means to indicate the houses where he had handed out leaflets. All over the country posters and placards appeared warning people to beware of Catholic attacks. Storekeepers used wrapping paper printed with warnings against Popish poison plots and other dangers. Many places were terrified by rumors that Irish servants were killing their Protestant masters with poison provided by priests. Many girls lost their jobs.

In Charlestown, Massachusetts, the shame of the Ursuline convent burning came close to being repeated. Hannah Corcoran, an Irish servant girl, was converted to the Freewill Boston faith by her employers. The Protestant press and the pulpits glowed over this snatching of a brand from the burning. Neurotic, disturbed by the publicity, on February 12, 1853, Hannah vanished. The newspapers gave credence to the rumor that she had been abducted by priests, although her mother said she had gone to Philadelphia to look for work—and to get away from a community where she had aroused so much controversy. On February 23, handbills were distributed:

SHE MUST BE FOUND

> All people opposed to religious oppression and the IMPRISONMENT of a human being for Opinion's Sake are requested to meet at Richmond Street, Charlestown, Wednesday evening, March 2.

The selectmen, fearing the crowd might attack a nearby Catholic church, called out the militia. Foiled, the mob managed to tear down one Irish home, and rioting shook the town for days. Then Hannah reappeared.

From their pulpits, all over Charlestown and Boston, Protestant preachers joyously heralded her return "still strong in the faith of Our Lord and Saviour, Jesus Christ."

She profited. She was showered with so many gifts that she quit being a servant and went off to school. Her escapade provided meat for sensational pamphlets and books: *Hannah Corcoran, the Missing Girl of Charlestown, the Mysterious Disappearance Unraveled. The Convent and the Confessor. Attempt at Abduction Foiled! A Full and Complete Report of the Riot at Charlestown.* Thomas F. Caldicott came out with *Hannah Corcoran: An Authentic Narrative of Her Conversion from Romanism; Her Abduction from Charlestown and the Treatment She Received during Her Absence.*

In 1852, the Pope sent a block of marble from the Concord Temple in Rome as a gift to the American people to be placed in the Washington Monument, just started. The Know-Nothings denounced this as an insult and a desecration. For two years they repeatedly flung armed guards about it, defaced it, and raised such a continuous hullabaloo, gathering petitions, holding mass meetings, publishing pamphlets, that work was halted, and the monument not completed for thirty years. The block of marble represented "a designing, crafty, subtle" scheme of the "far-reaching Power" that was "grasping after the whole world to sway its iron scepter with bloodstained hands over the millions of its inhabitants." Finally a mob broke into the shed where the Pope's gift was kept and threw it into the Potomac.

All this ignorance, bigotry and chicanery, brutality and violence, rising to a third crest of national hysteria, made rich pickings for demagogues. The country was ripe for a new Know-Nothing upsurge, and another crop of vociferous super-patriots made the streets a free-for-all and fought the older parties on their home grounds of underworld gangsterism. They made a cyclone of men's minds, a grab bag of politics, a growing chaos through which their single-purpose ambition drove along its determined path of ruin and self-advantage. They collected the human iron filings of doubt, indecision, prejudice, and fear with the strong magnet of their "pure patriotism" and their power-urge. Strong-arm methods became the rule of the day.

The persistent dark-lantern tactics of the Protestant Society and the OUA had attracted a dense swarm of night bugs. The fruits of their undercover crusade were beginning to ripen. They now had a host of imitators—some sixty secret patriotic societies, anti-Catholic, anti-foreign, in New York alone. One of the first—the most significant—was the Supreme Order of the Star-Spangled Banner (SSSB), or the Sons of the Sires of '76, organized in 1849 by Charles B. Allen. The first president, a journeyman printer, William L. Bradbury, died a few months later, and Allen took his place. Meetings were held around about in homes.

All members had to be white American-born Protestants, not married to Catholics, and had to swear to recognize no other authority in political affairs. Its initial strategy—as, lately, that of the OUA—was to attempt to control Whig and Democratic caucuses and conventions in behalf of "true Americans." Only SSSB-endorsed candidates were to be voted for by members.

The order cut little ice until schemers from the OUA took it over. The OUA had built up its vast membership on a non-political non-partisan basis. But the plums of concerted political action were now ripe for the plucking. As the OUA might be wrecked if it turned to politics, the leaders decided that political activities would be carried on better by a well-controlled auxiliary organization. The plot matured in Washington Council No. 2.

Some organizations, such as the Guard of Liberty, were merely armed Storm Troopers. The SSSB seemed just right, thoroughly secret, small enough to be easily captured—according to one account, only forty-three members, although apparently larger, for it had a number of chapters. The OUA clique headed by James Barker, with "Hindoo" Daniel Ullman and Thomas R. Whitney, of Washington OUA Chapter No. 2, moved in, were duly initiated, and staged a coup. Shoved aside, Allen led his minority out in a huff, and his council refused to recognize the new top command.

Later this was to cause the Know-Nothings headaches when the "authentic Firsters" organized their separate Grand Council and, in a few years, obtained a considerable following with more than a hundred councils in New York and thirty in New Jersey. Often they backed candidates opposed to those put forward by the Know-Nothings. It placed the whole secret apparatus in jeopardy. Secrecy could be a double-edged weapon.

Barker, born in White Plains, New York, December 5, 1805, had come to New York City as a dry-goods clerk. In time he set up his own small business, he was burned out, and for a year or so engaged in real estate before finally devoting full time to Know-Nothingism. In the 1854 municipal campaign the *Tribune* published a letter accusing him of having set fire to his own store in order to gull the insurance company. He sued for libel. The case was settled out of court, apparently without retraction. He had the closed mentality typical of so many small businessmen.

The OUA group pushed the expansion of the SSSB, and presently—in May, 1854—in super-secret top-flight conventions, Barker was named head of the state SSSB Council; and, three days later, of the national Grand Council. Under his aggressive leadership, with the backing of the OUA executive committee and under-cover aid from Fillmore's Silver Gray Whigs and the Protestant Society, the SSSB grew by leaps and bounds. Trusted OUA elements became the hard core of the new SSSB wigwams. Secret organizers quickly spread it across the land. By July 12, 1854—within a month of taking over power—Barker formed 152 councils; by August 1, there were 201; presently, a thousand.

Securing concentrated authority, he streamlined the organization for action—and personal power. He was given sole right of appointment of officers at local, district, and state levels. District deputies named by him chose their nine associates for each new local council, and he had a hand-picked band of precinct "superintendents" with wide powers of investigation and expulsion. Lukewarm or anti-Barker elements were ruthlessly purged.

This rigorous rule was maintained by three orders, plus what amounted to a fourth top ruling order. The members of the second and third orders were chosen by successive close screenings based on loyalty, fanaticism, and cleverness in anti-foreign, anti-Catholic work. Those initiated into the first degree were not even told the name of the organization, nor could they hold any office, a privilege of those admitted to the second degree. With exceptions, only third-degree members could hold public office. Those in the fourth tier had the only real power to make political decisions—there Barker ruled supreme, with iron hand.

For local elections Know-Nothing candidates sometimes were picked by the entire council rather than through arbitrary designation from above. In counties and legal districts, candidates were chosen by officers or by secret nominating conventions, although the choices were sometimes ratified by first-degree meetings. Beyond some local matters, the first-degree members had no voice at all.

Soon the secret decisions of the SSSB spread terror among politicians, who never knew how, when, or where lightning might strike. Great bodies of voters, not merely the Know-Nothings, derived glee from confounding old-line machines by voting for dark-horse candidates sometimes not presented until election-day morning. It hastened disintegration of both Whig and Democratic parties, already badly split over the slavery issue, temperance, Catholics, foreigners, pacifism, women's rights, and a score of dog-catcher dilemmas.

Blank pieces of paper, of different colors and cut to code shape, gave the place and time of meetings—which were held in barns, store lofts, creek bottoms, secluded halls, or locked lodge rooms. A red paper, usually heart-shaped, meant imminent danger and required immediate attendance. Only illness or absence from town was accepted as an excuse. A member meeting another who might not have seen the call, said, "Oh-oh-oh." The other replied, "Hio, hio, h-i-o," and the necessary information was imparted. The ordinary call was by means of triangular plain white sheets posted on fences and walls and strewn in public places between midnight and half an hour before dawn.

All secret SSSB matter, to the extent it was put in writing, was in code.

| A | B | C | D | E | F | G | H | I | J | K | L | M | N |
|---|---|---|---|---|---|---|---|---|---|---|---|---|---|
| 1 | 7 | 13 | 19 | 25 | 2 | 8 | 14 | 20 | 26 | 3 | 9 | 15 | 21 |

| O | P | Q | R | S | T | U | V | W | X | Y | Z |
|---|---|---|---|---|---|---|---|---|---|---|---|
| 4 | 10 | 16 | 22 | 5 | 11 | 17 | 23 | 6 | 12 | 18 | 24 |

The first initiation degree—"seeing Sam"—as of 1854, was: "You and each of you of your own free will and accord, in the presence of Almighty God and these witnesses do solemnly promise and swear that you will never betray any secrets of this Society, nor communicate them even to proper candidates except within the lawful council of the Order; that you will not permit any of the secrets of the Society to be written, or in any other manner to be made legible except for the purpose of official instruction; that you will not vote nor give your influence for any man for any office in the gift of the people unless he be an American-born citizen in favor of Americans ruling America, nor if he be a Roman Catholic; that you will in all political matters so far as this Order is concerned, comply with the will of the majority, though it may conflict with your personal preference, so long as it does not conflict with the Constitution of the United States of America, or that of the state within which you reside; that you will not under any circumstances whatever, knowingly recommend an unworthy person for initiation nor suffer it to be done if it is in your power to prevent it; that you will not under any circumstances expose the name of any member of this Order nor reveal the existence of such an association; that you will answer an *imperative notice* issued by the proper authority, obey the command of the state council president or his deputy, while assembled by such notice, and respond to the claim or *sign* or *cry* of the Order unless it is physically impossible; that you will acknowledge the state council of [*name of state*] as the legislative head, the ruling authority and the supreme tribunal of the Order of the State of ———————— acting under jurisdiction of the National Council of the United States of North America, binding yourself in the penalty of excommunication from the Order, the forfeiture of all intercourse with its members, and being denounced in all the societies of the same, as wilful traitor to your God and to your country."

The second-degree pledge was similar: "You and each of you of your own free will and accord, in the presence of Almighty God and these witnesses, your left hand resting on your right breast and your right hand extended to the flag of your country, do solemnly and sincerely swear that you will not under any circumstances disclose in any manner, nor suffer it to be done by others if in your power to prevent it, the names, signs, passwords, or other secrets of this degree, except in open Council for the purpose of instruction; that you will in all things conform to all the rules and regulations of this Order, and to the Constitution and by-laws of this or any other Council to which you may be attached, so long as they do not conflict with the Constitution of the United States nor that of the state in which you reside." A pledge to attend to all signs or summonses thrown out followed, and to support "in all political matters, for all political officers," all members of the Order in preference to any other person. Next came a pledge that if elected or appointed to any official position "conferring on you the power to do so," to "remove all foreigners, aliens or Roman Catholics from office or place, and that you will in no circumstances appoint such to any office or place in your gift." This and all other obligations previously taken "shall ever be kept through life, sacred and inviolate . . . without hesitation or mental reservation whatever. So help you God, and keep you steadfast."

The third or "Union" degree oath was almost identical but contained the further pledge "to preserve the Union." This concession to southern slaveholders was added by the secret National Council in Cincinnati, November 15, 1854, largely by two southern high-degree Masons, Kenneth Raynor of North Carolina and Albert Pike of Missouri; emphasis on "Union" was an effort to sidestep the slavery issue and short cut strife between North and South. The Massachusetts order, completely dominated by Abolitionists, flatly refused to adopt the "Union" oath or the third order.

The president's charge to new members for each degree stressed "the dangers which threatened American liberty . . . from foes without and from enemies within." For Degree One, it covered "the source and nature of our most imminent peril," and "first measures of safety." For Degree Two, it defined the means by which "assaults may be rendered harmless." For Degree Three, the charge reiterated the previous lessons—to provide against "a more remote but no less terrible danger from the domestic enemies of our free institutions." Here UNION was stressed with capital letters. "The unity of government which constitutes you one people is justly dear to you, for it is the main pillar in the edifice of your real independence, the support of your tranquillity at home, of your peace abroad, of your safety, your prosperity, even the liberty you so justly prize."

Meetings were protected by "out" and "in" sentries. At the outer wicket the member gave the password and then, for first-degree meetings, gave one sharp rap on the inner door. He gave his name, lodge number, his council, the general password, and the degree password.

Once inside, the member proceeded to the center of the room and addressed the president with the countersign: the right hand diagonally across his mouth. The president made the appropriate response, and the member took a seat.

On leaving, he was required to salute the president again and give the proper general or "term" degree passwords to the inner sentinel. This might go:

Member: "We are . . . ."
Sentry: "Term pass?"
Member: "Our country's hope."
Sentry: "Degree pass?"
Member: "Native."
Sentry: "Traveling password?"
Member: "The memory of our Pilgrim Fathers."

For second-degree meetings, two raps were given at the inner door; the password was "American." When the member reached the center of the room, he extended his right arm to the national flag over the president's head, with the palm of the hand upward. As the arm was dropped to the side, he uttered another ritualistic phrase, such as "Yorktown," "Sons of '76," or "Put none but Americans on guard tonight."

For a third-degree admission, the outer sentinel demanded, "You?" The member replied, "NI," and the sentry responded "ON." Three raps were given on the inner door, the password "Safe" and the personal information were provided. On entering the room, the member placed his hands on his breast, fingers interlocked, and bowed to the president, who made due response.

In third-degree initiation ceremonies, not less than five at a time were admitted, "to give more solemnity to the ceremony." All members present formed a circle about them, arms crossed over their breasts and firmly grasping hands to symbolize the linked unbroken chain of eternity. After due ceremonies, the degree was confirmed by the raising of the flag in the center of the circle beside the president, who administered the oath.

Outside the lodge room, the first-degree sign of recognition was to grasp the lapel of one's own coat with the right hand, forefinger extended upward. The other member answered in like manner, but with his left hand. An ordinary handshake was tendered, except that the first member drew his forefinger across the other's palm; the other did the same, and the handclasp ended with the ends of the forefingers hooked together. The first member then said: "Is that yours?"

"It is."

"How did you get it?"

"It is my birthright."

For second-degree members, the sign of recognition was identical except the middle finger was extended, the others folded. For third-degree members, the third finger was extended in the lapel gesture. At the handclasp, the forefingers were slipped over the top of the thumbs and the little fingers were pressed against the inside of the wrist. The words exchanged were:

"Do you know what that is?"

"Yes."

"What is it?"

"Union."

Another sign was said to be: to close one eye, place the thumb and forefinger formed into an "O" over the nose—a rebus meaning:

| EYE | NOSE | O |
|---|---|---|
| I | Knows | Nothing |

When a member spoke unguardedly in public, he was warned by the drawing of the forefinger and thumb across the eyes, the rest of the hand closed. If necessary, the words "Keep dark" were added. Other signals indicated that the eavesdropper was "a Papist" or "a Jesuit."

This all seems incredibly childish; it represents typical teenage gang cohesion. Any good textbook on ego involvement—such as that by Muzafer Sherif and Hadley Cantril

—describes the psychological and social processes involved in this type of voodooism, how gang loyalties supersede other moral and social obligations by drawing a magic circle, investing even criminal acts with noble phrases and high "moral" content.

The gang keeps the dread imagined enemy out, seals members together in a tight little self-righteous brotherhood. A chief task of the ego is the achievement of status. The hierarchical gang automatically supplies the precise superman status without struggle or soul-searching. The gang's supposedly superior attitudes supplant those of society at large, and are assumed to be the only proper attitudes for society and the nation. Race hatreds are determined, not by association with the hated race or opponent, not by knowledge acquired by free contact and interchange of ideas, but by blind acceptance of the herd attitude. The same goes for religious hatreds. Chauvinists live by emotions, prejudices, hatreds, blind loyalty to stereotype symbols, and they consider all change and progress to be dangerous, subversive, even immoral. Such gangs, and the ready-made slogans they live by, arise and gain unthinking vogue most frequently in times of confusion or crisis, at a time of intense economic, social, or national competition. The advent of the foreigner from 1830 on introduced keener competition. This was a creative process that added to the variety, strength, and happiness of the nation, but the Know-Nothings feared to grant to the foreigner his due rights under law or to permit him the status to which his abilities entitled him. The Know-Nothings sought to wipe out his upsetting presence and destroy him.

Involved here is the adolescent and ignoble wish to feel superior to other breeds. The secret order created a false superego. In the gang the member found a social identity and apparent love and friendship not felt in his home or in society at large.

Such gangs always have an iron-clad hierarchical structure. Members submit to a vertically integrated authority, and orders are accepted as divine edict—essentially a military concept, where men become obedient brain-washed cogs, and the organization, rather than the individual, acts as a unit. This mechanized discipline creates the inevitable dilemma that individual talent and initiative may be absent in a battle crisis requiring heroic individualism. But such militaristic gangs require the hierarchy of dictatorship, the concentration of power. The invariable feature of such fascist, military type of gangs is the permanence of the reign of the person or persons at the top.

But for each member in safe isolation and anonymity, personal security, plus an alleged noble purpose, were seemingly provided. The religious nature of this experience—all its intricate precise ritual—obeyed the unadmitted fear impulses that create all religious ritual. Hence the SSSB was not so dissimilar, ironically enough, to the Roman Catholic Church, which the group considered its worst enemy. All closed monopoly groups consider all other closed groups as potentially dangerous. Since the Know-Nothings offered nothing truly positive, except a false slogan of race superiority and "Union," enforced by brutality, the only possible road became rule or ruin.

The other face of this psychological dilemma was evasion and escapism. Most members were at heart, for all their ugly intolerance, weak vacillators, afraid to take an open stand on any matter—even hatred of Catholics and foreigners was a hidden conspiracy which came to life, except for the public barnstormers, only in moments of erupting violence.

Often the desire to sidestep the slavery issue was sincerely patriotic, but it could not be accomplished merely by head-in-the-sand avoidance—these were the people designated at the time as "dough faces"—or by frustrated aggressions against other groups. Like all thoughtless, cowardly, middle-of-the-road groups in crises demanding valiant decisions, the Know-Nothings made more inevitable and destructive the eventual catastrophe. Their position would have had moral and pragmatic value only if they had promoted a constructive program superior to the choice of "the lesser of two evils."

They found no such lofty, peaceful solution for the slavery controversy, none whatever. They merely ran away from it, mouthing phrases such as "States Rights," "Union," "No North, No South," with evangelical bravado, and blindly attacked foreigners and Catholics rather than indulge in the more dangerous pastime of attacking Negroes or slaveowners.

Everything was obscured, befogged by the incense of mystery, the mumbo jumbo of a pseudo priestcraft. Numbers of rhapsodical statements, pure drivel, some with an almost Paul Bunyan flavor, have come down to us. Kenneth Raynor of North Carolina (a Know-Nothing slaveowner rabidly anti-foreign and anti-Catholic, but a transcendental orator and a clever practical politician) left us this gem in the Richmond (Virginia) *Daily Evening Post:*

> There is a certain personage abroad in the land, at the sound of whose voice the shackles of party drop from the hands of our people, like those of Paul and Silas at the approach of the Angel. . . . Although the echo of his footsteps is not heard, yet to the demagogue and the party hack he is as able as an "army with banners". . .; the touch of his wand, like that of the spear of Ithuriel, causes the mask to drop from the face of hypocrisy and exposes selfishness and partisan bigotry in all their deformity. . . . They call him "Sam." But he is not "Uncle Sam.". . . He passes rivers at a bound, scales mountains at a leap, and through swamp and forest he never loses his way. He never stops, except to drop a tear on the grave of some revolutionary hero, for his heart is tender as his nerves are strong. . . . He carries in his hand the flag of his country. . . . The halo of freedom beams upon his countenance, and enemies of the Union fly at his coming, like kites and crows at the eagle's swoop.

When he strikes, "the edge of his claymore severs joints and marrow, and a hecatomb falls at every blow. The creed of his faith is the constitution of the country, and

Luther and Washington are his two great examples of religious liberty and civil freedom. . . . Convent walls cannot be built too high for him to scale."

The Abingdon *Virginian,* February 23, 1856, reported a Know-Nothing speaker:

> The noble and mysterious Sam, with sound head and pure heart—coming up from the fires of the Revolution, shaking his hoary locks of wisdom, and cleaving to the doctrine of our fathers—is seated upon his war horse and with sword in hand, is flying over the plains of the New World, bearing down all opposed with a purpose as firm as eternal granite that supports the earth, that Americans shall rule America. . . . Sam, Sir, is the embodiment of liberty. He has the soul of a lion, and carries the American Republic in the soul. His words burn the demagogue, and lash the black heart of political corruption like the sting of an adder. He has wounded both old parties, and left an eating ulcer . . . that breeds death, but he has established another, a National, an American Party, that will live forever. . . . His mind glides along in limpid and growing abundance, flowing up from the clear sparkling current of his unadulterated patriotism, an image far more lovely than a sleeping Venus; I mean Sam's own bride, the Goddess of American liberty.

Freud would certainly have had a field day with this effusion.

The Austin, Texas, *State Times,* March 3, 1855, showed equal softening of the brain:

> Like the wind we hear the sound of his approach, but no man can tell whence he cometh or whither he goeth. . . . In imitation of "Jack, the Giant Killer," he appears to be perambulating the whole country.

Reverend Brooks of the District of Columbia declared

"Sam" was "from the Garden of Eden; . . . he rode out of the flood with Noah in the ark; he was present at the building of the Tower of Babel; he wandered with the children of Israel in the wilderness; he was with Miriam in the inspired song and dance; he blew the loudest ram's horn trumpet when the walls of Jericho fell; he clothed John, the Baptist . . .; he held up the chains of Paul . . . before Agrippa. . . .

"He had a hard time with the Popes and the Inquisition, but it was he who pointed the young Luther to the dust-covered Bible on the neglected shelves of the old monastery. He brought the Bible with him across the ocean on the *Mayflower;* he laid the cornerstone of the first Protestant church in the colonies. . . ." Page Freud again.

A bit sarcastic, the Richmond *Penny Post* offered $100 reward for the capture "of the fellow called 'Sam' . . . prowling about in these parts. . . . Supposed to be a tall American, whose forefathers fought in the battles of the Republic, and came to this country many years before; as Mrs. Parrington says, 'to worship God and cheat the Indians according to the dictates of their own consciences.' He wears home-made clothes and contends strenuously that he has the right to read the Bible as much as he pleases—also that this is the greatest nation in the world and owes no allegiance whatever to the Pope. . . ."

The North Carolina *Weekly Standard* printed a Know-Nothing Bill of Fare:

First Course

Catholic broth Jesuit soup

Second Course

Roasted Catholic Broiled Priest

Third Course

The Pope's Big Toe, broiled

Fourth Course

Fried Nuns, very nice and tender

Dessert

Rich Irish Brogue Sweet German Accent

And so Barker, with his little top clique, had his gang, his church—kept well under his thumb by means of all the voodoo shindigs and semantic idiocy. An indication of his broad powers was his revocation of the charter of the State Council of Ohio when that body declined to support Fillmore, the 1856 Know-Nothing presidential candidate. He had built the SSSB into a strong national organization. His national council (less closely controlled after a time than the state council) was composed of seven appointed delegates from each state council, two from each territorial council. These delegates received three dollars a day and five cents a mile travel allowance. Thirty-two members from thirteen states constituted a quorum. The national council elected annually, a president [Barker], vice-president, chaplain, recording and corresponding secretaries. All had to be third-degree members. The national office received four cents a year from the twenty-five-cents-a-year dues of each member. This at the peak of the organization totaled $60,000 or better. California had no dues, and depended on voluntary contributions, but paid its national quota.

Recruits kept coming in in droves, many of them OUA or Protestant Society members. And violence mounted. In Louisville—stirred to rabid fury by the *Journal's* Know-Nothing propaganda—twenty men were killed and several hundred wounded in an assault on the German quarter of the city, a day long remembered as Bloody Monday. In Lawrence, Massachusetts, 1,500 "Americans" stormed the Irish section, destroying homes and churches. Philadelphia, Baltimore, Boston, New Orleans experienced near-civil war. In St. Louis, during the 1854 election, rioting brought out the militia to prevent continued loss of life. The Irish were hit hardest, and nearly every saloon from Broadway to Levee Street was looted, smashed, or wiped out.

In New York City, William W. Patten supplemented Know-Nothing violence by organizing the auxiliary Secret Order of Free and Accepted Americans, usually known as the Order of the American Star from its emblem of a five-pointed star centered by the numeral sixty-seven. This was made up wholly of teenage ruffians, nicknamed the "Wide Awakes," unable to gain status or quick preferment in the existing societies. Unlike the SSSB, the members did not conceal their identity but swaggered abroad provocatively, armed and wearing broad-brimmed white hats, and inciting street brawls with the Irish and other Catholics, who in turn took every opportunity to give the young hoodlums a trouncing. In 1854 or 1855, older persons were admitted, and Barker, Ullman, and other conspirators moved in and took over control as they had with the SSSB, in order better to direct its punitive activities for political purposes.

On the lighter side, such things as Know-Nothing candy, Know-Nothing toast, Know-Nothing toothpicks appeared on stands. Many Know-Nothing almanacs were published. One clipper ship and many stage coaches were named Know-Nothing. Great letters K. N. appeared in the dark of night on walls, houses, fences, hillsides. Even dogs appeared on the streets daubed K.N. A wag started an Owe-Nothing society.

As the SSSB moved toward power in state after state, the eyes of many intelligent people were opened to the dark conspiracy. Henry Ward Beecher lashed out against dark-lantern politics in the *Independent.* "One might as well study optics in the pyramids of Egypt or the subterranean tombs of Rome, as liberty in secret conclaves controlled by hoary knaves versed in political intrigue."

Henry A. Wise, statesman of Virginia, not without his own brand of demagogy and inconsistently an upholder of slavery, launched continuous attacks on Dark Lantern methods. His Senate speeches are among America's greatest documents of reason, freedom, and democracy. He exposed the "un-American" conspirators who monopolized the word "American" with remorseless logic, confuting Know-Nothing methods and program. As early as September 18, 1852, he rose in the Senate and delivered a memorable peroration on free and open democratic practices. Where political life was ruled by free discussion, he averred, there was no need to fear evil, for where Truth was free to combat error, sooner or later she would light up the dark wreckage with her torches.

Why, then, this conspiratorial secrecy, miscalling itself a political party? he demanded. A secret party caucus might be necessary and convenient, but even that was "reprehensible if carried too far." But this great national face-hidden organization, what was it? "Nobody knows. To do what? Nobody knows. How organized? Nobody knows. Governed by whom? Nobody knows. How bound? By what limitations and restraints? By what rules? By what oaths? Nobody, nobody knows. All we know is that persons of foreign birth and Catholic faith are proscribed, and so are all others who don't proscribe them at the polls. . . .

"Why should any portion of the people desire to retire in secret and by secret means to propagate a political thought, or word, or deed by stealth?" For what end? "If it be good why not make the good known? Why not speak it, write it, act it out openly and aloud? Or is it evil which loveth darkness rather than light?"

Congress, certainly, was impressed enough in the early 'fifties to look into the matter of political secrecy. A congressional committee on political secret societies reported, over the protesting screams of Know-Nothing congressmen, that "the pretended" Know-Nothing conspiracy (which it compared to the rule of Julian II, the Apostate Roman emperor) "should acquire supremacy over the American Union is as absurd an anachronism as would be the anticipation of a Carthaginian incursion or the subjection of the country by mail-clad warriors of a descendant of William of Normandy."

A satirical account of a supposed SSSB initiation pictured the novice being whirled around three times by a Revolutionary War veteran and required to swear that if Uncle Sam's farm were ever "attacked by South Pole cannibals or by Goths and Vandals," he would take up "arms, pitchforks, stovepipes, wooden nutmegs, and logs and swear by the great horn spoon to lick all creation."

A Missouri editor said the insigne of the Know-Nothings had finally been discovered: "An American eagle holding in his bill a furriner by the seat of his breeches."

Many fake rituals were published ridiculing the order, how the novitiate entered to discover everybody wearing a dunce's cap "at an angle of 45° about 18 inches in length. Every man has the right forefinger of each hand in his mouth and . . . tugs on the corners of his potato trap to see which can produce the most horrible grimace and the deepest guttural cavern, studded with the longest rows of bad ivory." The oath: "I pledge my most pertinacious logos, binding myself under a penalty no less than having my boots drawn off over my head, my hair twisted into a cord nine feet long, the skirts of my coat cut into forty-nine strips . . . and suffer myself to be rode on a three-cornered rail nine feet long over the railroad track of a Hamburg rocket at the rate of ninety miles per hour."

A widely printed account of the "Do-Nothings" appeared, with Tom Lazybones in the chair and Loaferson as vice-president. "Several idle men were present." Jim Vacuum, without moving from his seat, offered to make a motion that it was "a popular prejudice that it was the destiny of man to work." A new member was carried in on a four-poster bedstead. After giving the password, *Ex nihilo nihil fit,* he took the oath of "eternal laziness." Asked to repeat it, he responded "Ditto," then fell asleep. "He'll do," said the president approvingly. He was merely roused to pay his dues, but did nothing of the kind. Nobody did anything.

But neither attacks nor ridicule gave the fanatical party pause in its march toward power. It had become an orgy of revivalism. It was one of those emotional and mental fevers that periodically overtake the American democracy. Would it run its course and the patient recover safely? Or would the nation itself be locked up in institutional bars?

CHAPTER VII

# THE NEW DODGE

"OLD Fuss and Feathers," General Winfield Scott, was anxious to be president and felt he deserved it, especially as in 1848 brassy, blundering Mexican War General Zachary Taylor, "Old Rough and Ready," had beaten him for the Whig nomination and had won at the polls, despite the bad war record of the New England Whigs.

But now in 1852, both parties were shaken by bitter differences over whether the territory grabbed from Mexico should be carved into free or slave states. The 1850 Clay and Webster slavery compromise, after a long fervor of thanksgiving that God was in His heaven, had sharpened rather than assuaged ill-feeling. The Fugitive Slave Act had infuriated even northerners lukewarm to Abolitionism. Emerson, always carefully aloof from the slavery controversy, now called upon everybody to defy this evil law. Harriet Beecher Stowe's *Uncle Tom's Cabin,* appearing early in 1852, heightened antagonism to it. A Boston mob liberated one arrested slave.

The Whigs again in 1852 pinned much hope of success on Democratic dissensions. In New York, the "Hunkers," who wanted a "hunk" of the spoils, and the "radical Barnburners" debated angrily over reckless canal spending. The best chance to hang on to power, many Whigs believed, was to nominate another outstanding army man—the braid is always good for lots of votes—so Scott had strong backing among party bosses, particularly Seward. Scott's Know-Nothing tinge and his wishy-washy attitude on slavery scarcely pleased the New Yorker, but both were strong Manifest Destiny expansionists.

The real battle for control was between Henry Clay, who was backing President Millard Fillmore, and Seward, who had long fought Fillmore and his reactionary Silver Grays in New York, and in the national arena. Nor did Seward love Webster, also anxious to gain the nomination. Under Scott, Seward could take his pick of any cabinet post, although he denied he would do so.

The general had had a distinguished if stormy career. A West Pointer made brigadier general in the War of 1812, its outstanding hero, twice wounded when horses were shot out from under him; an Indian fighter; the man who had threatened South Carolina in 1832, when that state tried to secede because of Webster's high tariff law, and who had stopped New Brunswick and Maine from fighting over their boundary, he became army head for three years and led the Vera Cruz invasion of Mexico, fighting up to the capital, where he ran the Stars and Stripes up over Montezuma's halls.

In 1852, when he made a blunt-fingered clutch for the presidency, Old Fuss was sixty-six but he still had a thundering parade-field voice. His massive face sagged like an old St. Bernard's—a nose big as a plow, a pugnacious lower lip jutting out from a tight, nasty mouth, and a freight-car jaw, with a scraggly under-chin beard; a gray mane parted way down on the left side. Autocratic, bigoted, hating foreigners and Catholics, contemptuous of civilians, he was devoid of comprehension of economic, social, and political problems. Accustomed to roar at underlings, to turn purple at the slightest criticism, he had only one political forte: pompous spread-eagle patriotism.

He had become identified with Nativism as early as 1836, the year of Morse's flimflams. Angered by "foreigners crying, 'Down with the Natives'" (really the other way round), he issued a call for a new "Republican or Democratic American party." In 1840, he spoke at a Nativist rally at Astor House. He blamed the 1844 Whig defeat on foreign voters and as late as 1848 uttered ugly anti-Catholic statements. In December, in the *National Intelligencer,* he advocated the denial of suffrage to all foreign-born citizens. But he spent the next four years pulling wires with Whig bosses and trying to convince the world he had changed his stripes and loved everybody. But as one critic remarked, "To ask Irishmen to vote for Scott is to ask them to embrace a political vampire who for thirteen years has abused their character" and has "resorted to every means to rob them of political power."

The great Daniel Webster—"Black Dan," now sixty-eight—wanted the presidency as the crown of his long, brilliant career. But his reputation was badly tarnished. Long ago his drastic treatment of South Carolina's nullification efforts had antagonized the South. The high tariffs he had pushed through the Senate had favored New England manufacturers at the expense of the rest of the country. He was accused of taking payoffs from wealthy eastern interests. According to Congressman Charles Allen, Free-Soiler of Massachusetts, Webster had pocketed $50,000 to have the government borrow money at an unfavorable rate from favored financial interests: he was a servant not of the government but of bankers and brokers. Of late he had tried to placate the South, but his Fugitive Slave Law and other compromises had lost him respect in the North. His new hands-off "Union First" "States Rights" position—which would soon be taken up by the Know-Nothings—favored the slaveholders. "I wish to speak today not as a Massachusetts man, not as a northern man, but an American. . . . I speak today of preservation of the Union" —almost the precise Know-Nothing phraseology. His drinking alienated the fast-growing temperance crowd. Those years were not easy for politicians trying to please everybody. Webster had become opportunist, all things to all men, but he was still the greatest orator in the land.

He had avoided attacks on foreign elements, but his patriotic blustering had won the support of Nativists and like-minded Whigs. Particularly popular was his reply in 1850, as President Taylor's secretary of state, to Chevalier Hülsemann, Austrian chargé d'affaires, who had protested again United States meddling in Hungary and its quasi-recognition of the revolution there. Webster informed him that the revolution represented the same principles on which responsible popular government in the United States had been founded and added blatantly, "The power of this republic, at the present moment, is spread over a region, one of the richest and most fertile on the globe, in comparison with which the possessions of the House of Hapsburg are but a patch on the earth's surface." Such hairy-chest talk was music to the Manifest Destiny "Young Americans." Most people believed that Webster, in spite of his shady financial deals, would get the nomination.

The would-be candidate deserving most from party hacks, President Millard Fillmore, had taken over from Taylor during the "Great Debate" over the slavery compromise—just in time to get blamed for the defects of that tightrope juggling; nor did his rigid enforcement of the Fugitive Slave Act sit well in many states. Stiff, over-righteous, calm, he had little imagination and no particular courage, although his inflexibility sometimes was mistaken for courage. Born January 7, 1800, in Locke, Cayuga County, New York, he had started in politics with Seward and Thurlow Weed in the early anti-Masonic party in 1828, then had become a Whig in 1834, later breaking with both his friends as he mounted the ladder through legislature and Congress to the vice-presidency in 1849. He was a tall, robust individual, had a certain rough wit, and was relatively good-natured. Seward is said to have remarked of him, "I had no idea dictators were such amiable creatures." Fillmore had the knack of winning excessive adulation, a host of admirers "who followed him about like a little dog."

He had seemed to lack concern for American dignity when the governor general of Cuba—convinced that the purser of George Law's side-wheeler *Northern Light* (which had a fat mail subsidy) had peddled unpleasant news about Cuba—

ordered the vessel (or any other vessel on which said purser might be working) not to enter Cuban waters under penalty of seizure. Law demanded protection, but Fillmore sensibly refused unless the said purser were left home. Law blew this up into a big patriotic issue and defiantly sent the vessel on its regular run with the purser at his post. The Cuban governor decided to look the other way. Although the outcome was an anticlimax, the controversy gave Law, already scheming for the presidency (on the Know-Nothing ticket), considerable publicity as a "fearless red-blooded American." His interchanges with the President had been sharp; the two became bitter enemies, and the newspapers that Law had been buying up far and wide to push his future campaign did not spare Fillmore's feelings.

By and large this year's nomination, although few admitted it, hinged in good part on the slavery issue. The party bosses wished to placate both southern slaveholders and northern anti-slavery elements—an impossible feat, ever more impossible as the years rolled by. The Free-Soilers were in the running, too, this year, with candidates John P. Hale (New Hampshire) and George W. Julian (Indiana) pushing the slogan, "Free Soil, Free Speech, Free Labor, Free Men."

Scott was less hampered by the slave issue, but even with Seward's support he received two fewer votes on the first convention ballots than did Fillmore. Webster polled only twenty-nine. It took fifty-three ballots before Seward got Scott named.

Webster was then nominated by "Unionists" in Georgia and by mill ends of the American Republican party meeting in national convention in New Jersey. He declined and died, disillusioned, before the election. So did Clay. The Georgia "Unionists," not liking Scott, gallantly voted for Webster even though he was dead.

After prolonged balloting, the Democratic convention also pulled a general out of the hat—dark-horse Franklin Pierce of New Hampshire. Only forty-eight, the youngest member of the United States Senate, he was handsome, open-faced, with curly black hair, hazel eyes, and a winning personality. Unfortunately, he lacked firmness and decision. He had gained some publicity as a pro-Jackson reformer and a supporter of the admission of Texas "slave or free."

Not a real general, however. At the outset of the Mexican War he had volunteered as a private, but, being a reliable party wheel horse, was at once made a general on Scott's staff. Fortunately Pierce was never given any important field forces or assignments, and his name scarcely figured in war stories. He came back as he had left—merely a paper political general, but nevertheless a good title for campaign razzledazzle and the automatic vet vote.

Pierce made few campaign speeches—and these were dignified and straightforward—but sat quietly in Concord, New Hampshire, clinging to his aura of anonymity, and let Scott's hoarse-voiced ignorance and hollow platitudes hand him the election. Scott's speeches, although they tickled long-eared Know-Nothing and spread-eagle patriots, aroused widespread derision. A mud-slinging campaign. Pierce was called a drunkard, coward, Abolitionist, an opponent of religious liberty, and a Catholic because he had voted for a proposed amendment to the New Hampshire constitution (not passed) to permit Catholics to hold elective and appointive positions. "One piece with the church business of Philadelphia," growled the Nativist New Haven *Palladium.* However, this year, especially in Connecticut, the Whigs were catering to foreign voters. In an effort to get the votes of Germans whom the *Palladium* had long derided, the paper charged that Pierce was being backed by New York financier August Belmont, "the agent of Austrian despotism." On their side, the Democrats hammered away at Scott's Know-Nothing, anti-Catholic, anti-foreign record.

The Whigs rallied little support in the South where some liberalism was yeasting and the old citadels of the plantation oligarchy were falling. Traditional slaveholding representation at the expense of poorer non-slave settlers, everywhere in the majority, was being cut down. Maryland's 1850 constitution doubled Baltimore's representation while halving the improper voting power of the tidewater plantation slaveowners. Similarly the 1852 Virginia constitution broke much of the improper voting strength of the coastal slavery Whigs. Some Whig strength remained in North Carolina, Florida, and Louisiana. In Tennessee and Missouri they managed to elect half the congressmen and hang on to control of the legislature, and in Kentucky the party continued to control the state, except for the governorship.

Although the nationwide vote was fairly close, Scott won the electoral votes of only four states, and Democratic governors were installed in all thirty-one states. Spectacular enough to be called a landslide. Congressman Nathaniel P. Banks of Massachusetts, with strong Nativist sympathies, produced figures showing that the foreign vote held the balance of power in the nation and had elected Pierce and defeated Scott. But the Know-Nothing tide was now rising anew against the "foreign menace."

The SSSB, OUA, and other secret Nativist groups exercised considerable influence in the 1852 campaign, especially in New York City and Massachusetts. The following year, Barker held his free-speech meeting in behalf of rabble rouser Parsons and took full charge of the SSSB. The vast crowds turning out for Know-Nothing and anti-Catholic street meetings made New Yorkers aware that a great ground swell was in the making. New Nativist papers were issued. More and more speakers sprang out of the dark to attack foreigners and Catholics. Violence mounted everywhere, and wild stories spread of thousands of armed men drilling for unknown purposes. By mid-year Patton's new Wide Awakes spearheaded many attacks. The operations of the strong-arm Guard of Liberty came to light when a Catholic paper published its secret ritual, in the mistaken belief it was the Know-Nothing order.

The SSSB was carrying on active ward organization. Members were divided into electoral groups of ten, with defined obligations to canvas, propagandize, register voters, get voters to the polls and keep opposition voters away, by force if necessary.

On July 4, 1854, a parade of Irishmen in Ward Nine

REV. W. C. BROWNLEE
An outstanding anti-Catholic demagogue.

REV. WILLIAM HOGAN
Once head of the Catholic diocese of Philadelphia, Hogan later became an anti-Catholic propagandist. His books were best-sellers.

How young ladies were "seduced by priests" (according to William Hogan's *Popish Mummeries*).

National unity being whittled away—and cut in two at the same time *(Diogenes Lantern).*

A jab at George Law, who schemed to annex Cuba *(Diogenes Lantern)*.

Emblem of the Order of United Americans, as it appeared in the funeral cortege of "Bill the Butcher." The serpent represented the enemies of the nation and of Protestantism.

Anti-Papist, anti-foreign Presidential candidate Winfield Scott wooing the Irish vote *(Diogenes Lantern)*.

Satirical comment on Brigham Young, Mormon leader, and his alleged crimes *(American Comic Almanac)*.

DELICATE ATTENTIONS.

ESCORTING A LADY TO A PUBLIC AMUSEMENT.

Perils of the opera—hazards of going out in the streets of New York City in 1852 *(Diogenes Lantern).*

A Row in the Sixth Ward.

A Row in the Sixth Ward (contemporary sketch). Citizens crying "Watch!" mean "Police!"

**THE MARE'S NEST, or Cuba Preserved.**

AN EXTRAVAGANZA, IN ONE ACT.

*President of the United States*—MR. FILLMORE. *Chief of the Filibusters*—GEORGE LAW, *his first appearance in that part*
*The other characters by* MESSRS CONRADE, HUGH MAXWELL, BRADY, *and the whole strength of the Company.*

George Law versus President Fillmore in the Cuban controversy *(Diogenes Lantern)*.

The Democratic Hunkers and other gangs in a New York City election parade *(Morning Herald)*.

William Lloyd Garrison being dragged through Boston streets, October 21, 1835, with rope around neck (contemporary cartoon; New York Historical Society).

The Dead Rabbit barricade across Bayard Street (*Leslie's Weekly*, New York Public Library). Tammanies are holding off Bowery Boys (Know-Nothings).

Astor Theater riot, 1849 (contemporary print).

Opening of battle between Bowery Boys (Know-Nothings) and Dead Rabbits (Tammanies) at Elizabeth and Bayard Streets (*Leslie*'s *Weekly*, N. Y. Public Library).

was broken up. The Irish were damned for not being patriotic and twice damned if they tried to show they were. This riot resulted in the organization in that same ward of a new American Republican party, with the Bible-reading, anti-foreign, anti-Catholic program of Harper's 1844 party. But SSSB extremists moved in, insisting on more blatant anti-foreign proscriptions, and by October the party folded up. The SSSB and OUA leaders had other plans afoot.

Secret state and national SSSB conventions had been held in May and June, 1854. Thirteen states were represented. Flourishing state organizations existed in New Jersey, Pennsylvania, Maryland, Connecticut, Massachusetts, and Ohio. The press learned that James W. Barker became head of both the state and national organizations. A secret state nominating council was held in September, which set up a fusion ticket with the Whigs.

The New York *Times* ferreted out the program—an order resting upon "the grand principles of secrecy," forbidden to "appear before the public in any respect as a distinct body or known organization." Its policies and operations were directed by an inner clique of the inner clique of the Grand Council, which enabled Barker to rule even local wigwams with an iron hand.

On November 10, 1854, the *Tribune* first used the word "Know-Nothing" to describe them, and this became the accepted appellation, even after they organized as the American party. Merely "a new dodge of protean Nativism . . ." said the paper, "essentially anti-foreign, especially anti-Irish, and anti-Catholic."

Within a month, Barker doubled the number of local chapters and pushed organizers through the state and across the land. Thereafter the Order "multiplied like a family of rabbits."

Council members and sometimes others were frequently called before the ruling bodies and subjected to "The Test," a pointed cross-examination regarding the defendant's beliefs, voting record, activity and loyalty—very much like later communist purge confusions—and the slightest dereliction was punished, usually by expulsion, thus enforcing thoroughgoing discipline.

Through 1852 and 1853 the SSSB and OUA were busily trying to control ward- and city-wide caucuses of the older parties, and backed Thomas R. Whitney to organize a false-front Reform League in coalition with the Whigs. He and Daniel F. Tiemann helped engineer such a front in 1844 and it had successfully put Harper into office. The SSSB now forced the Whigs to drop two Irish candidates and to nominate Whitney (although not without a bitter fight) for the state senate.

He went considerably beyond the Reform platform. The Roman Church, he told the voters, wants "to substitute the miter for our liberty cap, the crozier for our Stripes and Stars. . . . We want Union from snowy Vermont to the teeming prairies of Texas. . . . Slavery is the result of natural laws which give mind supremacy over matter. If you free the blacks, then you should free the ox and the horse. . . . We strive not for the physical emancipation of a few blacks, but for the political and moral freedom of the whole human race. . . . Foreigners reel obscenely through the public thoroughfare, and bawling and the midnight scream have usurped the place of order, decency, and sobriety. . . . Foreign bullies at the polls with their bludgeons beat down gray-haired Americans like dogs in the highway: the suffrage rights of these old citizens are challenged by the ignorant and besotted refuse from European municipalities."

It was improbable that any European municipality had such vicious conditions as New York, but it was hardly the fault of the foreigners. However, enough people believed this claptrap to elect him, so Whitney won.

Although the Know-Nothings were also active in state caucuses that year, there was no similar coalition, and the SSSB presented independent candidates—six Whigs, four Democrats—on November 2, a few days before the election.

A Whig-Know-Nothing city ticket carried the election by a 66,000 plurality, and all Know-Nothing candidates were elected (although the Nativist ticket polled only several thousand votes).

More significant than the New York showing was the way the SSSB was roaring across the prairies and through the Spanish moss of the South. It was well on the way to becoming a nationwide organization. Fillmore, disgruntled at losing the Whig nomination, lined up his Silver Grays behind Barker's membership drive, as did George Law his Live Oak clubs. Sub-rosa help also came from many Hard-Shell Democrats. The Soft-Shell Democrats continued to denounce Know-Nothingism, although after 1854 they remained discreetly silent, even maneuvered to get their men on Know-Nothing tickets. Before 1854 was over, the American party—i.e., the SSSB, the Know-Nothings—claimed 5,000,000 members and new ones at the rate of 5,000 a week. Americans apparently were tumbling head over heels into the Know-Nothing swamp.

The election-front designation used by the SSSB was the "American party." The name appeared sporadically here and there on ballots and was officially adopted nationally by the 1855 national Know-Nothing convention. All candidates had to be third-degree (on occasion, second-degree) members. It began scoring victories everywhere, particularly in New York, Pennsylvania, Maryland, and Massachusetts, and in most large cities, north and south. It became a power in the land, a militant new marching force. Able to arouse emotional fervor and reckless mood in great crowds, its efforts often resulted in butchering and burning, explosions of violence that caused counterviolence, as in Baltimore, New Orleans, and San Francisco, where the Vigilante movement coincided with Know-Nothing rule, its debaucheries and failure to maintain law and order. The Know-Nothings inherited shameful conditions nearly everywhere they came into power, and their officeholders proved unable or disinclined to remedy them; in fact, they often utilized them, despite promises of reform, to feather their own nests. But, given the disintegration of older political forces, the new upsurge, promising political success, attracted a few prominent people, particularly Whig politicians and in the South many able Democrats—neither band knowing where else to jump as their own organizations weakened or collapsed. In the North, many Abolitionists, not wishing to vote for either old party and as yet without a political haven, joined up. Some newcomers were men of considerable ability.

By 1854, three major forces were undermining party lines: Nativism, the temperance movement, and the slavery issue, and of these slavery was the great Moloch. The SSSB leaders believed that the path to success was to avoid sectionalism, redirect hate into other channels, and harp on patriotism. Whig conciliation of the slave power failed to please the South and was not healthy in the North. The Know-Nothings sought to avoid the dilemma by standing on the *status quo*—i.e., the compromises already made: no rocking of the boat. There was much sentiment in the land favoring such a retreat from threatening strife. An ostrich-head-in-the-sands policy seemed to promise success at the polls as the only viable route to build a national party.

The political trick, as Webster had seen without much personal profit, was not to upset compromises already made or raise new slavery issues, but to stress states rights and constitutional union slogans on which much of both North and South could agree, although the first meant condoning slavery and the second was little more than an empty phrase.

This explained the adoption of the Third or Union degree at the November, 1854, SSSB national reunion at Cincinnati, a new revised ritual worked out by Kenneth Raynor of North Carolina, a prosperous planter and prominent Mason who had served four terms in the state legislature and five years in Congress. He was one of the ablest, most active Know-Nothings, a remarkable orator, a master of voice and gesture, using every trick of vocabulary from pseudo-logic to flamboyant eloquence. Bold in expressing his opinions, even at the danger of sacrificing immediate success, he never hedged. To prove his strong anti-temperance views, before addressing his audiences he would down a jigger of corn whisky before their eyes. Above all he was a rabid Protestant and a hater of Catholicism. Later, really believing in union above all else, he turned "traitor" and fought for the North, being later rewarded with a number of good federal appointments.

At the 1854 SSSB convention there was opposition to his new Union degree by northern delegates—omen of future divisions—because of the protecting cloak it threw over slavery and its downgrading of anti-slavery elements in the Order. All delegates present took the oath; but Massachusetts, where the Order was dominated by Abolitionists, refused to accept it then or later. Within a few months it had been conferred on all more promising second-degree members throughout most of the country—according to George W. Julian, at least a million and a half persons. Barker backed Raynor at every step, holding the New York delegation in line, although there were murmurs. Barker knew that the slightest taint of Abolition in the American party would lose the South. Also it gave him a stronger weapon against Seward and his pro-foreign Catholic toleration and his radical anti-slavery views. Now Seward could also be labeled "anti-Union," and demagogues could toss in the word "treason." But the main thing was that the Know-Nothings were given a better chance to inherit the power of the declining old parties. Even objective observers and enemy politicians began to believe the dark-lantern crowd had a clear road to national power and the White House.

Already the SSSB growth in the South was phenomenal. The southern Whig papers everywhere covertly or openly supported the Know-Nothings, and before long all came over to the cause. In some states, such as Missouri, this meant half the press. The Democrats labeled it variously: Temperance, Niggerism, Whiggery, Black Abolitionism, Red Abolitionism.

But nearly everywhere the American party was abetted by reactionary slaveholders, although more rabid elements among them, embittered against any movement having followers in the North, branded it as a "Yankee trick," the Trojan horse of Abolitionism in disguise, no doubt based on the Abolitionist make-up of the Massachusetts organization. Also, here and there odd political coalitions between Know-Nothings and Free-Soilers and Republicans were celebrated, a fact that obliged Lincoln to clarify his own anti-Know-Nothing position. However, the 1852 Free-Soil vice-presidential candidate, Julian of Indiana, considered Know-Nothingism primarily a plot of the slave oligarchy.

"Its birth, simultaneously with the repeal of the Missouri Compromise, was not an accident. . . . It was a well-timed scheme to divide the people of the free states upon trifles and side issues, while the South remained a unit in defense of its great interest. . . . By thus kindling the Protestant jealousy of our people against the Pope, and enlisting them in a crusade against the foreigner, the South could all the more successfully push forward its schemes."

Early in 1854 the Know-Nothings built a strong organization in Natchez, Mississippi, "a Cuban filibuster expedition," the friendly *Courier*, called it. The sentimental basis was strong; Mississippi had sent a big delegation to the 1845 American Republican convention in Philadelphia. In June, 1854, the *Wilkinson Whig* of Woodville, Mississippi, exulted, "Deride, scoff, malign and traduce; it will avail nothing. Ere many suns have sunk in the west, the 'Know-Nothings' will be the most powerful party in the land—the bodyguard of our liberties and rights." Although there were less than five thousand foreigners in the entire state and only a few Catholic churches, the new party, known locally as the Order of the Stripes and Stars, was rapidly introduced into every county. Brought to Oxford County by a Yankee piano-peddling Whig, overnight it had 1,200 members. The Know-Nothings easily carried Vicksburg. After the 1855 Philadelphia Council, an enthusiastic all-day rally was held at Alton's Springs outside Raymond on July 5 to celebrate "Liberty and Union"—slogans, empty though they were, that produced "a spirit of determination like the heroes of '76." A throng of 2,500 cheered and listened to General McNab's famous band circle the square in a carriage, plugging "Hail, Columbia"; it was the biggest barbecue ever known, and speakers harangued all day, each one holding forth for two or three hours.

A strong popular candidate, C. Fontaine, a former States Rights Democrat, was put up for the November gubernatorial race. He campaigned hard, meeting his opponent in a score of debates, and driving his buggy far and wide through swamp and scrub forest and cotton plantations. Feelings ran high; one Democratic candidate reported that it was a rare meeting when he failed to hear half-a-dozen pistols being cocked. Fontaine was defeated, and only one Know-Nothing was sent to Congress, but "Sam" was considered to be a growing power.

The American party was set up in Alabama in June, 1854, and presently 678 members were reported in Mobile; by the end of the year, more than three thousand. The Florence *Gazette* reported: "The infamous band of treasonable conspirators," like "the midnight assassin or the highway robber," were trying "to accomplish their unhallowed purposes by stealth." But they took over Montgomery by a vote of three to one. The 1855 campaign was characterized by some burning of Catholic property. The candidate for governor, George D. Shortridge, stressed state aid to railway companies, promising them a million dollars of the state's surplus funds and no tax increase, in order to appeal to speculative cupidity of voters along proposed rights of way, as in Selma, Mobile, and Tuscaloosa. At a 240-foot table great barbecues were held and enormous quantities of food were eaten. At Selma 4,000 ate, consuming 1,500 pounds of cake; one of the cakes weighed 170 pounds; three had good-sized flags baked inside them. Shortridge was defeated by 10,000 votes, but the Americans did win two of seven congressional seats and more than a third of the legislature and numerous local offices.

Their successes continued through the year following. Colonel John M. Withers, a West Pointer and veteran of the Creek and Mexican wars, was elected Know-Nothing mayor of Mobile by a big majority. Later he repudiated the party, but was enthusiastically re-elected as an independent three successive times; then, after the Civil War, in which he became a Confederate general, still another time. The 1856 campaign was featured by ugly epithets and much violent language. The Know-Nothings were branded as "midnight impostors . . . treason plotters . . . French Jacobins . . . Doodle Holes . . . Bear Fighters." Again the Americans lost.

The new party made its bow in Georgia in May or June, 1854, under the auspices of Judge H. F. Cone, and the influential Augusta *Chronicle and Sentinel* promptly opened its columns to its propaganda. Attacks were made on 2,200 "foreign-owned" grogshops. It spread rapidly through the rich Whig cotton belt and the larger towns and cities.

The traditional parties were enmeshed in factionalism —the 1852 vote for Webster had shown that—and new Unionist, States Rights, and Temperance parties were milling about. In October, in Griffin, a dark-horse Know-Nothing candidate, announced on election day, defeated both Whigs and Democrats. Throughout 1855 other victories were won, and enthusiasm blossomed on all sides. The massive Know-Nothing rally in Macon was typical: "Yesterday delegations from adjoining counties came in wagons, with banners in their ranks and colors flying from their wagon beds and horses' heads . . . drums and fifes upon the street!"

For governor the Democrats put forward—or rather he put himself forward, since he was their all-powerful boss—a strong States Rights Unionist, Herschel V. Johnson, who campaigned with whip and gun. Unpopular but a man of iron, he herded the party ruthlessly back to discipline and campaigned without quarter. Later he described how he had "exposed without mincing words the nefarious principles and policy and aims of Know-Nothingism . . . its hostility to the great ideas of American institutions—how it sought to fetter the freedom of speech, the press—and the right of religious toleration . . . the most wicked political organization that had ever existed in our country." By hushing up a bad scandal over Democratic thievery on the state-owned railroad, he won by a 10,000-vote majority. The Know-Nothings elected only two congressmen, although two others came within 70 and 600 votes each of winning. They controlled a third of the counties, and in 1856 won five more and took over Atlanta. Prospects seemed bright.

The first SSSB councils in Florida were started early in 1854, and in December the Tallahassee *Floridian and Sentinel* came out in support of Know-Nothingism. In Jacksonville a last-minute surprise candidate, who didn't even know he had been nominated, was elected. Numerous other minor victories were won. A state council was set up in April, 1855. The Know-Nothing state candidates lost, although a shift of 161 votes would have given them victory. They did win strong minority representation in the legislature.

In South Carolina—that state of high-handed rice-and-cotton Bourbons, of "landgraves and caciques," of concentrated minority plantation representation and power—the Democrats were overwhelmingly in control, and from the outset Know-Nothingism was attacked relentlessly and ridiculed. One prominent naturalized citizen called it "a very wretched affair. . . . A child of Calvinistic bitterness. . . . They want to combat Papacy with hatred, not conquer it with love, truth, and the gospel." Even so, by 1855 Know-Nothingism gained strength in the eastern rice and cotton country, where even its haughty detractors realized it might serve them to hold back the rising forces for high-country political rights, and it made headway in larger towns. After a few local victories, by late spring it elected mayors in a significant belt across the state, often on the Bible issue, in Greenville, Columbia (the capital), and Charleston.

Led by flamboyant Kenneth Raynor, the Know-Nothings really threatened to take over all North Carolina, which had played an important part in the 1845 Nativist movement. A Know-Nothing mayor was elected in Raleigh, where the *Standard* called it "Whiggery in disguise"; while *The Register* launched attacks on Catholics and foreigners. "Surprise" candidates were successful in numbers of communities. The following year they elected three congressmen.

Relations between the eastern and western portions of the state were embittered over representation on a "white basis," as desired by western settlers, or on a "black basis," which gave the rich eastern planters control of the state. By counting Negroes, the slaveowning area, although having a far smaller white population, had thirty-seven senators, all the rest of the state only thirteen. The Know-Nothing candidate for governor, John A. Gilmer, avoided this and all national issues. He was badly defeated, but the Know-Nothings won approximately a third of the representation in the Senate and House of Commons.

The "raw head and bloody bones" flag of Know-Nothingism came to Texas at the beginning of 1854. As early as May the Texas *State Times* of Austin, owned and edited by J. S. Ford, chairman of the Democratic Committee, told of "the friends of that ubiquitous *hombre*—Sam"—at work in Texas. The particular devil targets were Germans and Mexicans, in some places Catholics. The Galveston *Zeitung* (August, 1855) urged all German communities to organize armed guards for self-defense.

The Democratic party was disintegrating badly. Leaders wrote each other anxiously about the Know-Nothing growth, frequently hinting they might join the order. Senator Sam Houston, "the black eagle of Texas independence," "the hero of San Jacinto," and Ford took the plunge in mid-1855. Ford called for "a great national organization" to bind the states together "with hooks of steel" and to "silence forever the dangerous and hateful dissensions. . . . When our nation is threatened

> *"None but the Native proud and free born here*
> *Can fell the throb or shed the patriot's tear."*

When the Know-Nothings were defeated in San Antonio, Ford blamed it in his paper on the "corrupt, sneaky . . . Mexican Priesthood." "The Cross has been prostituted . . . to render futile the attempt of Americans to rule America. . . . Deluded hordes of Mexican *peons* have been appealed to by a squad of black-robed villains. . . . serpent-like they have entered into the *jacals* [huts] of their countrymen. . . . A horde of political lepers have crawled to the ballot box and there nullified the votes of thousands of your countrymen."

Houston attacked foreign immigrants. He worried lest immigration increase the representation of northern and western states at the expense of the South, thus giving Abolitionists "more power." The South should bend every effort to stop foreigners from coming in, and the naturalization period should be extended to twenty-one years. (Of course, he himself was a "foreigner" in conquered Texas.)

The Know-Nothing candidate for governor was snowed under, but the dark-lanterns forces won thirty assembly and nine senate seats, plus numbers of municipal and county offices, elected the entire ticket in Hays County, and mayors in Galveston and Austin. The Democrats were in fresh panic. The Know-Nothing future in Texas looked bright. Especially as the ramrod of the Democratic party and the hero of their wars and their former President were carrying the blazing torch.

Arkansas had only some three thousand foreigners and practically no Catholics. The old parties were defined and unified, and Albert Pike, a national Know-Nothing leader from that state, said (likely early in 1855) that no one imagined the Order could get a foothold there, for party allegiance was "so stanch and true and party prejudice so strong"; but in seven months, he added, they had seen their councils swell to "more than six in number, and our members between eight and ten thousand." But the intrusion of the Know-Nothings aroused considerably more denunciation than in many states. "Ignorant," "southern traitors," were expressions frequently encountered in the press. The Little Rock *True Democrat* called the American party "the contemptible, oath-bound, demagogic, principle-sacrificing, midnight-conspiring order formed against the constitution of the United States and against all men who desire to be free."

A legislative resolution asserted the unconstitutionality of any attempt to "proscribe any class of citizens or exclude them from office . . . because of their place of birth or religious belief." The lawmakers denounced the "secret society meeting clandestinely" as "abolitionist in its conception and management." However, the Know-Nothings soon became strong enough to get the offending "traitor" resolution expunged from the record by a vote of 37 to 28.

Know-Nothing James Yell, opposing the Kansas-Nebraska bill, ran for governor against Democrat E. N. Conway, who favored it. Each candidate accused the other of being an "aristocrat," a more telling criticism for backwoods "democrats" than anything that could be said on state or national issues. Yell ridiculed his opponent for going around in a silk velvet suit, ruffled shirt, and an oiled wig. He also exposed a real-estate bank scandal that had swindled Arkansas taxpayers out of nearly four million dollars. But he received only half as many votes as Conway. The Know-Nothings found some consolation in the election of a state auditor and in winning control of Little Rock in January, 1856.

In August, 1854, the St. Louis Missouri *Gazette* mentioned the new Order approvingly, for it would end boasts by the St. Louis *Anzeiger* that the Germans held the political balance of power. Whig papers increasingly printed Know-Nothing news, protests about foreign immigrants, and other propaganda. By March, 1856, the Whig press in the state, twenty-six out of fifty-five newspapers, was solidly Know-Nothing. Both old parties were divided. The Missouri Know-Nothings flouted the national order by abandoning secrecy and admitting Catholics, of whom there were some twenty thousand in the state. But the SSSB remained bitterly anti-foreign. Germans and more than one hundred thousand Irish made up 12 per cent of the state's white population and were a majority in St. Louis, although not all were naturalized voters. There were serious Whig "race" riots during the 1854 congressional race against "Benton's Germans," and the militia had to be called out to stop further killings. The April, 1855, St. Louis campaign was characterized by denunciations of "foreign policemen along Broadway" for drunkenness and by vast Know-Nothing enthusiasm.

The pivot of all controversy in Missouri was Thomas Hart Benton, whose popularity and strength cut across all party lines. But in spite of Benton's hammer-and-tongs opposition and German support of the Democrats, the Americans carried the city in the 1855 contest. However, they lost the 1856 state election to the regular Democrats, although two congressmen were elected. Benton, by then shoved to one side by his own party, ran as an independent and was snowed under, coming in third.

The border states were considered very significant by the Know-Nothings. There the sectional pulls of North and South were felt strongly, and they promised to be a good test of Know-Nothing ability to mollify both regions by compromise and evasion.

In Tennessee the American party was strongly backed by the Baptists. As early as August 26, 1854, the Tennessee *Baptist* predicted rapid success of the SSSB because of the "deplorably corrupt" picture of the existing political parties. It was high time, when "nearly one million . . . foreign Catholics and German infidels" were pouring into the country annually. "If the Catholics are ever in a majority, freedom will be dead."

The 1855 campaign was enlivened by the bigoted Methodist circuit rider Reverend William G. Brownlow, originally from Virginia, who had set up a crusading Methodist political paper, *The True Whig,* that gained considerable following. For many it was "an oracle" they looked up to with blind idolatry. The "Hell Hound," as his enemies called him, spewed forth his acid opinions against the Church, against Andrew Johnson, in print, from the pulpit, and the platform, far and wide, and in innumerable virulent books and pamphlets, such as *Americanism Contrasted with Foreignism, Romanism and Bogus Democracy, in the Light of Reason, History and Scripture, in Which Certain Demagogues in Tennessee and Elsewhere Are Shown in Their True Colors,* and *The Great Iron Wheel Examined.* He considered the American party "the most powerful and effectually organized . . . in the known world," and added in bold-face type, which he used lavishly in varying sizes for emphasis, that "the hand of God, . . . we sincerely believe, is visible in this thing." He *proved* that Washington and Jackson were Know-Nothings. The "silent scourge" would "reach into every farm and hamlet, until our country is saved from infamy and demagogy. THE HAND OF GOD IS VISIBLE IN THIS THING."

For governor, the Know-Nothings backed P. G. Gentry, a long-term Congressman of considerable standing (who denied Know-Nothing membership, perhaps as secrecy required). It was known that the Know-Nothings had 17,000 oath-bound members in the state. He was opposed by Democrat Andrew Johnson, the orphan tailor, one-time escaped indentured servant wanted by the law, later to become vice-president and president.

In Tennessee style, the candidates appeared sixty times on joint platform debates. At Murfreesboro (in Gentry's stronghold, the rich plantation area), Johnson bluntly analyzed Gentry's career to prove that he favored wealth, not the people, and a great national bank, that he had been responsible for high tariff bills that had increased prices for the common people. His efforts to get the federal government to assume state debts would injure Tennessee. With a slashing, rough-tongued attack, Johnson flayed the SSSB secrecy and its anti-Catholic bigotry as religious persecution. "The Devil, his Satanic Majesty, the Prince of Darkness who presides over the secret conclave held in Pandemonium, makes war upon all branches of Christ's Church." Yet the SSSBs themselves were a sort of denomination, "bound together by secret and terrible oaths, the first of which, on the very initiation, fixes and requires them to carry a lie in their mouths! Show me . . . a Know-Nothing, and I will show you a huge reptile, upon whose neck the foot of every honest man ought to be placed." Like the hyena, they "come from their lairs after midnight to prey upon Human Carcasses." He would prefer to join the gang of murderous bandit Murrell rather than that of the Know-Nothings.

Gentry replied mildly, and Reverend Brownlow, incensed, thundered that this would get him nowhere. Gentry replied that he would follow the rules of a gentleman rather than "degrade" his manhood. "If you wish me to go down to the level of my competitor, I beg you to hunt another to take my place." He preferred to lose the election rather than his "self-respect and honor."

Reverend Brownlow had no such Christian restraints. He called E. G. Eastman, editor of the Nashville *Daily Union and American,* "a dirty lying and unscrupulous Abolitionist, from Massachusetts . . . he edits a dirty scurrilous sheet; and like his master, Governor Johnson, never could elevate himself above the level of a common blackguard." Both were "Billingsgate graduates." "Decent men shun coming in contact with either of them, as they would avoid a night-cart or other vehicle of filth. As some fish thrive only in dirty water, so the Nashville *Union and American* would not exist a week without slander and vituperation." It was a fit organ for "the piratical flag of Andrew Johnson and his Progressive Democracy."

Thirty thousand people turned out for the American rally in Nashville. Johnson lost the entire eastern tier of counties and twenty-two out of thirty-three center counties, but got a majority of the popular vote. In the west, he won only seven out of eighteen counties, but again had a small popular-vote lead. He became governor by a scant 2,000 majority. The Know-Nothings elected five out of ten congressmen, and, through Whig coalition, control of the legislature. Government was stalemated. Johnson flayed the Know-Nothings remorselessly. They refused to confirm his nominations, and he vetoed all their partisan bills.

Kentucky was another crucial border state. By 1850 foreigners in Kentucky numbered 30,000, largely in Louisville; they made up 4 per cent of the white population. As early as 1845 Kentucky Nativists had begun attacking the "Godless Germans," and in Louisville, headquarters of the National Central Union of Free Germans, riot after riot had caused deaths and burnings. The slaveholders were determined to stamp out the German anti-slavery, Free-Soil program, by death if necessary. Protestant leaders were equally bitter over German opposition to Sabbath laws, compulsory Bible reading, and their advocacy of Free Thought.

In Kentucky, the SSSB, rooted in the blue-grass and

limestone regions, as early as May, 1854 (though according to Anne Carroll the first council was organized in June), sent a state delegation to the Know-Nothing Grand Council meeting of that same month. Actually some pro-American propaganda appeared in newspapers, such as the Frankfort *Commonwealth,* as early as May. In September in Louisville the Americans put forth a ticket the very day of election, and it won. Other victories occurred in Kenton, Carroll, Jessamine, Logan, and Breckinridge counties.

In May, 1855, the Kentucky Grand Council reorganized the Order, dividing subordinate councils into "Decades" composed of chiefs of ten or less "Clans," in order to check more closely on members' activities and facilitate the distribution of propaganda. The Clan (sometimes spelled "Klan") heads were responsible for having poll watchers check the voting. Local candidates for county and district were not to be made more than ten days before the election date, and candidates were not allowed to discuss publicly the principles of the Order, unless directed to do so.

The year had started auspiciously with Know-Nothing victories in Whig-controlled Lexington and Democratic-controlled Covington. In April, the Know-Nothings carried Elizabethtown and Louisville, where the Democrats placed only one school trustee and two councilmen, the elections being characterized by ugly rioting. In Louisville, John Barbee, the Know-Nothing candidate, had no opposition, for the incumbent Democratic mayor claimed his term was not due to expire for a year. He was upheld by the court, but the Know-Nothing city council refused to deal with him and made Barbee de-facto mayor. On August 5, "Bloody Monday," occurred the terrible riot, when anti-Papist Know-Nothings, stirred up by the Louisville *Journal,* marched into the German section. Twenty-two persons, nearly all Germans, were killed, several hundred wounded, and sixteen houses burned.

The first Know-Nothing nominee for governorship had to withdraw because of ill health, and Charles S. Morehead was substituted. A prosperous lawyer, planter, and slaveowner, Morehead had served for thirty years in state legislatures and in Congress and as state attorney general. Most of the rest of the ticket was made up of Whigs, who, after Scott's defeat, had left the party to become Democrats, then had roved into the mists of Know-Nothingism. Big rallies were held. That in Louisville November 27 brought thousands from all over the state and beyond, filling several of the city's largest halls. Speakers came from Massachusetts, Indiana, Mississippi, Pennsylvania, and Illinois.

The Know-Nothing ticket made a clean sweep by a 4,500-vote majority out of 135,000 votes, winning all offices, control of the legislature, and six congressmen. The Democratic legislators raised ned over election-day rioting, and for months little was done except wrangle over who was to blame, Know-Nothing toughs or Democratic toughs.

The Americans had failed to carry much of the eastern mountain section, the central knob-hill lands, or the western "Purchase" corner, where then and subsequently they did little to spread the Order or to campaign. But they gerrymandered the districts, and in the 1856 elections increased their power in the legislature to fifty-one, over thirty-four Democrats. Louisville (a second time) and Henderson turned in Know-Nothing victories.

Well before this, national issues were sharpening. Free-Soilers and Republicans were accused of supporting Know-Nothings, and vice versa. In local instances there had been definite coalitions; later on, more important statewide bargains. This gave grounds for attacks by rabid southerners that Know-Nothingism was Abolitionist, merely a "northern trick." It plagued the Republicans with charges that they were hypocritically truckling to the pro-slavery evasions of Know-Nothingism.

In August, 1855, Abraham Lincoln wrote to a prominent southerner, apparently a friendly slaveowner, to make his position clear beyond all doubt:

"The slave-breeders and slave-traders are a small, odious, and detested class among you; and yet in politics, they dictate the course of all of you, and are as completely your masters as you are the master of your own Negroes. . . . I am not a Know-Nothing, that is certain. How could I be? How can anyone who abhors the oppression of the Negroes be in favor of degrading classes of white people? Our progress in degeneracy seems to be pretty rapid. As a nation we began by declaring 'all men are created equal.' We now . . . read it 'all men are created equal except Negroes'! When the Know-Nothings get control it will read 'all men are created equal except Negroes and foreigners and Catholics.' When it comes to this, I shall prefer emigrating to some country where they make no pretense of loving liberty—to Russia, for instance, where despotism can be taken pure, and without the base alloy of hypocrisy."

Clearly Lincoln was not taken in by what Greeley's *Tribune* had labeled "the new dodge."

## CHAPTER VIII

# THE BLOOD TUBS OF BALTIMORE

KEN HARRIS, constable on night duty, June 10, 1850, in his little watchhouse, smaller than a privy, on Washington Street in Baltimore, was drowsing when a band of young toughs, sneaking through the murk of the unlit thoroughfare, gleefully put their shoulders to the frail structure and tilted it over, smashing his lantern that was hanging from a nail, and bruising his shoulder. They left him sprawled in the wreckage and the inky dark.

There were only a few constables to police the city, no regular patrols, and in all the state, except for several small volunteer companies, no militia. Citizens preferred to go out at night without hats rather than without a gun.

When riots occurred, little could be done to stop them. Often cannon were used. In the 1835 bank riots, mobs sacked and burned the homes of two leading lawyers, who had the finest libraries in the city. On occasion battles were staged between rival volunteer fire departments. They rioted in every election. On reaching a fire, they sometimes got into bloody rows while the building burned down. To make life interesting and their services more appreciated, firemen themselves, it was charged, set buildings on fire. Baltimore became known throughout the land as "Mob Town." It took a bit of doing for other cities to surpass it along these lines.

In 1834, indefatigable Samuel B. Smith, addressing his Baptist cohorts, was driven off the platform by Catholics in the audience. Thereafter several local religious pig stabbers kept blood running. In 1835, Reverend Robert C. Breckinridge and Reverend Andrew B. Cross, both Presbyterians, started the *Baltimore Literary and Religious Magazine* "to expose the *rotten* conditions of American Popery." Simultaneously Breckinridge organized a Protestant association, a local extension of Brownlee's extremists, delivering a lengthy address. "Belief in many of the fundamental dogmas of the Church [Roman Catholic] necessarily imposes an implicit submission to priestly domination, which is incompatible with the due exercise of either civil or religious rights. . . . The whole history of the Church sustains the position that a free government never did, and never can, be organized by, or perpetuated among, a people professing the faith of the church of Rome. . . . The last trench of liberty and Protestantism may be found in the United States, and if we do not now prepare for the contest, may be there surrendered. . . ."

For two decades Breckinridge—a great orator with national stature and a power in the national councils of the Presbyterian Church—and his fellow denominationalist, Cross—narrower, more bitter—kept up the anti-foreign, anti-Catholic crusade that helped convert Baltimore into a shambles of lawlessness and brutality. In 1839, stirred up by the two preachers and their publication, a great mob attacked the Carmelite convent for three days.

General Duff Green also began flogging the Papists and foreigners in his Baltimore *Pilot* (later *The Pilot and Transcript*). He had founded and edited the influential *United States Telegraph* in Washington from 1826 on. As a close friend of John C. Calhoun, he formed part of President Jackson's notorious "Kitchen Cabinet," with his fingers deep in the pork barrel. He broke with Jackson, who subsidized a rival paper; his dimensions shrank, and he was now back in Baltimore stirring up a hate campaign.

In 1841, the anti-Papist crusade was further supplemented by the *Sunday Visitor*. Soon after, Breckinridge changed the name of his publication to *The Spirit of the XIX Century* and prodded the Baltimore clergymen to set up the militant Society of the Friends of Reformation. Meetings were stepped up with firebrand speakers to secure funds and publish anti-Catholic books and pamphlets.

All this played into the hands of political demagogues. The first strong wave of Know-Nothingism hit Baltimore after the election of Harper in New York City and the Philadelphia riots. November 5, 1844—the day that Henry Clay was defeated for the presidency—the Baltimore *Clipper* came out in support of the new American Republican party and changed the paper's name to the *American Republican,* substituting a spread eagle for the Maryland coat of arms on its masthead.

American Republican units were set up in every ward. Special appeals were made to the working class, "the bone and sinew" of the city, who should have "greater influence in the administration of public affairs." On March 12, 1845, a body of party principles was set forth—considerably milder than those in New York, Philadelphia, and elsewhere. They disavowed "distinctly and unequivocally" any intent "to interfere with the religious opinions of individuals. Happily for the people of the United States, the Constitution has wisely guaranteed a perfect toleration of religious opinion." The party was merely "hostile to any combination between church and state . . . destructive of human rights and dangerous to civil liberty." A mouse program, indeed, after all the puffing and blaring and violence by Breckinridge, Cross, Duff, and others.

The Nativist softness about the Catholic issue was explicable. Many leading Maryland families had been Catholic for hundreds of years. Most were Whigs, and the Know-Nothing movement had found its happiest hunting grounds among Whigs. Why antagonize them? The new party also disavowed antagonism toward foreigners, or any desire to proscribe them "from the full and free exercise of privileges and advantages of our common country"; it merely opposed the corrupt use of them at the polls.

The national American Republican convention in Philadelphia, July 4, 1845, changed the party name to the "Native American party." The Maryland Nativists considered this a too narrow emphasis, nor would they curb the rights of naturalized citizens.

Foreign immigration—predominantly German—was heavy, and had come into Maryland since early days. Increasingly after 1730, Scotch-Irish and Germans had pushed across the Blue Ridge from Pennsylvania down the "Great Valley." There, after the Revolution, a great many Hessians—some were deserters who had been promised land—settled because of Maryland's free land provisions. As early as 1778 Maryland eagerly sought newcomers to open up the back country. All foreigners, upon taking the oath of allegiance to the state, were granted full citizenship rights other than holding public office. Official and private circulars in various European languages were widely distributed abroad, setting forth the advantages of coming to Maryland, which had the most liberal and enlightened provisions for outside settlers of any state in the Union. From 1820 to 1850, 134,266 additional foreigners entered Baltimore. At least 60 per cent were Germans, a percentage higher after the 'forty-eight revolution. By 1850, Baltimore had 52,497 foreigners (one-third Irish), 24 per cent of the entire black and white population.

In Maryland, foreignism and Catholicism had never been bracketed as enemies of the republic. If anything, anti-foreignism was strongest among Catholics, at least against Germans, for many Germans were Free Thinkers and opposed to both Catholicism and Protestantism—institutions that "represented a gigantic conspiracy to keep the masses in mental bondage and subject to political oppression." They are "disciples of the anarchist school of Heine," sputtered the Baltimore *Catholic Mirror*. These "Freimänner . . . have set up Thomas Paine as their apostle."

What was worse, the Germans held "radical" political and social ideas. They believed in human freedom. They were full-fledged Jeffersonians. Many dreamed of an ideal "Universal Republic" as, on a smaller scale, did the disciples of

Fourier among New England Perfectionists and Transcendentalists, not to mention the western Owenites. The newer German immigrants were educated; they started newspapers; they were vocal. Baltimore, thanks chiefly to them—in spite of its tawdry election methods—became one of the more enlightened centers of the continent.

The Germans also aroused the wrath of plantation owners. The foreigners were opposed to slavery; their papers, strongly Abolitionist—as, indeed, were German papers in Texas, Louisiana, Missouri, and Kentucky. The hardy upland settlers, many of them German, were against slavery in theory and practice. Devoted to general agriculture, producing wheat, corn, oats, and rye, raising hogs and cattle, they had to do their own work, and they, like the city mechanics, saw the slaves as competitors keeping wages low and farm prices depressed.

But political control was in the tight grip of the tidewater slaveowners, mostly tobacco growers, who had long resisted efforts to allow Baltimore or the Piedmont's big Frederick County—embracing three fourths of Maryland when organized in 1784 and with the bulk of the population—to have a proportionate share of state representation. Baltimore, with a fourth of the state's population, was apportioned only one sixteenth of the legislative seats. The tidewater gentry disliked alien customs, languages, and institutions. The non-Catholics among them wanted to maintain the Puritan Sabbath and Protestant education in the schools. Above all else, of course, they were determined to hang on to their landed property and their assets in human slaves. They feared true democracy, fought extension of the suffrage, and all public improvements that might bring higher taxes.

Thus foreigners, particularly the Germans, came into conflict with the tidewater folk very early. The slaveowners soon saw the advantage of backing Know-Nothingism, which kept people embroiled in hates and blind to the evils of slavery.

Political Nativism of the 'forties soon faded, although the secret OUA continued to flourish. Revived in the 'fifties, it became more virulent, more bitterly anti-foreign and anti-Catholic. The secret Sons of the Sires was set up in 1852. The SSSB penetrated Maryland a year or two earlier than any other southern state. The first group, perhaps soon disbanded, appeared in 1851, but by 1853 the order was firmly established. Simultaneously a branch of the secret United Sons of America (USA), originally started in Philadelphia in the 'forties and in good part responsible for the terrible riots there, was organized in Baltimore in April or May, 1853, and became very active.

Breckinridge's anti-Papist movement gained renewed impetus from these three secret groups, as it did also from Archbishop Francis Patrick Kenrick, who brooked no nonsense from anybody. It was he who had driven Father William Hogan out of Saint Mary's Cathedral, in a dispute over control of church property, and had turned Hogan into one of the loudest, angriest anti-Catholics in the country. In a violent controversy over religious issues, he had pulverized "the milk-and-water arguments" of Episcopalian Bishop John H. Hopkins. In 1842, he promoted a campaign to get the American Episcopal Church to return to the mother church, from which it had erringly strayed. His success in getting the Philadelphia public-school authorities to excuse Catholic children from Bible reading stirred up the hornet's nest of Know-Nothing mobs that burned churches and homes and killed civilians and soldiers. But he posted notices to the Irish there not to participate in the rioting, placards which the Protestant rioters tore down and made into cockade hats. He should have told them to fight, growled militant Bishop Hughes of New York. As far off as Boston, Reverend Edward Beecher attacked him ferociously.

In April, 1852, Alessandro Gavazzi, the apostate priest, stirred up a frenzy of anti-Catholicism in Baltimore by "exposure" of corruption. In 1853, during the bitterness in the entire United States against Papal Nuncio Monsignor Gaetano Bedini, the Baltimore *Sun* reprinted a Virginia and New Orleans broadside denouncing him as a "butcher," unfit to breathe "American air," and calling on all "freemen" to "drive this murderer back to his bloody master."

The Baltimore Germans joined in burning his mitered figure in effigy with "the most impious shouts," not realizing that they were merely preparing the ground for their own persecution. The house of the archbishop, the seminary, the orphan asylum, and the Visitation Convent were shot at by fiendishly yelling mobs. *The Protestant Critic* maintained that this was the work of "German infidels," that Americans present were merely "spectators."

Presently an educational controversy brought ugly naked hostility. Breckinridge had imposed the Bible in Maryland schools in 1839. However, Catholics had been able to secure the introduction of their own Bible with freedom of choice for students. This was not considered a satisfactory solution, for they looked upon the Bible as no proper textbook for young children, especially when interpreted by teachers who were Protestants or improperly trained. The Catholics, like most Protestant sects, had little choice but to set up their own schools. The first free school in the state had been opened in 1829 in a Presbyterian church basement. By 1850 there were thirty private schools—two were Catholic—taking care of 5,000 children.

For years the Protestants had pointed out that Maryland schools were incompetent "to provide a Christian education." In 1840, the Fourth Provincial Catholic Council, meeting in Baltimore, also complained of the quality of public education and the use of textbooks that sought, by "covert and insidious efforts . . . to misrepresent our principles, to distort our tenets, to vilify our practices and bring contempt upon our church and its members." The Protestants smelled a sinister purpose in this, and for years the statement was reprinted as a shocking proof of the Catholic desire to control public education and do away with Bible teaching.

In 1852, the legislature's school committee drew up the Kerney School Reorganization Bill. It provided that free orphan and private schools, if they conformed to state standards, should receive a proportionate share of tax money "to avoid duplicate burdens on parents." Actually many Protestant schools, even several Catholic schools, were receiving state grants although not on any equitable or uniform basis.

There can be plenty of arguments pro and con regarding the advisability of state subsidization of denominational private schools, but more than argument was stirred up. A clause in the proposed law providing for "non-sectarian" education was seized upon by Protestant ministers as cloaking a sly Catholic move to ban the Bible from the schools. The bill was a deep-dyed Popish plot to gain control of education and public funds, a vicious underhanded scheme to unite church and state. Nose-spite fashion, opponents, showing their great love for the welfare of the children, declared in *The Clipper* (May 22, 1852) that they would force the closing of *all* schools if the bill were passed.

By the following year, the controversy had become acute; on May 10, the USA ran an ad in *The Clipper:* "God and our Native Land. Foreigners will render our elections a curse instead of a blessing." The two major parties were "making concessions to the foreign power in our midst of a nature degrading to the American character." Some of the men sent to the legislature "have proven themselves like the viper which stung the bosom of its benefactor—servants of Pius IV, John Hughes, and all Papal Rome instead of servants of their master—the American people." The proposed education law and others were "the handiwork of foreign Jesuitism. . . . Enlist under the red, white, and blue banner of Native American principles and fight valiantly for those rights for which Schiffler and his seven compatriots fell martyrs in the bloodstained streets of Kensington."

In spite of the hullabaloo, Archbishop Kenrick and others petitioned the city under the Maryland Declaration of Rights, asking for a redress from double taxation, since it was impossible for children attending Catholic schools to utilize the inadequate public schools. The City School Committee at once attacked the memorial. In "letter and spirit" it came "from the heart of a foreigner . . . incompetent . . . by birth or education to understand the genius of American institutions," or that good government could "be conducted without the union of Church and State."

On October 1, the USA sent a letter to all candidates asking their views on the Kerney Bill and demanding preservation of "the proudest pillars of our republic—the system of popular education." Although Maryland education was scarcely anything to be proud of, the controversy spurred the Know-Nothing movement to new militancy, on to victories at the polls. The Kerney Bill was shouted down in anger. Nothing was done to promote better education. The net outcome was the raucous revival of Nativism.

The Know-Nothings were in something of a dilemma when it came to proceeding against both Germans and Catholics, who did not like one another. The Irish, being both foreign and Catholic, were an easier hate target. But gradually the Nativist program took shape. The first big SSSB mass meeting, in conjunction with the OUA and USA, was held in Baltimore's Monument Square, August 8, 1853. Five thousand persons attended. *Americans should rule America.* They should oppose any change in Protestant control of the schools, restrict immigration, oppose the union of church and state, prohibit secret organizations among foreigners. "Union of church and state" was just a straw man, said one Catholic after looking over the inebriate crowd; there was "far more likelihood of the Union of state and the saloon."

An SSSB state council, supported by the OUA, was set up October 14, 1853. Intensive organization work was carried on in every Baltimore ward and elsewhere in the state, and in 1854, two weeks before the municipal election, the Know-Nothings hurriedly called a secret caucus, five delegates from each ward, and nominated a full municipal ticket, headed by Samuel Hicks for mayor. Hicks, who had labor support, was an advocate of the rights of Protestant Anglo-Saxon workers against immigrant competition. The ticket was made public the next day.

The Know-Nothings did not leave all to chance. Although not yet prepared for the rough and tumble of Baltimore elections, they had considerable experience in violent methods, and on election day fought a number of pitched battles for control of voting places. According to the *Catholic News,* Protestant ministers were seen taking part in the strife and handing out Know-Nothing ballots. Each party supplied its own ballots. One trick was to print heavy colored stripes that could be seen through the paper, thus violating legal secrecy. The gang in control of a polling place could easily tell if the voter was depositing the right ballot or should be beaten up and chased away. The Democrats customarily used heavy blue stripes, and for this election the Know-Nothings —who in later elections used red stripes—did the same. Their ballots were unsuspectingly accepted, and before the day was over, the Democrats were convinced that the Know-Nothings were not getting any votes—only to discover to their amazement when the ballots were counted that the upstarts had walked away with the election.

The Know-Nothings were even more amazed, doubly so at winning such a smashing victory. Besides electing Hicks, the First Municipal Council would be composed of fourteen Know-Nothings and six Democrats; the Second Council, eight Know-Nothings and two Democrats. Victories were also won in Hagerstown and Cumberland.

In the later statewide elections, lacking effective organization outside of Baltimore, the Know-Nothings did less well. A Democrat, T. W. Ligon, was elected governor. But the coalition Whig-Know-Nothing ticket gained control of both houses of the legislature, and A. B. Sollers was elected to Congress. "Organized tyranny" had gotten control of the state, said one Democratic leader.

The Know-Nothing program as it unfolded, especially after the 1855 Philadelphia convention, suited Maryland slaveholders. The attacks on foreigners, naturalization laws, immigration, and Papal "aggression" diverted public attention from the slavery issue. Know-Nothing Sollers exulted in a House speech (January 4, 1855) that by sidetracking slavery discussion, which was destroying the old parties, and sweeping it under the rug, the Know-Nothing movement, a truly "national" party, was the "natural ally" of the South. He held his slaves by rights established by the framers of the Constitution and by the further right of the "naked sword" of necessity. The use of force was being rendered unnecessary, now that a new party, possessed of "all the strength of Hercules" and "knowing no North, no South, no East, and no West," had been born, ready to "stand by the Union as it is and the Constitution as it is"—neither pro-slavery nor Abolitionist—merely the *status quo*.

He was against foreign immigration, he told Congress, because foreigners, taking up fertile lands in the West, inevitably became anti-slavery advocates. He opposed all immigration into Maryland for the same reason—it menaced slavery.

At various times Archbishop Kenrick, never one to hide his light under a bushel, deplored slavery and laws against educating slaves, but he believed that militant Abolitionism, by "disturbing the whole fabric of society," ran the danger of "rendering the condition of the slaves worse." He reminded slaveowners that Pope Alexander III as early as 1167 had "forbidden Christians to be held as slaves and called for voluntary gradual manumission."

Early in 1855, the Know-Nothings won control of Williamsport and Annapolis. In June, the American party held its great national convention in Philadelphia, with every state represented. As before, Barker, Raynor, and others tried to sidetrack the slavery issue, but Article XXI, triumphantly imposed by the southern delegates, declared that the country "ought not to legislate upon the subject of slavery, within the territory of the United States." Delegates of twelve northern states withdrew and issued a statement calling for the restoration of the Missouri Compromise. The schism, though healed, boded ill for the future unity and effectiveness of the party.

For the first two days at the convention, Maryland delegate chairman William Alexander tried to have the SSSB membership ban on Catholics lifted, but was twice decisively voted down, and the convention adopted Article VIII. This opposed the "aggressive policy and corrupting tendencies of the Roman Catholic Church and called for the exclusion of all Catholic citizens from" all political stations—executive, legislative, judicial, or diplomatic.

How truly nefarious for Catholics to hold public positions, jibed the Catholics, pointing out that in the House of Representatives there were only two Catholics; Protestant ministers constantly took part in political activities and held office, as no priest ever did; repeatedly Protestants petitioned the government in matters not concerned with religion. Thirty-five hundred New England clergymen had memorialized Congress against the Nebraska Bill—not one Roman Catholic priest had signed it. In one city, the *Catholic Mirror* noted, there were fourteen elected Methodists, and two were preachers. Who were the ones meddling in politics?

Actually, of course, the SSSB position violated both the United States Constitution, of which they always spoke with such reverence, and the Maryland constitution, which set no barriers to officeholding except a declaration of belief in the Christian religion or a belief "in a future state of rewards and punishments." This proviso might be silly, but it let almost any office seeker slip through the bars of religious prejudices.

In order not to antagonize many conservative, wealthy tidewater families from whom they hoped for support, the Maryland Know-Nothing leaders wished to eliminate all anti-Catholicism, except for innocuous phrases, from the state program. Local units for some time had admitted Catholics, although it was difficult to understand why any Catholic would desire to join.

Another great rally in Baltimore's Monument Square took the decision out of the hands of the head men. Each ward marched there en masse with music, flags, banners, and transparencies, and such famous figures as Jacob Broom of Philadelphia, John Cunningham of South Carolina, Albert Pike of Arkansas, and A. R. Boteler of Virginia stirred up vast enthusiasm. The leading speaker was Congressman Kenneth Raynor of North Carolina. This meant a gloves-off harangue against "Romanism." As expected, he wiped up the floor with the foreigners. "The foreign population, which, like the serpent, through your kindness taken from the most abject poverty and warmed into life, repays your hospitality by stinging your vitals, by attempting to destroy your freedom."

He went on to attack nunneries. "We shall battle against them . . . as Americans and Protestants . . . we are fighting for the Bible and the right of religious liberty" against "the machinations of the Roman Catholic Church." We are fighting to put "a check upon . . . priestly aggression. . . . No man can be a true American and a true member of the Roman Catholic Church, for his allegiance to the priesthood is stronger than that which he bears to his country."

However, the Baltimore leaders were still cautious and made it plain in the columns of *The Clipper* that they proscribed only "*foreign* Catholics" from office, not American Catholics who disclaimed allegiance to the Pope in political matters. "Maryland Protestants and Catholics had lived in harmony until recently and would have continued to do so had it not been for the indiscreet zeal of foreign Catholics."

The Democrats (also the Whigs) of Saint Mary's County issued declarations strongly denouncing Know-Nothing bigotry. "Much as we have dreaded . . . the consequences that may arise from northern Abolitionism, we consider Know-Nothingism still more alarming. The former . . . can only divide our once happy country; the latter will make our country not worth dividing. Only universal chaos will cover all, through which no ray of patriotic hope will penetrate."

The October, 1855, election was high-lighted by riots before and during the voting. When it was over the startled Know-Nothings discovered they had lost their majority in the municipal council. They redoubled efforts to win the state elections the following month. The opposition was divided among Whigs, Democrats, and Unionists, and the Know-Nothings won thirteen out of twenty-one counties and an overwhelming majority in the legislature.

In his annual January message, the governor bitterly assailed the Know-Nothings and the American party. This legislature had been set up by "a conspiracy," and he demanded a full-scale investigation of secret societies. There was no excuse for such societies in the free American system, with "a thousand channels of communication with the people always open . . . all history admonishes us that a war of races and sects is the deadliest curse that can afflict a nation."

The legislature dutifully set up an investigating committee, but it was headed by Know-Nothing Anthony Kennedy, who was later rewarded with a United States Senate seat. The committee denounced the governor and demanded proof that any secret societies existed. The governor let loose another blast, dotted the i's and crossed the t's and asked for legislation to prevent and punish "any hindrance or obstruction . . . that prevented a voter from depositing his ballot."

The committee brushed this aside as an "insult." "The people of Maryland in the majority of their power" had furnished ample proof "of the purity of its [the American party's] principles" by electing a majority. "Every citizen has a right . . . of judgment upon the religious and political opinions no less than upon the character and capacity of any one who is submitted to . . . his vote." Republican freedom guaranteed "him inviolable immunity from all questions of his motive."

The minority on the committee disassociated itself from the Know-Nothing report, branding it as braggadocio presented with a *"tremendous flourish"* of a trumpet—as though "General Tom Thumb" were to be ushered on the stage. The majority had refused to call witnesses and challenged the minority's right to do so. However, nineteen Baltimore former members of the SSSB were quizzed and much of the secret ritual and password rigmarole was disclosed. In its separate report, the minority declared that if a majority grossly violated law and right, they were as culpable as one man would be. The chairman, a stanch Protestant, noted that Know-Nothing principles and the movement were the work of Protestants, and he "hung his head for Protestantism; it had been false to itself; it had disgraced itself; it had allowed bigotry to become captain of its forces. . . ."

All this time Cross had continued his tirades, and he

now petitioned the legislature for an official investigation of convents to determine if they were holding inmates against their will and whether they should be abolished. Legislator Merrick, a consistent champion of civil and religious liberty, denounced the petition as an "indignity" to the legislature, "a false charge against a large, pure, and respectable portion of our community." The petition was "intended as a firebrand, to excite malevolence, bitterness, and ill-feeling . . . for the vile purposes" of exciting "fanaticism," encouraging "bigotry and intolerance" and engendering "a war of religion and persecution. . . . Do you mean to go on in the diabolical work already begun in the United States of interfering in matters of conscience, invading private property, insulting defenseless women, and engendering strife which will desolate the land in misery and woe?" Why this "persecution" of persons who have meddled "with the affairs of no one . . . known only by their good deeds of charity; who acted at Baltimore in the cholera season [recently there had been a terrible epidemic of cholera and yellow fever] as nurses for the afflicted; who never disturbed the peace, but willingly sacrificed their lives for the public weal?" Were they now "to be hunted down, vilified, and persecuted because a malevolent foe" had made "a sweeping charge against them?" Somewhat shamefacedly, the Know-Nothing legislators backed water, and Cross's petition was laid on the table by a vote of forty-nine to thirteen.

The 1856 national American party nominating convention put up former President Millard Fillmore, a northerner eminently satisfactory for the southerners, but the assemblage split worse than that of 1855 on the slavery issue, a schism that boded ill for Know-Nothing success. The slavery question had become too overpowering for even the Know-Nothings to dodge any longer, although they strove mightily to keep it safely anchored in the nebulous never-never port of pompous platitudes. Hurrah for the Bible and the Constitution—a slogan "as appropriate for Chile as for the United States," said one critic.

But in spite of a party split and a bad setback in Virginia the previous year, Maryland Know-Nothing strength was growing, and every occasion was seized upon to hold mass meetings and parades. They celebrated September 12, Maryland's "Fourth of July," in great style. The numerous clubs that had sprung up—the Rip Raps, Tigers, Plug Uglies, Wampanoags, Eyebolts, Eutaws, Black Snakes, Rough Skins, Rosebuds, Ranters, Regulators, Decaturs, Washingtons, Thunderbolts, Little Fellows, Babes, White Oaks, Black Oaks, Blood Tubs, etc., some imported from New York City and Philadelphia—paraded openly. A riot broke out at Federal Hill, and shots were exchanged. Two persons were killed, twenty-six seriously injured.

The Democrats were not without their own roughneck clubs; the Ashlanders, Bloody Eights, Double Pumps, Calithumpians, Senior Mount Clares, Ferry Road Hunters, Peelers, Pluckers, Shad Hoes, Eighth Ward Black Guards, Butt Enders, Stay Lates. Nor could the Know-Nothings be accused of first introducing election violence, which had existed for a decade and more. Hordes of alcoholics and vagabonds, some imported, were rounded up and voted en masse. This "coop" system resulted in political clubs being called "coops." Usually polling places were located near the "coops" of the party in office, so that nondescript press gangs could be marched out and voted not once, but a dozen times. For days before an election, anybody who came upon the streets was in danger of being seized. In one instance the mayor himself escaped only because he had a fast horse. In October, 1849, Edgar Allan Poe, becoming intoxicated at a dinner with military friends, was captured, and voted at several booths on election day.

What the Know-Nothings did was to organize violence more effectively and to make a philosophy of rule by force—in the name of the democracy they constantly extolled. Mussolini told the Romans on entering the imperial city in 1923, "This day we have trampled on the prostrate form of Liberty, and we shall do so again and again!" But the Know-Nothings raped the poor lady, then told the world she was a cherished virgin whose purity they were ready to die to protect. In the name of "democracy" and "freedom" and "the Bible," they invented new weapons of terrorism and murder. The most shameful demonstrations of mob rule in the history of Maryland occurred under the Know-Nothing administrations.

By the 1856 municipal election, the Know-Nothing ruffians were determined to put Thomas Swan, former president of the Baltimore and Ohio Railroad, in as mayor, and from the first moment their thugs gained control of nearly all polling places, with clubs, bricks, knives, and guns. The Rip Raps attacked the Irish Fire Company in Lexington Market, routed the firemen, and wrecked the firehouse. Swan and a Know-Nothing Council majority were easily elected.

For the November election the Know-Nothings were active throughout the state. At a great pre-election rally in Frederick, it took bands, marchers, and 372 carriages more than an hour to pass. Leading orators from all over the country spoke simultaneously from different platforms. The people roared out their campaign ballad for presidential candidate Fillmore.

> *Fill high the cup with ruby wine*
> *And pledge a hearty health to him*
> *Whose name in purest light shall shine,*
> *Nor slander's broth shall ever dim.*
> *Fill up! Fill up, the sparkling cup.*
> *Fillmore! Fillmore!*

In the city, the campaign got off impressively with a rally of 6,000, addressed by Congressman W. A. Lake, a lawyer and rich planter from Mississippi. Appeals made by opponents, private citizens, and the governor for proper safeguards for a free election were brushed aside. In broad daylight, the Rip Raps and Wampanoags (named after a warlike Algonquin tribe) brought carloads of bricks to clubs and saloons near polling places, and set up cannon. Election day saw wounding, maiming, and killing. Open battles took place on five main streets. Gangs of fifteen- to eighteen-year-old boys roamed the streets, committing felonious assaults—also voting. In the Catholic Sixth Ward, the Know-Nothings moved in with cannon. The Democrats drove the Know-Nothings out of the Fourth Ward, but the latter came back with bigger forces and clobbered them.

Maryland was the one state carried by Fillmore. The national election returns were a bitter disappointment to the American party, but it consoled itself that Maryland was still a "bulwark of conservatism between two ultra-sectional fires" —"a rock adamant against ultra-abolitionism . . . and extreme nullification . . . both fanatical and equally destructive of the Union." Laudable and intelligent sentiments—except that Know-Nothing medicine was worse than the disease.

At the next year's municipal elections, the polling places were stuck in disreputable corners close to hoodlum clubs or hangout saloons, and again cannon were mounted. Most of the violence occurred when the Rip Raps and Blood Tubs tried to capture the Irish Eighth Ward, where the mayor provided no police protection. The Democrats hauled out a cannon from their Jackson Hall headquarters, a police sergeant was killed, and the Know-Nothings had to abandon the fight. Numerous houses were sacked and burned.

Before other polling places, the Know-Nothing Blood Tub set out tubs full of bloody water, into which they dunked German and Irish voters, then kicked and cuffed them down the streets. The sight of these gory apparitions pursued by ruffians frightened off respectable citizens.

The spectacle was so disgraceful that the governor made forceful proposals to Mayor Swan for maintaining order at the November elections. Rebuffed again, he proclaimed martial law, ordered the handful of militiamen at his disposal to be in readiness, and that six volunteer regiments of 600 men each be enrolled. He borrowed 2,000 rifles from the governor of Virginia.

Baltimorians were angered, their right of suffrage menaced on one side by lawless violence, on the other by bayonets. Nor did tension diminish when Mayor Swan appointed 200 special police in each ward and closed all liquor and gun stores. Everybody knew that his police and the Know-Nothing thugs would fight shoulder to shoulder against the militia and the Democrats. The Know-Nothing press riddled the governor fore and aft, and the city largely resented his decree.

The mayor was unable to get enough volunteers to form even one company and had to renounce force. Election-day rioting and bloodshed were less in evidence but fraud, sneak violence, and intimidation were rampant. The Know-Nothings carried concealed shoe awls, and whenever a voter refused to accept a red-striped Know-Nothing ballot, a crowd closed around him and he was jabbed in the legs and back.

Former Mayor Thomas H. Hicks was elected governor by a four-to-one vote. All other Know-Nothing candidates for state offices, a strong legislative majority, and four of six congressmen were elected also.

On leaving office, Governor Ligon lashed out at Baltimore lawlessness. "This is anarchy. . . . The final power it creates is an essential tyranny. It sways a spurious empire over a people despoiled of their rights, and its career must be in profligate antagonism with law, order, and good government."

The Know-Nothing legislature denied this libel on the "good people of Baltimore." Governor Hicks denounced Ligon's attempt to use force in the city and promised he would never call out the militia to control elections.

The 1858 election in the city was preceded by more menacing violence than usual, including an attack upon the *Deutsche Correspondent*. It was hoped, however, that the abolition of rival volunteer fire companies a month before the voting would reduce violence. The new paid firemen, of course, were tools of the Swan administration. The only important benefit was the sudden drop in the number of fires.

Election-day intimidation and disorder were so great (all polling places but one were seized by lawless Know-Nothing bands) that every opposition candidate withdrew by noon. Mayor Swan was re-elected by a five-to-one majority. Three fourths of the opposition vote was cast in the single Irish eighth Ward. Only two opposition councilmen went in.

At the 1859 Democratic state convention, Joshua Vansant of Baltimore bitterly condemned the murderous Know-Nothing clubs, ruffians armed with deadly weapons and having armories of muskets and rifles near the polling places, the waylaying and beating of opposition voters approaching the polls, the murder of those failing to deposit a marked Know-Nothing ballot. The crimes were abetted by the police, a mercenary force 600 strong, "that assaulted where it should have protected" and was "more to be feared than the bowie knife of the vile clubs."

Revolt manifested itself against the SSSB dictatorship. For the October municipal election a Reform group held a giant Monument Square mass meeting where it was voted to nominate city candidates and enroll 200 volunteer constables in each precinct. The Know-Nothings countered with a rival "reform" mass meeting and accused the "Reformers" of being "the only source of corruption." Mayor Swan denounced the proposed force of private "constables" which could result only in conflicts with the authorized police.

Prior to the election, four Know-Nothing toughs, of a dozen wearing colored handkerchiefs around their necks, were arrested for attacking Negroes on the bay steamer *Express*. The Negroes were knocked down, robbed, and stabbed, and colored girls were raped. The Know-Nothing judge told a *Sun* reporter he wished the thugs had also thrown the captain overboard for taking on Negroes as passengers. When the jury convicted three of them, he imposed on each a fifty-cent fine and two days' imprisonment.

The elections followed the usual pattern, bricks, guns, shooting, stabbings—the most ruffianly election so far. A new stunt to keep out unwanted voters was to sprinkle voting places with prickly cowhage. The Know-Nothings destroyed the Twelfth Ward ballot box after it had been temporarily lost and stuffed. Yet the Reform elements came within a few thousand votes of winning.

More extensive preparations, speeches, and parades

were made for the state election the following month. American Senator Kennedy and Congressman Henry Winter Davis made more incendiary incitements to violence. One Know-Nothing parade placard showed toughs with awls in their hands and Democrats and Reformers with bloody heads, with the straightforward warning:

REFORM MAN IF YOU CAN VOTE I'LL BE DAMNED

The Know-Nothing Rattlers advertised in the papers that awls were ready for distribution. Extra Know-Nothing thugs were brought in from Washington. Polls and adjacent clubs and saloons were equipped with alarm bells to call toughs into action if necessary. As usual, cannon were mounted. Know-Nothings, draped in the American flag, rode by on the tops of busses, taunting opponents, haranguing people on the street and at the polls. "Vote American! Vote American!" The terrorism was incredible. In the Fifteenth Ward, where voting was held in the Know-Nothing Watchman's Engine House, gunmen in upstairs windows fired on any known opponents. Two approaching Reform leaders were killed.

Attorney S. T. Wallis, testifying to election frauds, told how Erasmus ("Ras") Levy, an incumbent judge, collected thirty or forty vagabonds and ruffians in his home, who were marched single file to the nearby polling place—"a wretched set of creatures, filthy, stupefied with drink," some in sailors' clothes, some without shirts, one without shoes. The thugs escorting them shouted, "Clear the way. Make room for voters." Everybody else was shoved aside, and the ballots of the bums taken as quickly as the judge could handle them. They were then marched back to Levy's house, presently marched out to vote again—back and forth at least six times.

But in spite of the terrorism, the Know-Nothings lost their legislative majority, electing only ten of thirty-two senators and twenty-eight of seventy-four House members. The Democrats elected their entire state ticket and three congressmen. Maryland was slipping away from the Know-Nothing brass-knuckled grasp.

From Baltimore two Know-Nothing congressmen were elected. Their seats were contested. Sworn affidavits were secured from 5,766 persons who had been unable to vote because of intimidation or actual physical violence. But the efforts to invalidate the election proved futile.

The first act of the new Democratic-controlled legislature on meeting January 4, 1860, was to remove the police power from the mayor and put it under an independent Board of Police Commissioners. Mayor Swan contested the constitutionality of this, but was overruled by the Court of Appeals. It meant that rule by the clubs, by revolver, robbery, and murder was about over.

The 1860, fall elections were orderly, and a Reform mayor and an entire Reform Council were elected. By then the greater terror of civil war was hammering at the door of Mob Town.

## CHAPTER IX

# THE FORGOTTEN BATTLE OF NEW ORLEANS

KNOW-NOTHINGISM in Louisiana was partly an aftermath of the 1853 cholera and yellow-fever plague that swept away a sixth of the population of New Orleans. Know-Nothingism, to a degree, and the plague were both products of fantastic filth in a low, undrained city without sewers and ringed by mosquito swamps.

Although by 1840 New Orleans ranked fourth among American cities in population, even in normal years its death rate was double that of New York, Boston, or Philadelphia. Epidemics in the 'twenties killed a sixth of the population. In the 1832 plague, priests and ministers had been obliged to perform funeral rites for those who could be dumped at the cemetery gates all day and deep into the night. The 1847–49 epidemic took off 8 per cent of the population.

Five thousand immigrants—"great multitudes of jabbering and croaking Irish and Dutch [Germans]"—arrived that year of 1853, and yellow fever came in with a shipload of Irishmen. Everybody who could fled from the city, and a third of those left behind perished. Heaps of rotting bodies were left in the streets. That was the year Know-Nothingism took on renewed life.

The newcomers—although bitterly assailed by the Know-Nothings—effected considerable transformation in the city, digging ditches and canals, laying down gas and water mains, particularly in the American section, the Faubourg Ste. Marie, which materially, if not in grace, beauty, or fine living, was outstripping the French Vieux Carré.

The city was split among conflicting racial groups. Rough frontier Americans and haughty French and Spanish Creoles detested one another. The Creoles could not hope to outnumber the tide of traders coming down the Mississippi, the inrush of immigrants. The Negroes, of course, sometimes pampered, but mostly abused, did not count. With the political decline of the aristocrats, their wealth and splendid culture ebbed away also, in the face of American vulgarity, greed, and violence. Not that the Creole world represented justice or the rights of man; one could still grieve to see the inexorable march of history, the lust of man, the deadly brutality of the process, bringing nothing overtly better while it destroyed the romantic aura and the grace of pre-American days. Know-Nothingism was on the march, and though, presently, as a movement it was to perish, in a deeper sense it conquered.

But until the mid-'thirties, Anglos were still outvoted by the Creoles, who neglected the Faubourg Ste. Marie and utilized municipal tax funds chiefly to promote improvements and commercial supremacy in the Vieux Carré. The French quarter was connected by railroad to Lake Pontchartrain—the second railroad in the United States—to suck in trade, and it had the only good ship canal. The Anglos countered by using strong immigrant backs to dig a second canal from their quarter to the lake. They improved their streets and built better buildings.

In 1836, although outnumbered in New Orleans, they were strong enough in the state to get the legislature to divide the port city into three sectors, the Vieux Carré, the Faubourg. Ste. Marie and the Faubourg Marigny, with one mayor but separate autonomous councils, each having independent control over tax monies and public works. This led to tremendous rivalry. A separate town hall was built on Lafayette Square by the Anglos to rival the old Cabildo on the historic Plaza de Armas; they put up Hotel Saint Charles, said to be the finest in the land. The Creoles countered with the elegant Hotel Saint Louis, with great stately salons and dazzling dewdrop chandeliers. Even so, many French commercial houses, seeing the inevitable drift, moved over to the Anglo sector, setting up stores or branches on Saint Charles Avenue and adjacent streets.

But the division resulted in added corruption and confusion that worsened year by year. As early as 1843, the Democratic machine particularly began using Irish immigrants as "repeaters" at the polls and five years later imported Chris Lilie (a pugilist henchman of Captain Isaiah Rynders), who introduced Tammany rowdyism in perfected form. The independent voter could get no protection from the boss-controlled police.

In 1853, the city was reconsolidated, and the seat of government fixed in the Anglo section above Canal Street rather than on the old Plaza de Armas, now known as Jackson Square. The corrupt police department was shaken up, somewhat reformed. But soon corruption seeped back in and demoralization grew worse.

The answer was a shout of Nativism. At first the SSSB was hard put to it for an effective program. New Orleans was not a good place to peddle anti-Catholicism; too many votes were at stake. Nor could the Know-Nothings easily pose as pristine "Americans." They themselves were the immigrants —along with the Germans, English, and Irish, whom they could not afford to alienate although they did attempt to prevent unnaturalized immigrants from voting. Hence the pivotal Know-Nothing hates were softened by flowery patriotic catchwords, mostly slogans of civic righteousness and clean government. But they soon matched ruffianism with ruffianism. If a poison sometimes is a successful antidote to another poison in the human body, this is rarely true in the body politic. At bottom, it was a struggle for power and loot, a final phase of the rise of the conquering Anglos to ruling status, part of the "Americanization" process, the destruction of the existing "alien" culture.

By 1854, the Know-Nothings had a strong organization in the city and state. In New Orleans, in coalition with the Whigs, they supported an "Independent Reform" ticket. Anti-foreignism played a larger role.

The New Orleans *Daily Crescent,* March 21, 1854, bemoaned the fact that "a strong nation should, on its own soil, be governed by a comparative handful of foreigners, ignorant of its laws and seizing upon office while yet hardly speaking its tongue." The foreigners had turned suffrage into "a hell's holiday of drunkenness and perjury and bludgeons."

A gang of Democratic rowdies tried to drive off "Reform" leaders from one polling place and stabbed the policeman on guard. At another, rowdies shot Chief of Police O'Leary when he tried to eject Know-Nothings, who had come to inspect the voting lists in the Seventh Precinct, where 1,400 Democratic ballots had been cast with a registration of only 932.

Charles Gayarré, an Independent Democrat, a Catholic, made ferocious attacks on election corruption: "a dead foreigner was not dead as long as his naturalization papers could be found"—papers often fraudulent. Never had suffrage been riddled with such "barefaced and shameless" audacity. Men were toted from one poll to another in furniture carts, voted, and revoted. "An honest man's vote was worth one, while a rogue's was worth ten." Four thousand more votes were cast than the year before, although 10,000 had died from the plague, and 20,000 had fled the city.

The Independents failed to win the mayor's office, but won control of all branches of the city government, including the Council. This meant important patronage. Also, the victory stimulated further Know-Nothing gains elsewhere in the state. Auxiliary female organizations, called "Know-Everything," were started.

Anti-Catholicism, which had received its first hysterical impulse at the time of Papal Nuncio Bedini's proposed visit to New Orleans, when "the Butcher of Bologna" was warned to keep out, was growing stronger. The New Orleans

*Daily Crescent* and other papers began taking an anti-Catholic line. A fanatical Blue-Light anti-Catholic Know-Nothing faction was organized. Later the president of the national order revoked their right to establish subordinate councils.

In September, 1854, the Catholics gave credence to rumors that they were to be slaughtered by the Know-Nothings, and a great crowd of them armed themselves and gathered in Lafayette Square. The mayor tried to quiet them, but a druggist, Dr. J. J. Meighan, waving his gun, led them two hundred strong down Camp Street to defend Saint Mary's Church. A gun fight with a Know-Nothing gang resulted in two deaths and many injuries. The militia were kept on duty the following day and night. But a Know-Nothing mob attacked the coffee houses on Levee Street. Violence and death continued all week. The mayor deputized special police, but not until September 18 did the city quiet down. Know-Nothingism in New Orleans was now definitely in the lists against Catholicism.

In spite of this, Gayarré turned Know-Nothing and was chosen to lead the party's delegation to the national Native American convention in Philadelphia in June, 1855, but was there refused a seat because he was a Catholic, although the rest of his delegation was accepted.

The State Council, meeting in New Orleans, July 4, angrily talked of secession, but it was decided to stick by with a watered-down version on the Catholic question. This platform was ratified by 10,000 people in Lafayette Parish after addresses by Randall Hunt and Albert Pike of Arkansas.

In the fall elections, the gangs were out again with guns and bowie knives. Polling places were in closed courts reached only by narrow alleys, and, when the Democrats lost control, they set up rival ballot boxes.

One man was killed as he tried to push into a Know-Nothing booth with his naturalization papers in one hand and his pistol in the other. At Know-Nothing places, cries of "Clear out, you damned Dutch and Irish Sons of Bitches" were heard. A mob destroyed the second and ninth Democratic precinct ballot boxes, and the commissioners could make no returns. When they refused to obey a court order to do so anyway, a judge fined and jailed them.

With the 1856 spring election coming on, the Democratic papers called the Know-Nothings "murderers, thieves, thugs, orphan killers, brass knuckles, midnight assassins, widow makers, rowdies, bullies, plug uglies, house burners, dark-lantern ballot-box breakers." The mayor, preparing to avoid trouble, raided the *Courier* office and seized guns. The Catholic charity hospital was ransacked. Charges of misconduct of the nuns were circulated.

At the outset, the SSSB gangs seized control of crucial voting places. The police were powerless, for Mayor John L. Lewis disarmed them on election day. Many resigned. As election-day violence mounted, the mayor called for law-and-order citizens to come to city hall and be armed. Only twenty showed up. They were sent out at once to the worst trouble spots. There were numbers of deaths, a score wounded, plenty of broken heads. A disgraceful election of violence and bloodshed, the *True Delta,* June, 3, 1856, called it.

The Americans easily elected Charles M. Waterman mayor and all candidates other than two Democrats, who got under the wire as aldermen. Know-Nothing victories occurred in other Louisiana towns and parishes.

Governor Robert C. Wickliff, perturbed by the Democratic defeat, denounced "the acts of violence upon multitudes of our naturalized citizens" who had not "dared . . . to exercise the right of suffrage." He pushed through legislation creating a central board of elections for New Orleans Parish under the attorney general with a resident inspector of elections, empowered "to prevent and suppress riots, tumults, violence, disorder, and other practices tending to the intimidation of voters." Judge John B. Cotton, later a reconstruction carpetbagger, was put in charge. The expense was charged to New Orleans.

The *Delta* said furiously that this system gave the attorney general "as a reward for his prosecutions, 20 per cent of the money extracted from his victims." This revived "the days of Titus Oakes and other knaves, and no man is secure.

Give blood money to a public officer, and he invariably sinks into a bloodsucker."

In July, the mayor obtained an injunction prohibiting the Election Board from functioning. On October 13, Judge Cotton enjoined the mayor from naming polling places. Cotton got no cooperation from the Know-Nothing authorities or the police, controlled by them, and was threatened by Native Americans, who gathered in a mob outside his home. They withdrew on finding the doors and windows barricaded and that Judge Cotton and other men were ready with leveled guns.

All this maneuvering was a prelude to the November presidential election. The Know-Nothings were determined to whip up great enthusiasm throughout the state for Millard Fillmore, since a strong vote for the national ticket would help their local candidates.

At the Jackson rally in East Feliciana Parish September 13, the procession was two miles long, with 840 carriages and 5,000 marchers, two bands, "banners and flags in profusion, two cannon, meat and bread in great profusion, cakes, candies, ice cream . . . and other sweet things in abundance —and four of the best speakers I have ever heard."

The Know-Nothings won numbers of seats in the legislature. The lower house—Democratic—investigated contested elections, and held customary star-chamber hearings, not allowing the Know-Nothings to cross-examine witnesses or present their own evidence. It vacated several Know-Nothing seats. One deposed winner was re-elected overwhelmingly.

The Senate similarly vacated three seats, not even letting the Know-Nothing minority on the credentials committee listen to or see the testimony. A *Crescent* correspondent wrote: "Messrs. Editors: The blood fairly curdled in my veins when I saw the Rapides representative, a foreigner by birth . . . expounding American law to American senators, on the trial of three honorable Native Americans."

In the 1857 state Know-Nothing convention, held in Baton Rouge, Democratic misrule was denounced, as were failure to protect southern rights in Kansas and neglect of the schools. Protection for a free ballot, "a sacred American institution," was demanded, and freedom of religion—but not, of course, freedom for Catholicism. Candidates for minor state offices were named.

The Native Americans were decisively defeated this year. Only two state senators were elected. The showing in the lower house was better, thirty-eight Know-Nothings to forty-nine Democrats. Scattered parish and city offices were won. Only in New Orleans, where J. B. Cotton was not allowed to carry out his functions, did the Know-Nothings secure a clear-cut victory.

By the 1858 municipal election, Mayor Waterman, who had quarreled with the party leaders, refused to accept renomination and Recorder Gerard Stith, former pressman of the *Picayune,* was put up. Seeing no chance in the face of Know-Nothing violence, the Democrats and Whigs combined on reform Mayor P. G. T. Beauregard, an envious little man who had distinguished himself in the Mexican War (later a Confederate general), hoping to cut into any Creole support for the Know-Nothings. The SSSB toughs intensified their terrorism.

On June 1, 1858, Know-Nothing ruffians broke into the office of the registrar of voters and seized the registration lists. They were returned some days later with the names of all Whig voters struck off—which was startling, inasmuch as the Whigs had practically spawned the Know-Nothing movement. Why hadn't the Know-Nothings struck off the names of Democratic voters? Had a deal been cooked up between the traditional enemies?

This electoral piracy stirred up a Vigilante committee, composed of Whigs and Creoles, that set out to meet Know-Nothing violence with counter-violence. Headquarters were established in the university building at Commerce and Bayonne streets, just outside the Vieux Carré, four blocks from the city hall on Lafayette Square, a branch office on Dryades Street. A thousand men were armed, all so quietly that little was known about them until June 2, four days before the election, when they boldly took over the Cabildo in the Vieux Carré on the Plaza de Armas or Jackson Square, the calaboose on Congress Square, and the state arsenal on Saint Peter Street, which slanted down toward the river front. Muskets and small arms from the arsenal were distributed among the Vigilantes, and sentries were posted on all streets running into the square.

The operation was in the hands of a newcomer, Captain Johnson Kelley Duncan, a West Pointer and a Seminole War veteran, who in January had become New Orleans Federal Superintendent of Repairs in charge of the mint, marine hospital, quarantine warehouse, and the Pas à l'Outre Boarding Station. From the arsenal, he issued a proclamation that the Vigilantes, "resolved to free the city from the murderers who infest it," had assumed the powers of a temporary government. It asked "all good men and true to join up for active duty and to inflict prompt exemplary punishment upon well-known and notorious . . . violators of the rights and privileges of the citizens."

Mayor Waterman learned of the insurrection at 5 A.M. He summoned General John L. Lewis, now head of the First Militia Division, to city hall, and asked him to take steps to suppress the revolt. Lewis sent out a mobilization call for the Washington Artillery, the Southern Rifles, and the National and Continental Guards. The police, except for a handful, had not reported for duty, and the chief of police had no idea where his men were.

The mayor called a special 10 A.M. session of the Common Council. He was greeted by a great roaring Know-Nothing crowd, demanding suppression of the rebels.

The Council proposed arming the mob. The mayor opposed this and declined to publish the Council's resolution calling for the immediate wiping out of the Vigilantes. Tempers flared, and the councilors asked for his resignation. He refused. Disgusted, the Council gave him full disciplinary powers and adjourned. The whole thing was now his baby.

The Vigilantes moved sentries forward to Canal Street, where they patrolled along the Vieux Carré side, and threw up barricades of cotton bales and paving blocks on all streets into the French Quarter.

Mayor Waterman requested a parley with Duncan, the Vigilante leader, and went to the Cabildo with former Mayor Kent and General Lewis. They found many veterans of William Walker's filibuster expedition to Nicaragua under arms.

Duncan refused to disband his forces or give up any positions, unless all his men were sworn in as special police. The mayor returned to city hall, where he was cheered by the crowd for refusing to accede to Duncan's demands. He proclaimed to the city that "a lawless mob" had invaded the property of the city of New Orleans and taken possession of the state arsenal and military arms and ammunition belonging to the city and the state.

General Lewis had not been able to get volunteers for the militia units. He sent out a call for the First Brigade and Louisiana Legions, and the mayor issued a warrant for the arrest of Captain Duncan and his fellow officers, but the chief of police was obliged to return from the arsenal to city hall without arresting anybody. Presently he, too, vanished from the city. The Know-Nothings claimed he had accepted a $3,000 bribe to clear out.

The mob in the square shouted for the immediate storming of the Vigilante positions. Waterman reluctantly signed orders on a hardware and sporting-goods store for weapons. The Know-Nothings, now armed, returned to Lafayette Square, firing their weapons in the air and dragging several cannon taken from militia quarters. The guns were set up to command Saint Charles Avenue and Camp Street and at nightfall sentries were posted along Canal Street, across the street from the Vigilante sentries. The situation was tense, but no fighting resulted.

At 8 A.M. Friday, June 4, Waterman was informed by Lewis that fewer than one hundred and fifty militiamen had responded, not sufficient to dislodge the Vigilantes. Again, with Lewis and two prominent citizens, the mayor went to parley with the Vigilantes. It was a frightfully hot day. With sweat pouring down their faces, the emissaries argued with

Duncan all morning and on through the lunch hour. In the afternoon, the mayor signed on the dotted line, conceding all Vigilante demands.

General Lewis, assisted by Duncan and the two citizens present, was to replace Judge Cotton as election inspector. A proclamation to this effect was issued from the "Office Executive Committee, Arsenal, June 4, 1858. The Vigilante Committee . . . having organized with a view of freeing the City of New Orleans of the notorious thugs, outlaws, assassins, and murderers who infest it," has agreed "to disband as such, after being legally sworn in as election policemen under General Lewis . . . and to bring up for trial, under affidavits, the notorious offenders of the law . . . and free the city." The Vigilantes would retain present positions and occupy any others designated by General Lewis.

Waterman's announcement of surrender stirred the city hall crowd to fury, and he was threatened with hanging. After milling about, shouting, 300 marched down Saint Charles toward the French Quarter, vowing to drive out the Vigilantes. A shot from a Vigilante sentry wounded one Know-Nothing fighter on the cheek, and the marchers halted in confusion.

Acting Recorder L. Adams ordered the crowd to disperse. About half obeyed; the rest continued the march along Royal Street, as Saint Charles is named at that point, until they came up against Vigilante barricades and cannon. Then they broke and tore helter-skelter down side streets and along Saint Louis to Chartres Street toward the Plaza de Armas. Finding this also barricaded, they fled back to Lafayette Square.

The only casualties were two Vigilantes, one killed, not by the Know-Nothings, but by the premature discharge of a brass twelve-pounder being prepared for defense.

Adams again urged the Know-Nothing forces to store their weapons in the city hall. Most obeyed. Mayor Waterman was in heated conference with fifteen citizens, who wanted to make Duncan compromise on the agreement. Their plan called for the closing of all drinking places on election day, the dismissal and disarming of all regular policemen (though no one knew where any were), the disbanding of the Vigilante Committee and evacuation of all city and state property; the appointment by the mayor of a new police force of a thousand men for the election, with permanent jobs promised them.

The mayor finally agreed and went to Jackson Square with his chief adviser. There, however, he began swearing in the Vigilantes, as per the previous agreement. Fearful of going back to city hall with news of his treachery, he slept that night in the second floor of the arsenal behind the guns of the deputized Vigilantes.

When the Know-Nothings heard about it, they issued handbills attacking him for giving in to the "traitors," and the crowd in city hall plaza, some 5,000 now, shouted for his blood. All night they kept shouting, getting into fights, shooting their guns into the air, and listening to incendiary orators denounce the mayor and call for the extermination of the Vigilantes. Chief rabble rousers were Colonel Thomas Henry, a former Walker filibuster, and old William Christy, a War of 1812 veteran. Christy wanted to lead them to the Cabildo at once, but got little response when it came to a showdown.

While he was speaking, heavy firing came from the French Quarter. Fearing a Vigilante attack on Lafayette Square, a hundred men were posted about the building under the command of Justice Bradford. Actually the firing was due to the jitters of the Vigilantes, who had fired on a group of their own men coming down Saint Peter's Street, killing four and wounding nine.

Terror and apprehension rode the city. Except for a few liquor stores, all businesses except in the distant Fourth District were barricaded. The Know-Nothings roamed restlessly, committing depredations, looting stores, beating up "foreigners" and naturalized citizens. Government had collapsed; no mayor, no common council, no police, no militiamen, no nothing except two rival mobs.

During the afternoon, prominent citizens went to the arsenal to urge the mayor to return to city hall, but they were unable to promise him protection from the Know-Nothing mob. He authorized the Know-Nothing candidate for mayor, Stith, to enroll a special police force, but revoked it a few hours later as being an illegal delegation of his own powers. By then Stith had already sworn in 250 men.

The Common Council came to life again at 6 P.M. on June 5 and adopted impeachment articles against the mayor for abandoning his post and failing to terminate control by "an unlawful and armed organization." "Recreant in his duties," he had "failed, neglected, and refused to enforce the laws of the United States and the ordinances of the city."

Stith and three citizens called on the mayor to get him to return to city hall and defend himself. Duncan and other Vigilantes warned him that his life would be in danger, but he set forth—as far as Hotel Saint Charles. He told Stith to inform the Council that if requested by that "honorable body" he would wait upon it.

The Council did not send for him, and for the next two weeks he remained isolated in the hotel. The council asked H. M. Summers, president of the upper Council, to act as mayor. He agreed, if provided with "all the sinews of war," and taking over Waterman's duties, he revoked the appointment of the Vigilantes as special policemen, issued a proclamation that they constituted a lawless mob, and called upon them to disband.

Fifty federal soldiers came down from Baton Rouge; for a moment it was thought they had come to fight the Vigilantes, but they marched only to guard the mint and other federal properties.

The following day Summers replaced the vanished police chief with Colonel John A. Jacques and ordered all policemen back on their jobs. Enough responded to restore some order. But no action could be taken against the Vigilantes. Both bands continued to patrol on opposite sides of Canal Street.

Sunday passed calmly, and the election was held per schedule—Monday, June 7. Before the polls opened, Acting Mayor Summers swore in several hundred special police and additional election commissioners. As election inspector, General Lewis advised Vigilante leader Duncan that he would call on him only in case of an emergency.

It turned out to be one of the quietest elections in the city's history. The Native Americans captured every office except for three minor posts. They were more strongly intrenched than ever.

The Vigilantes began evacuating their positions as soon as the polls closed, abandoning bedding, food, and the weapons stolen from the arsenal. Only about two hundred remained until morning in Jackson Square. These Duncan marched to the United States Army barracks, where they were disarmed and told to go home. Those caught were beaten up. During the previous night a large number, mostly "foreigners," fearing such treatment, had slipped across the river and hid in the swamps below Algiers until, almost starved, they surrendered to the police. They were released at once, along with others previously arrested. More prominent, wealthy Vigilantes escaped from the city by steamboat, and the authorities considered swearing out warrants to bring them back, but nothing was done. The coroner held inquests over eleven bodies "slain within the entrenchments," but his findings were never published.

It took several days' hard scrubbing by Negroes to clean the blood, mud, and filth from the arsenal and Cabildo.

In the 1859 election, the New Orleans Democrats were split into innumerable factions: Hard Shells, Douglas Democrats, Anti-Douglas Democrats, Old Jackson Democrats, Union and States Rights Democrats, Old Whig Democrats, Sidelians in Easy Circumstances (the most fanatic pro-slavery crowd), Sidelians Who Haven't Been Paid, Opposition Democrats, Independents, Ex-Know-Nothing Democrats, Calhoun Democrats. But they coalesced before election day and carried the state by 9,000 votes. The Know-Nothings put up no state ticket but elected one congressman from a New Orleans district. By 1860 the party, except for New Orleans, had almost disappeared, but in the city it held on to power grimly and easily elected John T. Monroe, a prominent labor man, mayor.

Crime and murder, regular diet in New Orleans, grew worse under the long Know-Nothing rule. An English tourist noted, January 27, 1857—after Waterman had been in office a year—that there were pending fourteen cases of murder and nearly four hundred for shooting, stabbing, assault and battery. The city, said the *Bee,* a year and a half later, was infested by "desperadoes who shed innocent blood and spread terror and consternation." Murder continued, said the *True Delta,* a year later. "The record of one deed of blood has hardly dried upon the paper when another recital of crime" followed, "each chapter a brutal and bloody continuation of the preceding." During the succeeding two years under Know-Nothing Mayor Monroe, the coroner held a murder inquest once or twice a week, 132 in all—but few killers were ever punished; nothing was done to check the continued surge of crime.

Two thirds of the swamp and underworld murders never even were reported to the police. This covered much of the city, which teemed with gin mills, dance halls, whore houses, low taverns, concert saloons, and barrel houses. Even on Saint Charles Avenue, between Canal and city hall, there were forty-five saloons. A great part of the population spent most of its time drinking and brawling.

Not until the Civil War, when Admiral Farragut brought a fleet up the river and took over the city for the Union, did Know-Nothing power come to an end.

*CHAPTER X*

# *THE NATIVE SONS OF GOLDEN CALIFORNIA*

*The miners came in forty-nine*
*The whores in fifty-one*
*And when they got together*
*They produced the native son.*

*I came from Quakerdelphia*
*With my washbowl on my knee;*
*I'm going to California*
*The gold dust for to see . . .*
*Oh, Anna, don't you cry . . .*

THE first Native Sons were the Indians; by all accounts, probably prejudiced, they were a shiftless lot, although they gave the first Spanish missionaries some bad moments.

The second Native Sons were the Mexicans, who arrived several centuries before the Anglos, founded missions, presidios, and landed estates, and established a frontier society that, whatever its worse aspects, had leisure and grace.

There was neither grace nor decency in the greedy swarms who came to win fortunes—not merely the gold hunters, but the saloonkeepers, gamblers, desperadoes, ex-convicts, speculators, and fancy females. The newcomers were mostly Americans, but Chileans, Peruvians, Europeans, Australians,

Japanese, and Chinese came also. Overnight San Francisco grew into a filthy town among the masts of abandoned ships, mostly tents and shacks, a few flimsy wooden structures, and some solid Spanish-American buildings. At night, when lamps were lit, and showed through the semi-transparent canvas and burlap, the city on its hills resembled cubes of sunlight stacked up like gold bars. Gambling hangouts, saloons, dance halls, whore houses ruled nearly every street and Portsmouth Square—to this day known as the Uptown Tenderloin. There were no sewage facilities. The streets, even Market Street, the main thoroughfare, were so deep with mire that they were "not even jackassable," so one humorous sign warned. Drunks who fell in suffocated before they could be rescued.

From the start there was hostility by the Anglos toward all foreigners, particularly toward the Mexicans, whose properties were being stolen as rapidly as possible. Often they were killed and their women raped. The Chileans and Peruvians—who brought to Frisco its permanent heritage of "Pisco Punch"—were subjected to raids, arson, and murder. Such was the backdrop of Know-Nothingism in the Golden State: heartless persecution, abetted by the authorities and by General Persifer F. Smith, United States Army commandant, of Spanish-American "greasers" in the gold fields, on their ranches and in cities and towns. They were driven from their claims, their farms, and homes, and he who refused to evacuate was strung up pronto. At Downieville, the Anglos made a carnival of lynching a Mexican girl for stabbing an American miner who broke into her cabin to rape her.

A San Francisco alcalde, one of the first elected Americans, who hated cigarette smoking, tried a Mexican accused of horse stealing:

> JUDGE. "Do you smoke cigarettes?"
> PRISONER. "Sí, Señor."
> JUDGE. "Do you blow smoke through your nose?"
> PRISONER. "Sí, Señor."
> JUDGE. "Constable, take this fellow out and shoot him. He stole the horse sure enough."

This sort of brutality was aggravated first by the OUA, set up in 1850; later, by the SSSB. From the start, the Nativists were backed by newspaper editors, who berated the original Mexicans and the Chilean immigrants as trespassers on the public domain. The public domain was anything not owned by an Anglo-Saxon.

Such brutalities produced counter-violence. Daring eighteen-year-old outlaw Joaquin Murieta (alias Carrillo), a circus horse trainer, and his wife Rosa Felix, who rode with him in male attire, hair cropped close, performed exploits soon celebrated in Spanish, even English, ballads. They were the terror of all "white" land thieves, and Murieta considered himself a true patriot, called to free his "native" countrymen. He was the futile Aguinaldo, the Sandino, of the raped province of the West. He was finally betrayed for a few hundred dollars, by his friend, gambler William Burns.

The race-hating Nativists were the Hounds, "The Regulators," who proclaimed that California had been "preserved by Nature for Americans only, who possess noble hearts." They beat Spanish-Americans, robbed them, stabbed them, killed them. They broke into their homes, raped their women, time and again burned down their tents, cabins, and houses and, on occasion, half the rest of the city besides.

"With the coolest impudence," wrote Bancroft, "the Hounds asserted their determination to protect American rights against Spanish-speaking foreigners, and sometimes claimed to have instructions from the alcalde to extirpate the Mexicans and Chileans." The Mexicans were, of course, theoretically American citizens.

The Hounds were mostly Colonel Jonathan D. Stevenson's regiment of New York volunteers—originally Plug Uglies, Bowery and Atlantic Boys, "true Americans" all—recruited in the war against Mexico and stationed in California. Most of these patriots had been well trained in stealing and brawling as members of New York volunteer fire companies and Know-Nothing gangs, hence were well schooled as spread-eagle Americans for street forays. So began the tradition that persisted in California for half a century—the worst New

York Bowery riffraff running the great commonwealth. Stevenson's regiment was discharged on the scene, October 1, 1848—all who had not already deserted to the gold fields. They caused trouble in every mining camp, town, and city.

In San Francisco, Sam Roberts, a private in Stevenson's regiment, assumed the rank of full lieutenant and wore regimentals and organized his fellows for action against the "foreigners." They continued to wear army uniforms or more outlandish uniforms. Mostly they hung out in the Shades Saloon on Kearney Street. Their official headquarters, a large tent at Kearney and Commercial streets, near the later Barbary Coast, was called Tammany Hall. A big drum called them together for hoodlum forays.

They drilled regularly with muskets and swords and paraded each Sunday with fiddle, fife, and drum. Usually the day ended in a brawl in Chilean town on Telegraph Hill or in the Portsmouth Square whore houses. Pets of Nativist politicians, the Hounds were used for controlling voting booths and were employed by steamship companies to shanghai crews.

The big voice behind the Nativists was political boss David S. Broderick, a former New York saloonkeeper and Tammany hireling, who received a 50 per cent kickback on all fees and municipal salaries. Typical was his henchman, Charles P. Duane, who shot A. Fayole, owner of the French theater, for not letting him in free.

Growing bolder, the Regulators demanded support from merchants. Those who refused were smashed up and robbed. In taverns and restaurants they left without paying, telling the owner "to collect from the city." If he objected, they smashed up his place or set it on fire. They pushed men and women off the sidewalk. One Negro, who accidentally jostled one, had his ears cut off. A Mexican pedestrian who failed to obey an order in a servile manner had his tongue torn out.

On July 15, 1849, the Hounds descended en masse on the Chileno tents and shanties and displayed their "noble American hearts" by plundering them, beating the occupants with sticks and stones, and knifing them. Recklessly they fired into the homes amid the shrieks of terrified women, one of whom was murdered, and the groans of wounded men.

This occurrence was too shocking to be ignored. Sam Brannan and Captain Bezar Simmons laid down the law to the alcalde, T. M. Leavenworth, and obliged him to issue a call for a citizens' mass meeting in Portsmouth Square.

Big Sam Brannan, California's first millionaire, was one of the most extraordinary characters of his time. A Mormon elder, Brigham Young's New York representative, he had grown embittered by official and private persecution of the Mormons. On February 15, 1846—the same day Young led his Mormons out of Nauvoo, Illinois, on their long march to the promised land of Utah—Brannan set sail from New York on the *Brooklyn* with another band, about three hundred—to set up a colony on the Pacific Coast where the United States would have no jurisdiction. Ironically, the *Brooklyn* sailed through Golden Gate three weeks after Captain John B. Montgomery and sailors from the U.S.S. *Portsmouth* ran up the Stars and Stripes on Mexico's flagpole atop the adobe customhouse on Yerba Buena's main square—at once renamed Portsmouth in honor of the American sloop of war and soon to become the focus of a brawling tenderloin. That flag was the first thing Brannan saw when the *Brooklyn* moved toward the Embarcadero. Enraged, he hurled his hat to the deck and yelled, "There's that damned rag again!"

After settling his flock in tents and adobe houses near Yerba Buena cove, Brannan went to Utah to try to persuade Young to bring the rest of the Mormons to the beautiful Eden of California, but Young refused to settle in a rich area that was bound to attract other, non-Mormon settlers. Brannan returned to San Francisco and told his band they'd be fools to go to dreary Utah. With numbers of his followers, he settled near Swiss John Sutter's fort in the Sacramento Valley, and there started a store near the big log blockhouse. When gold was discovered on the American River, he went and personally led all but seven of San Francisco's 900 inhabitants off to the foothills.

Sutter was overwhelmed by the rough, mad rush, but not Brannan. He had his store and he was still collecting tithes from his Mormon followers, and he made a quick fortune by selling supplies to the horde of invading gold seekers. Furthermore, he installed a scales and a safe and bought gold dust at discount with drafts on eastern banks, and lo, he became a banker.

But Brannan is better remembered for his leadership of the Vigilantes than for his piled-up gold. At the big Portsmouth Square rally, his great whiskers rattled and his booming voice rolled forth from the rooftop of the alcalde's building in invective of the Hounds. His "vigor of vituperation . . . had rarely been equaled." He enumerated the killings and burnings in the city: he pictured the horrors of the assault on Telegraph Hill and the plight of the Chileno families and called for contributions to help the destitute. Sacks of gold dust and gold nuggets and gold slugs overflowed the hats. Two hundred and thirty volunteers were armed to extirpate the Hounds.

Most of the Nativist desperadoes took to their heels, fleeing to the interior or frantically taking to the bay in small boats. Some twenty were captured—including Roberts—on the road to Stockton. The prisoners were lodged in the brig of the warship *Warren,* and two days later were tried by the mayor and two Vigilante judges. Roberts and another were sentenced to ten years at hard labor, the rest for shorter terms, and heavy fines were imposed. But within a few days politicians quietly released them, and they left the city.

The Hounds' role of terrorism was taken over by the Sidney Ducks, deported or escaped British and Australian criminals who had settled on Kearney Street, on the Devil's Half Acre, later known as the Barbary Coast. They, too, were used by politicians at election time and by shipowners. Sidney Town became the chief center for whore houses, lodging houses, gambling joints, dance halls, saloons, "hives of dronish criminals," shabby little dens with rough, hangdog fellows lounging about the doorways. If an arrest had to be made, the police never ventured there without a small army. "Little better than the Five Points of New York or Saint Giles of London," said the leading daily, the *Herald,* a paper that later sold itself to underworld politicians. "Unsuspecting sailors and miners are entrapped by the dextrous thieves and swindlers . . . always on the lookout." Often victims were drugged. "These dance groggeries are outrageous nuisances and nurseries of crime." Drunkenness, fornication, robberies, fights went on day and night. For a pinch or two of gold dust, the whores would stage indecent exhibitions. Herbert Asbury tells of the "Bear's Head," where a regular feature consisted of copulation by a boar and a woman, and of the "Fierce Grizzly," where a live female bear was used in sexual shows.

A criminal, "English Jim," and a companion–both Sidney Ducks–blackjacked a Montgomery businessman and stole $2,000 in gold. That was killing too close to home for Brannan's comfort, and he aroused 8,000 Vigilantes to take action. To the assembled crowd he roared out, "I'm . . . surprised to hear people talk about grand juries or recorders or mayors. I'm tired of such talk. These men are murderers, . . . and . . . I will die or see them hung by the neck."

Unfortunately, the Vigilantes convicted the wrong men.

In May, 1851, a Sidney Duck set fire to a paint shop on Portsmouth Square. As the flames spread, devouring three fourths of the city, the ruffians swarmed over the hills looting and shooting. DeWitt and Harrison on Commercial Street saved their establishment by dousing on 80,000 gallons of vinegar.

Sam Brannan called a meeting at his office and again aroused the Vigilantes. A few days later, they seized a thief and after a summary trial, hanged him at two in the morning from the gable of the customhouse on Portsmouth Square. It was a moonlit night.

Then in July they caught the real "English Jim," who "confessed." Although somewhat stunned by their previous mistake, the Vigilantes hanged him from a gallows on Market Street Wharf. A few weeks later, balked by the sheriff from lynching two more Sidney Ducks, the Vigilantes burst into jail and strung them up from two redwood beams stuck out the windows of their headquarters at Battery and Pine streets. A vast crowd sent up a paean of rejoicing.

But the real crescendo of criminality, corruption, and vice was to recur under Know-Nothing rule—and remedial action was taken by the Second Vigilante Committee. Out of such disorders, Know-Nothingism—one piece with the aims and operations of the Hounds if not always the Sidney Ducks—emerged with the false slogan of "Reform."

The OUA was started in 1850 by Robert D. Hart, W. Ackerman, and Charles M. Yarwood. By 1857 it had nine chapters. The first SSSB organization, according to *Alta California,* appeared in May, 1854, and headquarters for a "Native American party" were set up on Sacramento Street. The *Chronicle,* practically a Know-Nothing sheet, reported in June that rules and regulations were expected by the next ship. If the Know-Nothings would be able "to stop drunkenness and fighting at elections" they would deserve credit. The paper was pleased that the order had also appeared in interior towns.

On August 5, 1854, the Stockton *Argus* wrote: "Where are they?" They were meeting every night and increasing in numbers. But "nobody seems to know where their headquarters are. How the devil do they increase their numbers so fast when nobody can find the right door to knock at?"

That same month the *Alta California* commented that the administration had "stirred up the political cauldron in all the states" until it had "bubbled and boiled over," and that the Know-Nothings in California had their candidates ready to be launched at the opportune moment. They had "a good chance" to win, for the Whigs had little strength, and the Democrats were fighting over spoils—a split between "Tammany" and "Chivalry," a hint of sectionalism that might become decisively destructive.

The two Democratic groups were also known as the Electionists (the ins) and Anti-Electionists (the would-be-ins). From the latter, two more factions split off, the "Bone and Sinew" and the "Rose Waters." Thus five tickets would enter the mayoralty race. More would soon appear. For the electoral situation was incredibly confused. There was disaffection because public officials were stealing right and left and doing little to provide the necessary improvements and services needed desperately by the fast-growing city. Nor did they provide adequate law and order, because they were tied in with the worst ruffians and criminals.

The Know-Nothings branded the whole caboodle as "riffraff candidates" and called for a "Citizens' party"—men who would "administer the government with economy and a desire for the welfare of the people." But according to historian Bancroft, the Know-Nothing lawyers, judges, and fire-eating politicians were the scum of the state—"thieves, gamblers, murderers, some . . . living on the proceeds of harlotry." The president of one Know-Nothing convention was the leading racetrack owner. The Know-Nothing "Citizens' Reform" ticket was named in secret convention and disclosed four days before the election, September 2.

Two days later, the membership refused to ratify the choices, chiefly because names had been put on the ticket by "the same corrupt mode of bargaining, selling, and swapping" as on other tickets, and the candidate for mayor, Lucien Hermann, was a Roman Catholic. The day before elections an open nominating convention met in Metropolitan Theater, 760 members present, and put up a new ticket headed by S. P. Webb for mayor.

The discarded Hermann roundly denounced "the bigotry and intolerance" of members of the order who had opposed him "because of his religious faith." He remained in the race at the head of an independent "Cuidado" ticket, with a platform of "equal rights to all . . . no proscription on account of country, religion, or politics." By then an amazing number of tickets popped up—not to mention various candidates running on no ticket. The list included: Electionist Democrats; Anti-Election Democrats; Rose Water Democrats; Anti-Election Bone and Sinew Democrats; Citizens' Reform (Know-Nothing); Cuidados; Anti-Slavery; Independents; Y. I.'s Pine Tree Club; Independent Citizens; Anti-

Anti Know-Nothings; Know-Somethings; and Independent Union.

To keep order, Mayor C. K. Garrison, running for re-election, reinforced the police by sworn-in citizen deputies, chiefly recruited from the Sidney Ducks. Ironically, most had been bought off by the Know-Nothings with cash, promises, and guarantees of protection.

The *Chronicle* described Montgomery Street election-day scenes: bankers passing out slugs (fifty-dollar gold pieces); newsmen stealthily taking notes; the bars and billiard rooms jammed with a host of gentlemen and seedy loafers, 200 candidates and their multitudinous friends. All day long they drank and smoked, chewed and spat, and drank again. Everybody "speculated" and "nearly everybody belched forth perpetual volleys of oaths which like the discharge of unshotted guns meant nothing save impotent fury." Noise! Smoke! Stench! At least half of those electioneering were passing out Know-Nothing ballots.

Things went fairly peacefully until near closing time, when in the First Ward "shoulder strikers" tried to steal a ballot box. The Know-Nothings fought them off, wounding three and killing one. In the Second Ward, where a judge was absent, the Irish were shouting "No Know-Nothings!" until a wedge of SSSB thugs hit them. Police Captain North lost his gold star and was badly cut on the head. The roofs were black with spectators.

Twenty cops and armed Know-Nothings kept perfect order in the Third and Fourth wards. There was a fist fight in the Fifth, where a tax collector tangled with special cops and Irishmen "Do-Nothings." In the "Bloody Sixth," Mayor Garrison angrily tore off the badge off one of his police, who was "electioneering" for the Know-Nothings, but the SSSB thugs sent up their "Ay Ay Ay," for help, and the mayor got badly roughed up when 300 men poured in. The Second Ward "Mulligans" (Know-Nothings) marched in a body to the Sixth Ward where, the *Chronicle* remarked mildly, "they did not contribute to peace"—at least immediately. The Know-Nothings kept the Seventh Ward deadly quiet. In the

Eighth, controlled by the mayor's crowd, there was one interesting dogfight and one less interesting human scuffle.

The Know-Nothings won easily. The vote from the First Ward was never counted, and the returns from the mayor's strong Eighth Ward—800 ballots—were held up for a week. But no doctoring could cut down Webb's lead, 47,739 to only 4,200 for incumbent Garrison, mostly from the Eighth. All the new aldermen were Know-Nothings, except those from the First and Eighth wards.

It was immediately after this Know-Nothing success that Alderman Henry Meiggs fled to Chile, leaving the banks holding $800,000 in forged city warrants, and businesses and banks began folding up, leading up to the terrible Black Friday of February 13, 1855.

In March, Mayor Webb informed the city that when the Know-Nothings took over they found an $840,000 deficit —more or less the total of Meiggs' stealing—and an accumulated debt of $2,000,000 created since 1851. By legislative act, the entire debt was scaled down to $300,000, an easy solution but one that hit the banks and honest creditors, not the thieves, and aggravated the financial crash.

After Brannan's 1851 Vigilante activities, which had lashed at Nativist elements, crime and violence had been relatively muted. Now, under the Know-Nothings, it rose to a new crescendo, first under Webb, then under his successor, James L. English. Between 1849 and 1856 1,000 murders were committed in San Francisco, few of them ever solved. The Know-Nothings retained Sheriff David S. Scannel, a Broderick man and a former Bowery saloonkeeper; and his assistant jail keeper was none other than little Billy Mulligan, the Bowery thug, ex-convict, killer, and ardent patriot who had chased big Morrissey with a billiard cue. He ran a bunch of thugs for Broderick to control elections in the various wards, at the service of the Know-Nothings.

In March, 1855, a Know-Nothing Grand Council for the state met in San Francisco with 200 delegates; every county was represented except Los Angeles and Siskiyou.

The Democratic convention May 3, 1855, had denounced Know-Nothingism and secret organizations. "The Democracy of California abhors and repudiates as un-American and anti-republican the proscription of a man for the accident of his birth or for his religious opinions. . . . Universal democracy is a doctrine of equal rights to all under the constitution and the laws." The Sacramento *Journal* (anti-Know-Nothing), opposed to the Sacramento *Tribune* (pro-Know-Nothing), called the movement a hoax, and dubbed the Know-Nothings "Hindoos." (It was being charged that the "American-born" Know-Nothing New York gubernatorial candidate had been born in India.) The paper brooded over the cryptic utterance of the initiated, "Sam is out; the Gayascutus is loose." Already there were signs of northern Know-Nothingism with its Abolitionism, and southern Know-Nothingism with its anti-Catholicism. The dilemma of sectionalism could not be sidestepped even in California. "God is with Democracy," concluded the paper.

All during June, parades and meetings were held throughout the state. Turnouts in Duane Springs and Placerville were notable and boisterous. A monster Know-Nothing campaign meeting was held in Sacramento on June 24. It was addressed by Senator Wilson D. Flint, a wealthy warehouse commission man; famous David S. Terry, Supreme Court justice, a close friend of Boss Broderick; and former Governor Henry S. Foote of Mississippi. The Democrats were "unmasked."

Special Know-Nothing conventions were also held June 30 and August 22 to take a stand against Mexican land grants and in favor of "native born"—i.e., non-Mexican—settlers who were stealing land from the Mexicans. The nominating convention was held on August 7 at the First Congregational Church on Sixth Street in Sacramento, after a big mass meeting in front of the Orleans Hotel. Three hundred and seventy delegates were present. The permanent president was James W. Coffroth, owner of the Tia Juana race track.

The platform adopted included "Union" and "Constitution and Law," revision of naturalization statutes, universal religious toleration but no union of church and state, and "inflexible opposition" to the "appointing or election of officials acknowledging allegiance to any foreign government" —indeed, the election of only persons born in the territory of the United States. It called for an end of sectionalism, of high costs of government, of fraud in government, for ballot-box purity, and a railway from the Pacific Ocean to the Mississippi. It wanted a liberal legislature of "settlers," meaning one that would uphold Anglo land steals. Voters were urged to disregard party labels and judge candidates according to their principles. The criterion should be: "Is he capable? Will he support the Constitution?" Just how voters could ascertain this when Know-Nothing candidates were usually presented on election day was not explained. The *Journal* observed that the platform was clever pussyfooting, arranged by the former Whig, Henry V. Crabb, to sidestep Catholic and slavery issues and to focus on "good government."

John Nealy Johnson, president of the previous year's Whig convention, was put up for governor. A grand public ratification rally was held in front of the Orleans Hotel on August 9. A Supreme Court judge was attacked for upholding Mexican land titles.

At the September 5 election, Johnson and the entire Know-Nothing ticket were elected by a 5,000-vote majority, along with a K-N majority in the legislature. The Know-Nothing state treasurer Henry Bates promptly stole $124,000, a feat discovered by a later Democratic legislature, which convicted him.

The following year, a secret anti-Know-Nothing order, Freedom's Phalanx, which admitted naturalized citizens, held a mass meeting in the United States Hotel in San Francisco and put a ticket into the field to fight "the Yankee Mackerel-Snatchers." The municipal Know-Nothing ticket was given out on April 2, the morning of election day. Whigs and Democrats began withdrawing, and the Know-Nothings easily elected James L. English mayor; they lost only one alderman's seat.

Prior to that, a full delegation was sent to the February 22, 1856, Know-Nothing convention in Philadelphia, which nominated Fillmore. The national candidates and platform were endorsed by a Sacramento reunion of 140 delegates from twenty-five counties on May 13. A pro-slavery view prevailed. The Republican party was denounced.

A few days later, Governor Johnson was embroiled in the second Vigilante fracas in San Francisco, which resulted from the shooting of James King, editor of the *Bulletin,* by Johnson P. Casey, editor of the *Sunday Times,* a protégé of various Know-Nothing politicians and particularly of Boss Broderick. King, who started his paper October, 1855, fought crime and political corruption and was a thorn in the flesh of the Know-Nothing administration. King exposed the fact that Casey had served a term in Sing Sing for grand larceny. After an extremely savage attack by King, on May 14, Casey lay in wait for him at the *Bulletin* doors. King came out at five o'clock when the streets were full of people, and Casey shoved his pistol against his chest and left him writhing in blood on the steps.

Casey was lodged in the county jail, and by 7 P.M. an angry lynch mob of 10,000 people howled outside the stone walls and kept it up all night. They were held in check by the entire police force and two hastily mobilized militia companies. The morning newspapers called for a citizens mass meeting at the former Know-Nothing headquarters on Sacramento Street. Tom Coleman, right-hand man of Brannan in the first Vigilante efforts five years previous, was made head of a new Vigilante committee. Coolheaded, energetic, by noon he had assembled 1,000 armed volunteers. (Twenty years later, he headed a third Committee of Safety to put down the terrible anti-Chinese riots, instigated by the laterday ruffians of the Nativist White Caucasian League, the Native Sons, and the Sand Lots Labor elements.)

Events now took a strange turn. The militia companies resigned and marched out to join the Vigilantes. Other mass meetings in half-a-dozen interior towns denounced the shooting of King and offered armed help.

Nearly all the politicians, especially the Know-Nothings, were against the Vigilantes, but many responsible citizens also deplored mob usurpation of justice. The citizens who had failed to use their energies and votes to clean up the long-standing mess, now roared into the streets over a shooting between two editors.

Boss Broderick had no love for the Vigilantes—Casey was his man—but, a wise politician, he slipped out of town and took the occasion to build up his fences for future control of the entire state. Secretly, however, he gave considerable money to a rival Law and Order group, and subsidized the leading newspaper, the *Herald,* to support them and attack the Vigilantes. The Law and Order force, among whom was Supreme Court Justice David S. Terry, a famous and fearless duelist and a prominent Know-Nothing, was organized to uphold the constituted courts and the authorities against Vigilante "mob law."

For several days, while King lingered between life and death, thousands waited in front of his home and mobs continued to threaten the county jail. The Vigilantes bought up every gun in the stores, seized all rifles, pistols, swords, two cannon, and much ammunition from the state armory on Grant Street and began drilling.

Governor Johnson hurried down from Sacramento and parleyed with Coleman and the Vigilante committee. He agreed to allow a small Vigilante contingent to camp inside the jail walls, and so instructed Sheriff Scannell. They feared that Casey's friend, jail keeper Billy Mulligan, would arrange for his "escape."

At the same time Scannell served court orders on citizens in the streets to appear at the jail and resist the expected Vigilante attack. Only 50 obeyed the summons, and these were mostly Broderick lawyers and henchmen who felt safer inside the jail than out.

At nine o'clock Sunday morning, May 18, the bell at Monumental Fire Engine House on Washington Street on the north side of Portsmouth Square near the city's first theater, Washington Hall, called the Vigilantes to assemble there. Guns were passed out to all who showed up; by noon, there were some 2,600. Coleman surrounded the jail with them and demanded the surrender of Casey and the gambler Charles Cora.

The previous November 18, 1855, Cora had killed United States Marshal General W. H. Richardson, in the Blue Wing Saloon after the general had abused him for bringing his mistress, who passed as Bella Cora, and Madame Arabella Ryan, keepers of a super-fashionable Pike Street whore house, to a public performance of *Nicodemus.* Arabella, the daughter of a Baltimore clergyman, was now providing the most beautiful and most highly skilled girls at premium prices. At his wife's instigation, the general ordered the theater owner to throw the two girls out but the man refused to do so. Cora and the general bumped into each other at various bars and quarreled. Richardson threatened to kill him on sight. When he came into the Blue Wing, where Cora was drinking at the bar, however, the gambler drew his gun first and shot the general. Cora had powerful backing and was defended by a battery of first-rank lawyers. He might have gone free, except for King's constant demand, in the pages of the *Bulletin,* that he be hanged. Rumors spread that the jury had been bribed with $40,000, also that his escape was being engineered by his friend, jail keeper Billy Mulligan. "Look well to the jury," warned the *Bulletin.* "If the jury is packed, either hang the sheriff or drive him out of town. . . . If Billy Mulligan lets his friend Cora escape, hang Billy Mulligan or drive him out of town." He kept this up every day: "Hang the sheriff . . . Hang Billy Mulligan!"

The trial two months later resulted in a hung jury after forty-one hours of deliberation. The *Bulletin* stated baldly that crooked men had been put on the jury . . . "depravity . . . crime . . . cannot be prosecuted in San Francisco. He [Cora] may go through the farce of a trial [again], but nothing more." At the time King was killed, Cora was still waiting for his second trial.

The sheriff, now facing Coleman with less than one hundred men, was obliged to hand over the two prisoners. They were taken handcuffed to hastily improvised cells at the

Sacramento headquarters, where 300 men maintained guard around the clock.

King died on Tuesday. Twenty thousand men and women participated in his funeral and the burial, in Calvary Cemetery on Lone Mountain (Laurel Hill), a sand-dune graveyard set up the previous year. That same day, Casey and Cora were "tried," condemned to death, and hanged. Cora was given an hour's reprieve, at the request of the attending priest, to marry Bella.

The Vigilante Committee continued to parade and patrol the city, arms in hand. Governor Johnson proclaimed the metropolis in a state of insurrection and ordered the Vigilantes to surrender their arms and disband. He appointed William T. Sherman, who had a heroic Mexican War record, to be major general of the nonexistent militia, and called all local units to duty.

Defying the governor and Sherman as well, Coleman moved his Vigilantes to quarters near the water front, where they installed cells, a guardhouse, courtrooms, and fixed up a flag-decorated meeting room. A stone wall was hastily built in front, and beyond that, sandbag breastworks ten feet high and six feet thick. The two cannon were mounted on the roof and manned night and day. So was Fort Gunnybags created. Only artillery could dislodge the Vigilante force, and there was none except at the federal presidio and at Mare Island Navy Yard. The governor and the Law and Order leaders called on the federal forces for aid, but this was refused, and the refusal was upheld by President Fillmore.

Less than one hundred men responded to the governor's mobilization orders. Sherman garrisoned them in the state armory and at strategic points. But when no more help was forthcoming by the end of the week, he resigned. The governor replaced him with Volney E. Howard, a former Texas congressman, and sent Reuben Maloney, a Broderick henchman, with a large quantity of arms and ammunition on a flatboat down the Sacramento River to Howard and the Law and Order party. The Vigilantes boarded the vessel and also intercepted another shipment hidden under bricks on a small schooner. They toted everything to Fort Gunnybags.

A Vigilante deputy, Sterling A. Hopkins, and two assistants were sent to arrest Reuben Maloney, whom they found accompanied by Judge Terry in the office of Dr. H. P. Ashe, a United States naval agent. Terry and Ashe refused to allow Maloney's arrest, and all three left for the state armory to put him under Law and Order protection. A block from there they were overtaken by Hopkins, reinforced by more Vigilantes. In the ensuing brawl, Terry stabbed Hopkins in the throat with his bowie knife and got Maloney to the armory. Ashe returned to his office.

The Fort Gunnybags bell rang. Within an hour 2,000 armed Vigilantes surrounded the armory, and the Law and Order group surrendered. The Vigilantes seized all arms, then released everyone except Terry and Maloney, who were lodged in cells at Fort Gunnybags.

Maloney was deported from the city. Terry was held for a week, till Hopkins recovered, then put on trial for stabbing and other alleged affrays. The trial lasted seven weeks. Broderick secretly paid *The Herald* $200 a week to defend Terry and blast the "lawless Vigilantes." They burned the papers and terrorized businessmen into withdrawing their advertisements. Within a month the paper had to suspend publication.

After hearing 150 witnesses, the Vigilantes declared Terry guilty on three counts, and demanded he resign as Supreme Court judge. This he refused to do. The Vigilante court then announced that the "usual punishments" in their power to inflict were not "applicable in the present instance," and he was released.

On July 29, 1856, after a quick shotgun trial, two other men involved in shooting affrays were hanged. One went insane two days before his execution, which he faced with bloodcurdling shrieks. The committee deported twenty-six persons from the city. On August 18, they marched through the city, 8,000 strong, deposited their arms in Fort Gunnybags, and disbanded. On September 1, the sandbags were removed, the flag lowered, and the last guards left. On November 3, the weapons were formally surrendered to the governor, who withdrew his proclamation of insurrection.

Know-Nothing rule of state and city had become one big uproar, and the end for the patriots was in sight. In the 1857 state election the Know-Nothings fell to third place, pulling fewer votes than the Republicans.

## CHAPTER XI

# CONFUSION IN THE EAST

ONE of the Know-Nothing clergymen elected to the Massachusetts legislature in the American party sweep of that state in October, 1854, declared: "My brethren, Paul was a Know-Nothing, for he said, 'I determined to know nothing among you'— Let us be like him."

Whether Paul, had he come to life in Massachusetts eighteen centuries later, would have approved of such literal Bible interpretation, coupled with ludicrous punning, may be doubted, but as a Know-Nothing he would have been popular in the Bay State that year 1854. The hate victory put in twenty-four Know-Nothing Protestant clergymen as senators and assemblymen on the platform of no union of church and state, all anti-foreign, all imbued with fears of Catholic meddling in schools and politics, and quite insensitive to their own meddling.

It was a voter's cyclone that year. The Know-Nothing legislature of 376 members was almost solid, only one Democrat, one Whig, one Free-Soiler. "Our Praise-Bare-Bones Parliament," the Catholic Boston *Pilot* called it sarcastically. Wags also quoted the Bible: The legislature should take as its election-sermon text Job 8:9, "For we are but of yesterday, and know nothing." Unfortunately the word jugglers had none of Socrates' wisdom and modesty: "All I know is that I know nothing."

Nearly everybody in Massachusetts had become Abolitionist, and this profession of faith was demanded of every candidate. The Know-Nothing aspirant for governor, H. J. Gardner, a former arch-conservative Whig, evaded most issues, but was believed to have anti-slavery sentiments. He rolled into office by a crashing majority of 50,000, against an opposition mostly Whig, the Democrats and the new Republican party polling negligible votes. Rabid Abolitionist Henry S. Wilson, temporarily inscribed in the Know-Nothing party, was sent to Washington as senator.

Governor Gardner abolished all Irish militia companies. To the legislature he proposed Know-Nothing reforms, including exclusion of pauper aliens. Only toward the end of the session was the matter referred to a committee, but nothing was done about it. The same fate befell nearly all Know-Nothing and other legislation. A proposal for a literacy test for voting, curiously, was voted down. In the final hours, a bill was hurriedly passed that barred anyone who had not lived in the country twenty-one years from voting (palpably unconstitutional) and another forbidding office-holding to all but native-born Americans (equally unconstitutional). Both were repealed by a later legislature. A bill requiring Bible reading in schools "in the common English version" was passed.

The outstanding accomplishments of the Know-Nothing legislature were to vote its members increased salaries and to set up a Nunnery Investigating Committee—"the Smelling Committee"—something that anti-Catholic propagandists had been demanding for some time.

Headed by Legislator Joseph Hiss, "Grand Worthy Instructor" of a Know-Nothing Council, the Nunnery Committee was authorized to visit "theological seminaries, boarding schools, academies, nunneries, convents, and other institutions of like character. . . ." The grand tour began in March. The Jesuit Holy Cross College in Worcester was the first victim. Perhaps to establish a preliminary reputation for impartiality, or because the wines of the community, imbibed copiously and charged to the state, were so fine, the institution was given a clean bill of health. At Roxbury Girls' School, the seven committee members, joined by thirteen additional curious legislators, tramped boisterously through the building, treating the nuns and pupils with scant respect, poking into closets and corners for possible dead babies, frightening children badly, and generally disrupting the place.

The Boston *Daily Advertiser* described the lawmakers' adventure: "The gentlemen—we presume we must call members of the legislature by that name—roamed over the whole house from attic to cellar, . . . [without] respect for the common courtesies of civilized life. . . . The ladies' dresses hanging in their wardrobes were tossed over. The party invaded the chapel and showed their respects—as Protestants, we presume—for the One God whom all Christians worship, by talking loudly with their hats on, while the ladies shrank in terror at the desecration of a spot they hallowed."

Afterward the party adjourned to a banquet with champagne, a beverage that was illegal, all charged to the taxpayers. At Lowell, where another convent school was investigated, the committee charged not only its heavy banquet and liquor bills to the state, but also expenses for fornication with a Mrs. Parker—a notorious prostitute—not an unreasonable fee, to be sure: only $1.25; but another claim was put in for $71 stolen from a member's pocket when, allegedly, nuns got him drunk. The whole junket blew into a sordid scandal as other newspapers took up the hue and cry.

The legislature, badly frightened, called Hiss in to report. In spite of the crude manners at Roxbury, the committee was exonerated of charges of ill-treating the nuns and pupils. What might have been considered proper treatment by back-slapping legislators appeared considerably different to women and children. However, the morals charges against Hiss were too much for even his fellow party members to disregard. He was expelled from the committee and from the legislature by a vote of 137 to 15. Two hundred and twenty-four members sneaked out to avoid casting a vote. The dark-lantern Know-Nothings were brave only in the murk of secrecy.

*One after one the honored Bay-leaves fade,*
*And ancient glories wither in the shade;*
*The solons of the state, at duty's call*
*Have hissed a loving member from the hall;*
*Take courage, Joseph, in thy great ado*
*The world has hissed the legislature, too.*

In spite of the stigma of the Nunnery Committee and the fact that this legislature had cost more and accomplished less than any other in Massachusetts' history, another Know-Nothing lawmaking body was elected the following year, although only about a sixth of the previous members were repeaters. They accomplished little more, perhaps less, than the previous legislature.

Delaware, New Hampshire, Rhode Island, Connecticut, Pennsylvania, also went Know-Nothing in 1854, although in Pennsylvania the first victories were coalitions with the Whigs, later with Republicans. Strength in Maine was shown by a Supreme Court decision that Catholic school children were required to read the Protestant Bible.

Rhode Island had had a stormy career. The Dorr Rebellion, crushed after a fashion in 1842, had widened the suffrage beyond wealthy property owners. Soon the anti-slavery movement became strong. Temperance forces were given an impetus by the Maine dry law of 1854. The local Know-Nothings were anti-slavery, in spite of the Union oath; many were teetotalers.

Anti-Catholicism in this one-time province of religious tolerance had appeared in the early 'thirties and had been aggravated by provocative reactionary church statements. Thanks in good part to the bigoted Providence *Journal*, nuns were subjected to insults on the streets, often were in danger of being attacked. In March, 1854, mobs converged on the Sisters of Mercy Convent "to save an American girl" in response to handbills "Arms to the Rescue," although she had denied she had gone there or was remaining there against her free will. Fortunately the rioters were driven off.

The foreign-born numbered nearly a fifth of the state's population and had aroused much ill-feeling. The SSSB intrusion into the state was most secret and mysterious. "When it came, no one can say, what it saw can only be imagined. Its proceedings were too secret and its records too few to betray much of its existence." In July, 1854, it showed considerable official influence, for the Democratic Providence *Post* protested when the governor issued arms and uniforms to 2,000 "Guards of Liberty," composed entirely of "native-born Americans."

*The Spy,* a Worcester, Massachusetts, Know-Nothing paper, remarked, "From all we can learn there are pretty certain indications that Rhode Island will, at the next election, place itself on the side of Massachusetts on the American question, for it seems that 'Sam' has marched across the disputed boundary." Actually, a number of local surprise Know-Nothing candidates and a state assemblyman won office in 1854. "Sam" stood for "temperance, restoration of the Missouri Compromise, total abolition of the foreign influx, whether in the name of the Pope of Rome or of Bishop Hughes of New York."

In 1855, nominations were secretly made by the SSSB Grand Council. No campaign was waged, not a single public meeting, but the Know-Nothings won the elections by a five-to-one vote over the Democrats, who salvaged only two towns. Both branches of the legislature became strongly Know-Nothing. The movement had no newspapers. Why should it, was the retort, when it could depend for full support from both the *Journal* and the Providence *Tribune*?

But its record in office was not bright, and the following year the Republicans took over the state.

The first SSSB branch in Connecticut was started in July, 1853. A state council headed by Nehemiah D. Sperry, a New Haven stonemason who came from a prominent family, was set up in November. According to the Hartford *Times* (February 26, 1856) its aim was to resist "the murderous policy of the church of Rome, and all other foreign influences against the institutions of our country," and put into office "none but native-born Protestant citizens." By mid-1854, the SSSB was visibly influential in town elections. On June 6, allied with Whigs, it brought startling change to New Haven, overwhelmingly Democratic, with considerable foreign and Catholic votes, by electing Know-Nothing-Whig Charles Jerome by a two-to-one victory—an eye opener. Often it was not clear whether Know-Nothing triumphs were owing to Nativist beliefs or to the boiling issues of temperance or bitterness over the Kansas-Nebraska Bill and the continuing injustices of the Fugitive Slave Law. The Free-Soil vote dropped by thousands to support the Whig-Know-Nothing coalition. Until bolstered up by the Know-Nothings, the blue-stocking Whigs had considered their party lost.

The Hartford *Times* sounded the warning and aligned itself against the forces of bigotry: "We are among those who believe that secret societies are an evil in society," especially "secret organizations got up expressly to oppose any religious sect. Let religious and political abuses be corrected in an open manner. Let free decision have its way." It would be wrong to let any "Native who cannot possibly be more than two or three steps from original foreign stock connect himself up with any secret society to wage war in the dark against any religious sect. It is not republican. It is not the way to win a good cause." The outcome would be "jealousies and riots and bloodshed." No foreigners were contemplating injury upon native citizens. "The Irish Catholics have no idea of the kind. They are as devoted to the liberties and institutions of the country as any other class. Our army was composed, in some of its regiments, of a majority of Irishmen when it invaded Mexico, a Catholic country. . . . In a generation they will be Americans—'Natives.' "

In the October town elections throughout Connecticut, Know-Nothing-endorsed candidates, Whig or Democrat, were elected in more than twenty towns. Twenty-eight other towns—and some represented Know-Nothing victories—fell to the Whigs, as did Meriden and Bristol.

All this political action was done "in the dark," complained the Hartford *Times,* as "in despotic countries." The people were "kept ignorant of all initiatory steps. . . . The Order does not meet its political or religious opponents in an open face-to-face manner. . . . We abhor the practice of appointing foreigners, Catholics, Baptists, Methodists, Congregationalists, or Free Thinkers merely as such and to catch votes."

The November 27 Hartford election revealed the confusion and fear. Twenty-three tickets (several duplicates) were placed before the voters. The Know-Nothing ticket, which was to be kept secret until election day, was chosen November 20. But within hours, the *Times* got hold of it and published it. This leak caused the Know-Nothing Grand Council to withdraw it and present an entirely new one election-day morning. All the choices, Whig or otherwise, were persons favoring the Maine Temperance Law. Actually there was a secret pact between the Know-Nothings and the Temperance party.

The *Times* described the election. It "developed the proportions and aspects of the mysterious 'Sam' who had been . . . dodging about like a jack-o'-lantern among the fogs of Know-Nothingism for the purpose of drawing in such Democratic votes as can be induced to follow his deceptive light." The Whigs were wholly "subordinate to the Know-Nothing and Maine Law elements." And so Hartford was captured by the Know-Nothings.

The 1855 Know-Nothing state convention met in Odd Fellows Hall, Hartford, on February 22, Washington's Birthday, with 450 delegates. A former Whig, William T. Minor, was nominated for governor.

The Democratic convention held earlier in New Haven (February 14), had made a slashing denunciation of Know-Nothingism. "Foreigners have contributed to the growth of the Republic and to the fraternity of its inhabitants." The existing laws were "essentially part of the honest

American policy which . . . has signalized our beloved country as the home of the exile and the oppressed."

The Whigs met February 28. The *Courant* editor tried to get them to endorse Know-Nothing Minor but, though accepting the rest of the Nativist ticket for governor, they put up Henry Dutton of New Haven, another ardent Know-Nothing—and announced that they did not want the votes of "ignorant prejudiced foreigners" (apparently only those of ignorant prejudiced Whigs) but sought "to preserve America for Americans. . . . We advocate Temperance, Freedom, and Americanism." The party's temperance stand did not win over the Temperance party, which made a behind-doors deal to support Minor; in addition, an estimated 7,000 wet Whigs huffily went over to the Democratic party. The Free-Soilers endorsed Dutton, but for lieutenant governor chose the Know-Nothing candidate.

The Hartford *Courant* at once launched a virulent anti-foreign campaign and in the April election Minor squeezed through by a 788 majority. The Know-Nothing victory in the legislature was overwhelming: Senate, 18 to 3; House, 161 to 65. Know-Nothing Sidney Dean was sent to the United States Senate, and all four congressional candidates were elected. Thus the American party absorbed both the Whig and Temperance parties.

On inauguration day, Hartford bubbled with flags and enthusiasm. An enormous military parade, with almost every company in the state present, conducted Minor from the station to the State House. Music, bells, and cannon added to the jubilant uproar. The best-drilled, best-uniformed company was the Irish Emmet Guards, Company F, which preceded two Know-Nothing companies—after protests that almost caused a clash.

Minor's inaugural address referred to the "pernicious influence of foreign immigration"—aliens imbued "with the social infidelity of continental Europe—very many of them blind followers of an ecclesiastical government—a large number . . . without correct ideas of the duties appertaining to the citizens of a republican government and by early prejudices totally unfitted to learn them—differing in language, in national customs, and feelings. . . . From among them . . . comes a majority of the inmates of our prisons and asylums. . . . Our taxes are largely increased for the support of our foreign population. . . . Yet these people were admitted to citizenship after five years!"

He attacked the social, political, and military associations of foreigners, most of which should be forbidden. "A very large number are members of a church, the spiritual head of which owes no allegiance to our government or its laws—yet exacts the most implicit obedience from its members. . . ." Then, with looking-glass logic: When the American's "right to worship his Maker according to the dictates of his conscience . . . is seriously invaded" the "downfall of American liberty" will have begun. Because of the aliens' alliance to the Church and their manipulation by demagogues, he demanded a longer residence before any could be naturalized.

He wished to restore the American government "in its pristine purity"—whatever that meant; the first 1639 treasurer of New Haven, a church elder, was ousted for stealing money and land. "Nationalize our army and navy," he insisted, "cement the bonds of our national union," and thus "make the country great and prosperous."

Among the first acts of the Know-Nothing administration was to vest all Catholic property in the hands of the congregations, instead of the hierarchies. Religious property being held by a person or persons in ecclesiastical office was to revert to the incorporated congregation or to the state to be held in trust until time of such incorporation. But the law exempted five non-Catholic denominations: Episcopal, Methodist, Presbyterians, Shakers, and Jews. This, the *Times* judged, singled out the Catholic Church for attack—and in a flagrantly unconstitutional way.

A second Nativist legislature presented a constitutional amendment for a voter's literacy test, in the hope of excluding naturalized voters. The Democratic minority countered by offering an amendment to prohibit any member of a secret political organization from becoming a voter or holding office. "Secret associations and orders, conducted by a system of cabalistic signs, winks, grips, and passwords exist in this state" and "secrecy in public affairs is proverbially a badge of fraud and crime; the whole history of civil government shows that no such political association was ever formed for any other than a seditious, wicked, or treasonable purpose." "The Hindoos" were pushing the literacy law merely to try "to weaken the Democratic party." The proposal was "anti-Democratic and consequently anti-Republican and should be consigned to oblivion."

But it was passed (without the amendment) and plenty of non-alien citizens were also deprived of the suffrage—i.e., were punished for the deficiencies of Connecticut public education.

In August, Minor discharged six militia companies made up of foreign-born citizens, but not the German-manned New Haven city guard. Adjutant General Hodge refused to carry out the order, was ousted, and a pliant substitute was sworn in. The *Courier,* ever the patron of backwardness, rejoiced at the ending of "The disgrace of seeing bands of foreigners on our streets, armed and organized as such, paid from the Treasury of the State."

However, the Middletown *News,* on the adjournment of the "harmful" legislature, found that the running of Connecticut by a secret oath-bound society was "a disgrace to the state and its government, and shame upon the intelligence of the people." A prominent Protestant minister wrote in the *New England Magazine,* "We do not see a great deal of danger in the number of foreign voters. We apprehend there is more to be feared from native demagogues."

What was peculiar, the Know-Nothings were hawking an old-time America that was vanishing. By 1850 Connecticut was third in industrial production, perhaps higher on a per capita basis. It would soon produce more than 50 per cent of all American firearms, most of the country's clocks and watches, nearly all its carriages and wagons, most of its springs and ball bearings. This created a continuous labor shortage.

Actually for three decades Connecticut had been declining in population because of the westward movement, and needed immigration, not exclusion. The old rural Connecticut was disappearing. Its soil, always inferior, was leached out. Manufacturing and commerce were becoming the chief industries.

The Know-Nothings were simply obstructing inevitable transformation. Their real concern should have been over just labor, health, and housing laws, the establishment of a proper balance between industry and agriculture, the city and the countryside. But the Know-Nothings were haters of progress, whether good or bad—with dug-in heels. Their kind always appears whenever there is a change people do not understand and hence are afraid of.

So the introduction of a less stable population, a small part of it alien, permitted the demagogues to roil the waters and attract the dismayed and frightened old-timers. Naturally the loss by westward migration of old Connecticut stock, the steady population decline in rural areas (a 20 per cent drop between 1850 and 1860), the growth of cities, the Puritan population becoming overshadowed by newcomers and new wealth, were of serious concern to staid congregations. They bore heavily on many local Protestant churches, which were declining in numbers and influence, while new Catholic churches were being built in the municipalities. In 1850, there were only five organized Catholic congregations in the state; by 1852 there were thirty-seven, and seventeen edifices and nineteen priests—still not many; but by 1855 there were Catholic congregations in sixty towns. By then New Haven had two Catholic churches, three Catholic schools, two Catholic orphan asylums.

Bewildered long-term residents tried to fight for the perishing order. There were many acid comments about the serious decline in the caliber of Congregationalist leaders. Know-Nothingism in part represented a blind effort to affect the diminishing influence of the congregations. For several decades, the force behind the movement had been building up through the Dwights and other blue-blood Yankees who clung to the era of Puritan ascendancy, now giving way in the face of new developments. Nativism in Connecticut was being tested in the hot crucible of success.

By 1854 the Know-Nothings were almost ready to make a bid for power in New York State, where politics were more complicated. There, as elsewhere, the temperance question was becoming troublesome to politicians. Nor could the slavery issue, though not so pressing as in New England, be ignored. These and other questions, some local, caused much squirming and twisting, the basic aim of the politician being not to support principles but to get elected.

The New York Know-Nothings, given the fission in both old parties, had a good chance to cut a considerable figure, and they kept a close eye on the 1854 proceedings of the old-line politicians. For all practical purposes there were two separate Democratic parties, the Hard Shells and the Soft Shells. A similar split in the Whig ranks might bring out two tickets, backed respectively by Seward and Fillmore: the Wooly Heads and the Silver Grays. There was less chance for Know-Nothing beliefs to come out on top in either Democratic faction—although the Hard Shells might be amenable to nominating a number of SSSB candidates. As the Barker clique saw it, their best chance was to drive the Seward faction out of the Whig party, goad the seceders into separate action, and impose a complete Know-Nothing slate on the legitimate Whigs, who would then be largely made up of Fillmore's Silver Grays. If Seward forces could not be eliminated, then the wiser course was to keep all Native Americans off the Whig ticket. The Know-Nothings were concerned about Seward's power, even more than about the Irish-leagued Soft-Shell Democrats. Seward, too, enjoyed "foreign favor" and Catholic sympathy, and was outspoken against Know-Nothing bigotry, puncturing their emotional slogans and blown-up arrogance. He had hammered at them as recently as July 12 in a Senate speech.

First came the Hard-Shell convention (July 12). The platform worked out was silent about Nativism and Temperance, and so evasive about slavery as to be meaningless. Party nominations were non-committed persons, who had never taken a firm stand on anything. Caution was the watchword, wait and see the policy. They were hopeful that the Silver Grays and the Know-Nothings—sure to be rejected by Seward—would be forced to turn to them.

On August 16, anti-slavery elements showed that the parties would have to take them into account, by holding an enthusiastic anti-Nebraska convention. They were dissuaded from putting up their own ticket by numerous Sewardites present, who promised their cause would be taken care of in the Whig platform.

The Soft-Shell platform, adopted at their September 17 convention, was more outspoken. Enjoying support from Irish and Catholic voters, they opposed liquor restrictions, disapproved of Nativism, and supported Pierce's veiled pro-slavery position. The last insured support from wealthy manufacturers.

Many Know-Nothings went as delegates to the Whig convention in Syracuse September 20, to do battle, along with the Silver Grays, against the Sewardites. Even so, in spite of Seward's forthright position, many Know-Nothings were enlisted behind his banner out of intense personal loyalty. However, the burning desire of the Know-Nothing leaders was to write Seward's epitaph. Only he had the strength to hold the dying Whig party together and prevent it from dissolving into the mists of Know-Nothingism.

But the Seward forces, it soon became evident, controlled a solid two-to-one convention majority. This was the ideal moment, according to Barker strategy, for the Know-Nothings to withdraw, but the Silver Grays were reluctant, still hoping to pull out some plums by making last-minute deals. Many Know-Nothings, too, in view of the Democratic split and having nowhere else to go, preferred to ride the Whig gravy train for whatever crumbs they could pick up. In secret caucus, they decided to back whichever Know-Nothing candidate got the most votes on the first ballot.

Seward was canny enough not to antagonize the Know-

Nothings in his own group or to throw away all Know-Nothing support. He indicated his willingness to make room for Know-Nothing candidates who could swing sizable voting strength. Behind-the-scenes negotiations resulted in naming for governor a third-degree SSSB man, though one fanatically loyal to Seward—Myron H. Clark of Ontario, a strong antislavery man. Similarly a man openly friendly toward Nativism, Henry J. Raymond of the New York *Times,* a paper consistently cordial to Know-Nothingism, was picked for lieutenant governor. Instead of the Know-Nothings splitting the Whigs, Seward split the Know-Nothings.

However, he stuck stanchly to his own ideas for the Whig platform. It was outspoken against slavery, but made no reference to Temperance or Nativism, although a slight concession was made by striking out phrases considered derogatory to the Know-Nothings.

Right down the line, Seward was in the driver's seat. The humor of this situation would be that Seward and Barker, who hated each other beyond measure, would be working for the same candidates. Seward would be supporting candidates whose personal doctrines he despised; Barker would be supporting agreeable candidates running on a platform he did not want.

This thoroughly uncomfortable position put the SSSB and Barker in a secondary role. The Know-Nothings were unable to announce it as a coalition ticket and were left without bargaining power. Barker called a special Grand Council for October 4, but gave no intimation of his plans. Most members believed it was to endorse the Whig candidates, or if not, the Hard-Shell Democratic ticket. They did not know that two days prior to the reunion the SSSB and OUA executive committees worked out joint plans to put up an entirely new American party ticket. Open Know-Nothing opposition might well bring about Clark's defeat, and the high command preferred to smash the Seward Whigs, even if it resulted in an Irish-Catholic Soft-Shell victory.

Barker had worked frenziedly to pack the SSSB meeting. Overnight new paper locals were given charters—a device later used by labor leaders and doubtless by many others in the long history of political *chantage* in this world. Only nine persons were required to form a new council, and since Barker named all local deputies, they could easily pick nine members out of any council. Five black balls could keep out any anti-Barkerites. Each of these new councils could send three delegates to the Grand Council, with as much voting strength as any older council with hundreds of members. By the day of the Grand Council reunion in New York City's Odd Fellows' Hall, the number of state councils had been puffed up to 563. When the assemblage came to order under the pound of Barker's gavel, 515 councils were listed as wholly legitimate and needing no scrutiny of the admissions committee.

Routine organization was taken up. The first hint of brewing trouble came when the Canandaigua Council delegates were challenged on the ground of being an illegal secession group which had gotten hold of the Order's secrets merely to advance the interests of a number of "political demagogues." Myron H. Clark, the Whig gubernatorial candidate, was a member of this group. The Canandaigua charter was revoked and the lodge thrown out, which automatically expelled all its members. This meant that the Know-Nothings no longer had any obligation to support Clark, quite the opposite.

This maneuver, according to Barker's back-door planning, now made it almost requisite for the Grand Council to put out an independent ticket. The resolution to do so—a bolt out of the blue for most delegates—resulted in pandemonium on the floor. Present were many Whigs and Hard Shells who did not wish to be bound by a Know-Nothing ticket; they wanted endorsement of their own party. Nor were Silver Gray elements present too pleased. Clearly a separate ticket was unpopular with the organization. But Barker, it soon was apparent, controlled the assemblage.

He pounded the session back into order and threw the whole weight of his monolithic personality behind the move for a new ticket. The prolonged debate was bitter, with many crude personal insults. Time and again Barker brought the members back into line, then choked off the growing discord by recognizing only a motion for a roll call, advising members that they were obliged to abide by the desires of the majority.

The motion barely squeaked through. Pandemonium broke out again, and nearly half the delegates withdrew. Stone-visaged, unswerving, immobile except for a little lashing movement of his tongue, Barker watched them depart. Better to clear the decks now; more purges would follow.

When the hall had been cleared of all opposition, Barker calmly reiterated his faith in the basic strength of the Order, quieted the anxiety of the 514 delegates remaining, and called for nominations. The inner SSSB clique already had its slate chosen—it was an effort to parcel out future jobs to Seward Whigs, Silver Grays, Hard-Shell and even Soft-Shell Democrats on the basis of party and geographical influence, in the hope of attracting votes from all factions. Along with others, Attorney Daniel Ullman, Barker's long-term friend from OUA lodge Washington Number 2, a Silver Gray Whig, was put up for governor. He won a plurality on the first ballot, but failed to get a majority. Barker whanged the gavel and declared him the party choice. Ullman jumped up with alacrity and accepted.

Gustavus A. Scroggs of Erie, a Hard-Shell Democrat and a militia officer, was chosen for lieutenant governor. The candidate for canal commissioner, an Ithaca capitalist, Joseph B. Williams, not a member of the SSSB, never a spokesman for Nativist ideas, was selected because he was a Seward Whig. He was not present and after long delay declined the nomination.

A strong resolution was passed reminding all members of their sacred obligation to vote only for Know-Nothing candidates or face immediate expulsion. No platform was issued, only an address to subordinate councils (published in the *Herald,* October 31), a windy bit of rhetoric, with banal bits of flag-waving verse and denunciations of Romanism "trying to divide the American people, create party strife, and destroy their cherished institutions." There was no mention of foreigners. The OUA executive committee promptly endorsed the American party ticket.

The seceders met a few days later in Utica, passed far stronger anti-Catholic resolutions, and put out feelers to set up an independent order, sending circulars to every Know-Nothing council, accusing Ullman of being a German Jew born in Calcutta, not a native American at all; as a child he had spoken broken English, when in Harvard he had claimed to be a native of India. Strong statements were included about the steam-roller nominations tactics of the Grand Council. The Utica reunion called for general secession and the setting up of a genuine Know-Nothing order, independent of Czar Barker.

The Barker group fought back in appeals to the councils and the membership. It denied charges of "infamies" in choosing the ticket, denied there had been "a conspiracy." It sent out affidavits, secured by Ullman, that he was born in Delaware, not India. But gibes continued and during the campaign occasioned much hilarity that the Know-Nothings should put forward a foreign-born candidate. They were dubbed "Hindoos," a satiric epithet that spread across the country.

At another Utica secession reunion October 20, a new organization was effected, with about thirty SSSB councils and Alfred Cobb as president. This occurred at a bad time in the election campaign, especially as the "Firsters," the Charles B. Allen Know-Nothing crowd, had been growing with the general upsurge of fanaticism, until it now had 157 New York and 30 New Jersey chapters, all supporting Clark. Both groups were bitter against the Barker Know-Nothings.

The election was heated. The Whigs had secured the endorsement of the Temperance party, the Anti-Nebraska organization, and the Free Democrats, a small but vigorous splinter group. These accessions of strength were hardly offset by the support of the Know-Nothing ticket by the New York City Protestant Irish and the Albany Negroes. The Know-Nothings concentrated chiefly on discrediting Seward.

Initial upstate returns from towns and cities indicated a smashing Know-Nothing victory. But within two or three days, the rural vote, strongly pro-temperance, drifted in, and the Clark vote began to climb. In the final tally it totaled 155,000. The Hard-Shell Democrats polled only 44,000, but the Soft Shells, who rolled up a big east-county vote, got 133,000, leaving the Nativists in third place with only 120,000. The Know-Nothings were not discouraged, however, for the previous year they had polled only 4,000 in New York City. One third of the Know-Nothing vote came from the southeast counties, another third from the Fillmore-controlled westernmost counties. Forty-five Know-Nothings, belonging to the OUA or SSSB, were sent to the state legislature.

Presently Barker was defeated for mayor of New York City, after which he worked harder than ever to tighten up the organization while making some concession to the rank and file by adding a state committee composed of four-man delegations from each judicial district. But its powers were purely advisory, and it was pro-Barker. Actually he increased his own powers by securing the right to revoke the charters of refractory councils.

"Tests" were made more rigorous to detect and punish "treason." Starting with the Grand Council, a general inquisition was held up and down the order. Council heads, after passing the test, carried on a member-by-member examination, first of local officers, then of the rank and file. There were a few sputterings. A few officials were tossed out and a few charters were revoked. But iron-clad discipline was established from top to bottom. Barker's grip on the state and national organization was now all-powerful.

Barker, Ullman, et al. were also moving in on the Wide Awakes, as earlier they had moved in on the SSSB. They had persuaded the youthful organization to accept older members, and were preparing a coup so that the punitive armed forces of the Order could be directed more consistently toward political purposes. A number of other secret patriotic organizations were also invaded. Barker was working toward a new supreme patriotic unity to increase the striking power of the SSSB, his own power, and the impact of the entire American party. Nor did the pre-election secession visibly stop the SSSB growth. By early 1855 the number of chapters was more than doubled.

The state legislature convened January 3. Instructions went out at once to the Know-Nothing representatives and all other Know-Nothing members holding seats "to get Seward"—i.e., prevent his election to the United States Senate. Barker felt confident that with the Know-Nothing bloc, plus Know-Nothings in Seward's own entourage, plus the Silver Grays, Hard Shells, and Soft Shells and others, this could be done. The Know-Nothing nose count showed that Seward was a dead, dead duck. They were assured of at least a forty-five-vote majority against him. That seemed too much of a lead to be overturned. Barker set up a lobby of agents from each assembly district, to pressure the legislators, also to make a checkup on corruption and misconduct. The Albany *State Register* became a regular Know-Nothing organ to attack foreigners, Catholics, the education bill and, above all, Seward.

Every member of the legislature was bombarded with attacks on him. Even a Know-Nothing novel, *Stanhope Burleigh,* by E. Edward Lester (using the pseudonym, Helen Dhu), was rushed through the presses to burlesque Seward and Boss Thurlow Weed, Greeley, and other enemies of Know-Nothingism. It was widely circulated, and a copy given to each legislator.

The Sewardites were not idle. Thurlow Weed masterminded the counter-intrigue, and he was a superb shuffler of cold decks in back rooms. He moved every lever, applied every pressure. He handed out promises, favors, jobs, patronage, even to out-and-out Know-Nothing representatives.

The bitterness of the pre-election SSSB split was now fanned into a new flame. By this time the seceders had about fifty locals. They held a special Grand Council meeting of 125 members in Schenectady on January 10, passed militant anti-foreign, anti-Catholic resolutions; then, at Weed's instigation, hurried to Albany to lobby for Seward, seeing no inconsistency in toiling day and night in behalf of a pro-foreign, pro-Catholic personage. Weed also rallied the Temperance and anti-slavery forces against the Know-Nothing plot.

So, at the final roundup, the Know-Nothing leaders were outsmarted, outgeneraled. On February 6, Seward squeaked through by a majority of four votes. It was incredible. Barker and his group were utterly stunned. Barker went over the lists in cold fury. Twelve Know-Nothing representatives had voted for Seward. Thirty-seven of the secret Know-Nothing representatives, elected as candidates of other parties, pledged to vote against Seward, had not done so. Every last one was put on the carpet and raked fore and aft. Many were thrown out of the Order. The rest were put on probation with the warning that the slightest sign of deviation would result in expulsion. At the February Grand Council meeting, one assemblyman who had gotten out of line was mobbed, beaten up, and tossed out on his head.

In spite of schism and political setbacks, the SSSB continued to roll up strength, and by the May 8 session of the Grand Council Barker was able to report 1,060 councils and 178,000 members. Had the elections occurred half a year later, the Know-Nothings easily would have captured the state. Already the old parties were so demoralized by the new thrust that in smaller places they failed to hold caucuses. Local struggles became a crude show of strength between Know-Nothingism and anti-Know-Nothingism.

At that triumphant May reunion, which selected delegates for the forthcoming national convention in Philadelphia in June, Barker's key address set forth the unflinching aims of Know-Nothingism.

First: Americans shall rule America; second: The Union of the States; third: No North, no South, no East, no West; fourth: The United States of America as they are, one and inseparable; fifth: No sectarianism in our legislatures or the administration of American laws; sixth: Hostility to the assumptions of the Pope, through the bishops, priests, and prelates of the Roman Catholic Church, here in a Republic sanctified by Protestant blood; seventh: Thorough reform in the naturalization laws; eighth: Free and liberal educational institutions for all sects and classes with the Bible, God's Holy Word, as a universal textbook.

These patriotic, sectarian, nationalistic generalizations were not much worse than the shibboleths usually presented by politicians. Barker probably knew that unthinking millions are always swayed by blah-blah slogans. The Know-Nothings were preparing to reap the harvest of power from those unthinking millions—the honey of the buzzing hive.

In the Midwest, the Know-Nothings had made no great headway, although strong everywhere and, in Wisconsin, in spite of the German population, held the balance of power, a chief reason the state went into the Republican column.

Above all else the Know-Nothings this May of 1855 centered their hopes in Virginia. Nowhere else had the SSSB shown more phenomenal growth than in the South. Virginia would be the first serious test of the effectiveness of the new Union, States Rights, and constitutional slogans. The Know-Nothings had control of most major southern cities, and they already had won in Kentucky, but that was a mixed border state, whereas Virginia was the cream of the South.

The Americans had reason to be hopeful of winning the state election. The SSSB first appeared in Charlottesville, probably in April, 1854. By July it had won Norfolk, where it was backed by the *Era*—although Virginia had no secret ballot, only open-voice voting. Hundreds of councils sprang up, until nearly every village knew "Sam." Early the following year, Know-Nothings took over Richmond and Alexandria overwhelmingly. Half a dozen other important cities were captured. In addition to Whigs, numerous leading Democratic politicians had joined the Order and had provided notable national leadership. Division in the Democratic party was deep. There was sullen reaction against the implacable bossism of Henry A. Wise.

He was a remarkable personage and a remarkable orator, energetic and fearless. Although a slaveowner who ignored human rights for Negroes, he believed otherwise in bona-fide individual freedom and in open political controversy and opinions openly arrived at. He considered democracy and the American system, as well as his own political future, seriously menaced by Know-Nothing dark-lantern methods. Already he had blistered the secret order in and out of the Senate in speeches that add up to some of the finest examples of oratory on basic democracy and justice and enlightened Americanism ever delivered in this country. Much of the antagonism against him in Virginia was not owing to his bossism; the slaveholders were frightened by his liberal pronouncements and by his backing of the 1852 constitution that sheared away some of their rights in favor of poorer western farmers.

Nevertheless, by steam-roller methods, he was able to impose himself as the Democratic candidate for governor. His fellow senator, R. M. T. Turner, shrugged: Wise had "the bit in his teeth," so let him run head on into the forward-moving wall of Know-Nothingism and get smashed. The Democratic forces could then be reunited, and another election would tell a different story. The Virginia Know-Nothings followed their usual tactics, not nominating a ticket until late in the day.

Wise knew he had a killing fight ahead, and he took the stump early, promising to visit every county in the state, something no candidate had ever done. He ignored all personal attacks, and concentrated on hammering at Know-Nothingism; the conspiratorial secrecy; the poisoning of honest open politics; the absurdity of anti-foreign, anti-Papist diversionary tactics; dark-lantern dictatorship, based on subversion, hidden intrigue, and fear. His words fell on many willing ears. There was little anti-Catholic hostility in Virginia, except in Richmond, although some feeling had been stirred up in the 'forties by Presbyterian minister William S. Plumer. There were few immigrants. Know-Nothing fears seemed absurd—and even to many Know-Nothings, for two state councils had been set up, differing on these issues, but otherwise united for the campaign. Yet even some Democratic papers such as the Richmond *Examiner* were as anti-foreign as the Know-Nothings. "Every vagabond and adventurer escaping from jails . . . and poorhouses of Europe is not fit for sovereign citizenship the moment his dirty and stinking carcass touches our shores."

Wise was clear, simple, had a devastating power of satire, and was a remarkable phrase maker. He usually spoke three and a half hours and always held his audiences spellbound. Getting hold of the secret Know-Nothing ritual, he read from it at every meeting, ridiculed it, tore it to shreds, showed how its initiation oath forced members to become liars, how it turned members into blind, obedient sheep, not free men; how it sought to destroy open controversy and substitute force and secrecy and bury honest democratic methods. The Know-Nothing party was "evil, foul, its talk of Unionism merely a blind for deep-rooted black abolitionism." Wise knew how to hit straight punches—and also how to hit below the belt.

The Know-Nothing papers hotly defended the Order against his onslaughts, but were at a disadvantage. This time their surprise Blitzkrieg of last-minute nominations backfired badly. They had no candidates in the ring fighting, whereas Wise was getting himself across to 100,000 illiterates who never read newspapers, whom the Know-Nothing press could not reach. For those who could read, the Democratic press was savage in its denunciations. The editor of the *Democrat* (Abingdon, Virginia) called the rival Know-Nothing editor "a miserable scoundrel," "a turkey buzzard," "a polecat"—typical election language the voters loved.

The belatedly named Know-Nothing ticket was chosen with a sharp eye for success. Some candidates were not Know-Nothings at all and said so publicly, but believed this to be their one chance to get into office. The candidate for governor was an outstanding Whig lawyer and former congressman, Thomas S. Flournoy, the most beloved personality in the state, except for the northwest counties. A blue-blooded aristocrat by birth and association, a smooth, brilliant orator, his great personal following extended far beyond Whig party lines. Nor did he have to spend a cent on the campaign. His host of loyal friends worked hard for him, opened their purses, turned over their homes for meetings, hired halls, arranged parades, bought advertising space. He had little sympathy with Secessionist sentiments now growing up in the South and by conviction was a strong Unionist, so much so he was sometimes called a "northerner" and "a friend of Abe Lincoln," and only his blue blood diverted animosity in reactionary slave-holder quarters.

The Know-Nothing choice for attorney general was also picked to appeal to the old-line chivalry. As early as 1848 he had denounced Nativism as "Hell-born and Hell-bound," was openly cynical about his nomination, and right after his nomination told a Richmond church, "I don't belong to this secret organization . . . never belonged to a secret organization in my life, although most of my family were Masons." He had too great "scruples and fastidiousness" to go messing around in "secret engagements."

Still a third candidate was put up to appeal to the homespun northwest, where aristocrats such as Flournoy were distrusted.

In the short time left, the Know-Nothings threw swill buckets of vituperation at Wise. He was "a ranting demagogue, an unprincipled renegade, a truculent bully . . . a brawler, a foul-mouthed slanderer," using the "scrapings and refuse of political style." They imported Kenneth Raynor, who tore Wise's speeches to pieces bit by bit. Wise's magnificent truisms, such as the Sermon on the Mount and the Magna Charta, he pointed out, merely beclouded the issue. How did these documents prove that secret organizations were evil and dangerous? But the Virginia voters had no interest in reasoned rebuttal—if it could be called that. In the mounting passions of the moment, Raynor's voice was lost, the words of this most eloquent man fell flat.

Wise never bothered to refute even the most dastardly lying attacks; he barged ahead, driving home his dark picture of the Know-Nothing menace. His policy, he stated, "from first to last was to strike so fast and thick at 'Sam' that he was kept on the defensive all the time. The man who defends his policies is half-whipped. . . . The enemy was surprised that I never stopped to defend a position, but kept pressing constantly until he was broken." It was, he admitted, a well-nigh hopeless battle. As late as February he expected to be beaten by at least 20,000 votes. "Nothing but Napoleonic tactics could save the day." He supplied the Bonaparte drive.

Especially he went after the newly enfranchised vote in the western counties, the result of concessions in the 1852 constitution, and he promised to broaden their voting privileges still more, to abolish "the mixed basis" which gave added representation on the basis of the number of nonvoting plantation slaves. He promised also to do away with property qualifications. The western counties had been long neglected. Wise promised to redress the balance.

Flournoy and the other Know-Nothing aspirants, instead of trying to reach the new voters, accused Wise of selling out his "eastern" opinions for "western" votes. Clearly the Know-Nothings wanted not more but less democracy—that less to be controlled by a plantation hierarchy and by secret processes.

When the smoke and bad language cleared away, Wise had won by a 10,000-vote margin and carried into office his whole ticket and a majority in the legislature. The Know-Nothings elected only six senators, fifty-six House members, and one congressman.

Not that they were overly discouraged. They had a pivotal representation, they continued to rule large Virginia cities, as in much of the South, and in Washington they had seventy-five members in Congress.

But national opponents were gleeful, believing that the party could be definitely checked. After the Virginia election, the pat saying was "The Know-Nothings won't be able to win a single southern state." If they were unable to win in the favorable situation existing in Virginia, if their leadership was so poor, their tactics so bungling there—and they were—they would run a cropper everywhere. The Know-Nothings, if disappointed, still believed quite as strongly that their countrywide success in the near future was inevitable.

## CHAPTER XII

# ONE FOOT IN THE GRAVE

PRESIDENT BARKER hammered the gavel convening the secret assemblage of the American Party National Council in Philadelphia, June 5, 1855. It was a climactic moment of dramatic power when the Order that he, more than any other human being, had created, seemed destined to take over the country. In spite of the Virginia setback, it was growing more influential everywhere. He looked upon delegates from every state and the District of Columbia.

All were third-degree members, except the stubborn Abolitionists from Massachusetts, who considered the Union oath a concession to slavery. Some other states had been slow in adopting the Union oath, and the Ohio and Mississippi delegates had been initiated into the third degree after their arrival in Philadelphia. Other states had abandoned secrecy, something soon to become an issue everywhere. Some, such as Alabama, Virginia, California, and Louisiana, had refused to exclude Catholics. In Maryland, although Catholics were not admitted, the issue was glossed over.

The first rift in the optimistic assemblage came precisely over the Catholic question. The Louisiana delegation was headed by a leading Catholic, Charles Gayarré. After a passionate diatribe by Raynor, he was disqualified, although his Protestant confreres were seated. Wearied by this discord, the convention admitted the Alabama delegation, which also contained Catholics, without dispute.

Other fireworks exploded. A. R. Boteler of Virginia, formerly a leading Democrat, launched a savage attack on the Massachusetts delegation, headed by Senator Henry Wilson. Admission to the convention of an out-and-out anti-slavery delegation would overbalance slave-state representation and destroy the impartial States Rights position of the Order.

The evidence was nose plain. The Massachusetts SSSB had been making election deals with Abolitionists and Free-Soilers. Owing to such a combination, Wilson himself enjoyed his Senate seat. He was reported to have boasted he would convert the Know-Nothing party into an anti-slavery organization or destroy it. His convictions were known and implacable.

A versatile politician, with rigid ideas but weathervane adaptability, he had lodged in the SSSB as a refuge from party disintegration and a means of climbing into office before the Free-Soilers had become strong enough to provide sufficient backing. Just as Boetler was determined to keep Massachusetts out and promote southern control over the party, Wilson was equally determined to exclude the proslavery District of Columbia delegates. Here was a debatable issue, for the District, which legalized slavery, did not come within the States Rights doctrine. To put an end to the bickering, which promised to be eternal, Barker and the top brass imposed a compromise. Massachusetts would be admitted without opposition if its delegates would accept the District of Columbia delegates.

Southern delegates sniped at the Massachusetts delegation on every occasion. One of its members was accused of violating the secrecy rule by spilling these inner controversies to the press. To head off a new storm, William H. Burrell of Virginia jumped to his feet and admitted he had done likewise. The matter was dropped.

Barker spoke disapprovingly of efforts to raise the slavery issue in the party. He reminded the delegates that the party stood for Union and States Rights, not sectional controversy. Throughout the conference, he held the New York delegation sternly in line in support of this *status quo.*

Already attacks had been made on him for this. Greeley of the *Tribune,* increasingly Abolitionist, charged that Know-Nothingism had become an ally of slavery. "The interest and growth and ascendency of Nativism . . . require the submission to the exactions and behests of the slave power." The Abolitionist *Jefferson Democrat* branded Know-Nothingism as "a southern plot to divert the North from the slavery question by an appeal to religious prejudices."

Actually, Barker's policy of lining up the New York delegation solidly with Raynor and the southern viewpoint gave the southern bloc the whip hand in the convention. With Barker's support, the southerners were able to run the show. Once in the saddle, they were unwilling to have a northerner, however friendly, as president, and put up E. B. Bartlett of Kentucky, a Know-Nothing state. By now Barker had antagonized many northerners. The Order was moving into a broader arena, and his iron-clad dictation was increasingly resented. Bartlett, though a southerner, was not a slavery fanatic, but a man of some breadth and distinction. He was easily elected. Barker, by putting the southern delegates in full control, had cut his own throat.

Raynor followed up this sectional victory with flaming oratory and a resolution that the three great principles of the American party were to secure native-born-American control of the government, to fight the Catholic Church, and to maintain and preserve the Union. He could not foresee that the third slogan, after southern secession came, would come to have an entirely different meaning and potency—but he believed it, to the extent of deserting the South and fighting for the North during the Civil War.

Raynor ended his oration with the words, "We do therefore declare . . . that the question of slavery does not come within the purview of the objects of this organization."

Wilson fought this. Many southerners wanted even more assurance that the party was not a mask for Free-Soil machinations. But the resolution was voted down.

Nor was the Catholic issue settled. On the ninth day of the sessions, William Alexander of Maryland, chairman of the Committee on Ritual, advocated allowing American-born Catholics to join the Order. In his state, founded by Catholics, they had played a distinguished role during independence and had shaped the Bill of Rights. Notable east-shore families were patriotic, American beyond cavil.

He was backed by John Minor Botts of Virginia. But most delegates saw no way to separate Catholic sheep from Catholic goats, and bitter anti-Papists, such as Raynor, loudly opposed the change. Alexander's resolution was twice defeated by big majorities.

Once more, in spite of efforts to sidetrack the matter, the platform committee became embroiled in the slavery question, and split down the middle along sectional lines. Various accommodations were proposed on the Missouri Compromise, Kansas and Nebraska, squatter sovereignty, the Fugitive Slave Law. All mediation was rejected by the combined vote of the extremists on both sides.

Feelings ran so high that a "National Union" get-together banquet was held. Raynor never spread his oratorical wings in a greater golden blaze about the old Union and the glorious future of *the* Union.

The platform committee finally reported out with two contradictory resolutions supported respectively by eighteen and fourteen states. (The numbers of electoral college votes commanded by the two groups of states were, correspondingly, 145 and 140.)

The majority report was drawn up by Burwell of Virginia. "*Resolved:* That the American party having arisen upon the ruins and in spite of opposition of the Whig and Democratic parties, cannot be held in any manner responsible for the obnoxious acts or violated pledges of either; that the systematic agitation of the slavery question by those parties has elevated sectional hostility into a positive element of political policy and brought our institutions into peril." To guarantee peace to the country, perpetuity to the Union, since extreme opinions were irreconcilable, "the best guarantee of common justice" required that the existing laws on slavery be maintained as "a final and conclusive settlement." Congress possessed no constitutional power "to legislate upon the subject of slavery in the states," or to exclude any state from admission to the Union because her constitution did or did not recognize slavery as part of her social system. Nor should Congress interfere with slavery in the District of Columbia, for this would violate the compact by which Maryland had ceded the area to the United States.

The minority report, opposing this hands-off view, advocated the repeal of the Missouri Compromise as "a violation of the plighted troth of the nation."

Three days of hot debate ensued. In spite of secrecy rules each side, growing more embittered, leaked its version to the newspapers, which flared with dramatic headlines.

Barker stanchly defended New York's conservatism, fought Massachusetts' fanaticism, and supported the southern position. Thereby he gave the southern states full final control. But at the moment it seemed to mark the only road to national victory. If all slave states supported the 1856 Know-Nothing candidates, New York's thirty-five electoral votes, plus ten more, regardless of what most other northern states did, would put a Know-Nothing president into the White House.

The minority report was defeated 92 to 52, and the majority report adopted 80 to 59 as Section XII of the party platform. Various fringe states, also California and a few northern states, including New York, split their votes.

Some southerners grumbled that the resolution was too namby-pamby. Others, such as Botts of Virginia, believed that to ram even this much down the throats of northern delegates was a blunder that would result in "certain and inglorious defeat" for the party. The southerners had broken down the last barrier on the slavery issue. Did this really mean the national defeat of the Know-Nothings? Better had the delegates asked: Does this mean civil war? Part of the answer came at once.

Most northern delegates—all those from Massachusetts

—not only refused to vote for Article XII, but withdrew from the hall. Wilson called a caucus for the following morning, June 14, at which all free states except New York were represented by at least part of their delegates. An "Address to the People" favoring "Nativism and Anti-slavery" was issued; at the same time they agreed to return to the convention if it would pledge itself to demand the restoration of the Missouri Compromise.

Not all those at the caucus locked the door. Many continued in their convention seats and participated in subsequent proceedings. The split was not yet an irrevocable break. Yet, basically, it ran deep into the integrity of the organization. Not even the older parties, each composed of contradictory northern and southern elements, although playing dirty politics with the slavery issue, had had such open dissension at the national level. The party trying to sidestep the controversy, to salve it over the most, was the hardest hit. Many predicted the prompt disruption of the organization.

Behind the scenes, two presidential aspirants already were pulling wires, both from New York, former President Fillmore, who had just joined the Order and been given the third-degree initiation, and George Law, the big shipping tycoon; they had no love for each other. Both wanted southern support, which partly accounted for the convention's decisions. Law had bought up newspapers as far away as New Orleans. He was being harshly attacked by Fillmore supporter Vespasian Ellis, a super-conservative editor of the Know-Nothing *American Organ* of Washington, D. C.

The big question was: Would state organizations back home accept the new party platform, particularly Article XII? Throughout the South, in spite of some extremists and some secessionists, in Alabama and Mississippi, there was little difficulty. In Virginia, a ratification mass meeting in Lynchburg, October 19, interpreted anti-Catholic Article VIII of the Philadelphia platform to suit itself and opened SSSB membership to all, Catholics or not, who professed to owe no allegiance to any foreign power. The following January secrecy was abolished. In Ohio part of the Order split off, forming the anti-slavery Know-Somethings, a secret group that spread to California and to New York. Massachusetts repudiated Article XII.

Barker and his fellow delegates called a big mass meeting in City Hall Park three days after the Philadelphia sessions closed, and their eloquence easily carried the day. Upstate, however, a few lodges surrendered their charters and disbanded. There were signs of a ground swell of remonstrance against both slavery and the Barker clique, especially now that the leader had lost his national halo. This opposition—although Fillmore had always been conciliatory to the slave interests—seemed particularly strong among the Silver Grays. Barker smelled treachery, and coolness developed between him and Fillmore. He prepared to back Law for the presidential nomination next year.

The New York State Grand Council meeting at Binghamton August 28 enjoyed poor attendance. The delegate report on Philadelphia was received without enthusiasm and referred to the platform committee. Two resolutions were presented. Neither directly mentioned Article XII. One favored the moderate southern position and retained the neutralist New York position, declaring that the issue had "no rightful place in the platform of the American party." The other, definitely anti-slavery, condemned the repeal of the Missouri Compromise.

As adopted, the platform was a repetition of Barker's eight points of the previous May; then the two contradictory resolutions were added. It was a curious way of avoiding dissension. Face south or face north—take your choice: you were still a Know-Nothing. But from any angle, it was a slap in the face at the Barker clique.

In spite of this, the Know-Nothings were never more powerful, now claiming 185,000 members. Besides that, the OUA, with 30,000 members, was reorganized along SSSB lines for intensive political support. The Wide Awakes (the American Star), with 10,000 members, was also overhauled to bring it into line with SSSB purposes. Its new head was Jacob B. Bacon, a close ally of Barker. Its secrecy was tightened up, and the society reorganized on the basis of eighty-four temples, each pledged to support only the American party. Thus the Know-Nothings, in spite of some overlapping membership, totaled well over two hundred thousand, a punitive force of great power. The work of these orders was further coordinated at a secret joint executive meeting on July 13, a super steering group for the American party.

In contrast, the Democratic party showed no signs of healing internal differences. The Whig party was in complete disintegration. The Seward wing had crumbled; in rural districts it had been mostly taken over by the Temperance party, with some anti-slavery elements thrown in. Something had to be done if the Know-Nothings were to be blocked in the autumn state elections, when all offices except that of governor would be up for auction. Seward began picking up the pieces.

The Kansas-Nebraska organization had split the previous year over the question of becoming an independent party. Those favoring this seceded and by May, 1855, coalesced with the Free Democrats to form the new Republican party. Thus in July, Seward was able to pull together a working coalition of Whigs, Republicans, and Temperance party, plus two secret societies, the Choctaws (the 1854 Know-Nothing seceders) and the Know-Somethings (headed by William C. Parsons). Both were strongly anti-slavery, had eliminated anti-foreign doctrines, but were still anti-clerical. Would this combination be able to halt the Know-Nothings?

Despite Know-Nothing numerical strength, there were signs of lessened enthusiasm in the Order and among the public. The slogans of anti-foreignism and anti-clericalism were wearing thin, especially after the Catholic bishops, in May, jointly declared that Catholics owed no allegiance to the Pope in civic affairs. After all, the Catholics were a slim minority, and even in New York they were vastly outnumbered. Furthermore, the novelty of secrecy was wearing off; indeed, by now the oaths, ritual, and mumbo jumbo were widely known, and wrangles behind closed doors were apt to be aired in the press.

The Know-Nothings had learned some lessons since 1854. This time they tried to adapt themselves more to democratic controls and to customary political practices. Although the September 25, 1855, convention at Auburn was still exclusively SSSB in origin, the 320 delegates had been freely elected by subordinate councils, and rules had been revised to permit the convention to be run by officers elected from the floor. Nominees were to be similarly chosen.

Barker, acting as temporary chairman, handed the gavel over to elected State Senator Erastus Brooks, leader of the *Express,* and of the most conservative wing of the Order. The previous year he had staged a notable public controversy with Archbishop Hughes. The American party had become almost a bona-fide party.

Its "principles and objects" were clearly set forth. Those issued by the Twelfth Council of New York City's Thirteenth Ward, of which a brother of Thomas R. Whitney was a member, were interesting because they added an explanation of former secrecy. Without secrecy, the first "efforts at Union" could never have withstood the assaults of the "crushing power of old party combinations," their talent in "persuading the weak . . . overawing the timid, and . . . flattering and controlling the most resolute." Know-Nothingism would have been strangled in the cradle. Now it was strong enough to stand openly before the world. So ran the rationalization.

The ticket was again composed of Whigs and Democrats from every section of the state. The nominee for secretary of state, Joel T. Headly of Newburgh, a former minister turned author, was a strong anti-Seward man.

The subsequent Republican convention at Syracuse was dominated by Seward. He, too, named Democrats as well as Whigs. This was too much for the old-line Whigs, who bolted, held a mass meeting in New York City, then a convention. It condemned the Republican choices, then faded away. It was the last kick of the dying mule. A few crept back to the Seward fold; the rest dissolved into the haze of Know-Nothingism.

In the campaign the Sewardites could not attack dark-lantern politics, because they had the support of the Choctaws and Know-Somethings. The Americans hammered on "Union . . . Union . . . Union." The politicians, they alleged, had inflamed North against South and vice versa, until they had "brought even our sacred Union itself into jeopardy." The only gods were power and patronage. But the American party had come to restore peace "by a fresh invocation of national spirit." Anti-foreign diatribes were mostly muted, although campaign literature warned against immigration—"half a million strangers annually"—pouring in a "flood of ignorance, vice, and crime," bringing "distinct and ungenial nationalities into the heart of the city," an ever-swelling tide of outlanders "ignorant of our language" and our "sentiments." They banded "into combinations . . . apart from our long-known and familiar masses of native citizens," and remained untouched by America's peculiar and "complicated system of freedom." Public lands should be kept out of their hands; native labor should be given preference. Also, the "paramount attachments" of Catholics were likewise foreign, and their moral if not political allegiance was foreign. The Church sought to change the social constitution of the natives. For "nine tenths of our people" it was "essentially a foreign power."

The Americans carried the state by a 12,000 plurality over the Republican coalition, but failed to gain control of the legislature, electing only seven senators and forty-four assemblymen, partly owing to vote losses in the Silver Gray counties, which further convinced Barker that Fillmore either would not or could not control his old-time backers.

Half or more of the New York congressmen went to Washington as Know-Nothings, and interest focused on the opening of the December session, where sat 43 out-and-out-Know-Nothings, and more than twice that number in both the other two parties, a goodly batch among the Democrats; and actually 70 of the 108 Republicans, who had the largest bloc. Thus the Know-Nothings, even with their dyed-in-the-wool minority, had the balance of power, and no legislation could be passed without their aid, not even a speaker could be named. The result was the longest deadlock in the history of Congress. Not that the Know-Nothings were united; they merely created chaos. Greeley of the *Tribune* growled: "They are as devoid of persistence and coherence as an anti-cholera or anti-potato rot party would be."

Both the Democrats and the Republicans put up Know-Nothings for the speakership—Humphrey Marshall of Kentucky; Nathaniel P. Banks of Massachusetts—hoping to win Know-Nothing support. Under the chairmanship of floor leader William R. Smith of Alabama, seconded by Thomas R. Whitney of New York, the Know-Nothing caucus decided to back H. M. Fuller of Pennsylvania. But only six New York Know-Nothings stayed in line, and most northern Know-Nothings supported D. Campbell, an out-and-out anti-slavery man. Marshall dropped out on the twenty-eighth ballot. The Democrats and southern Know-Nothings were determined to block Banks—an overt Abolitionist, anti-Catholic, anti-foreign. Had the Americans held together at this point they probably could have forced Fuller across; at one time he was well ahead. But the Know-Nothing votes wavered and veered, came and went. There was no holding them solid. The matter dragged on for two months, during which Smith and Whitney, L. M. Cox of Kentucky, and Jacob Broom of Pennsylvania, made prolonged, violent speeches against Catholicism and foreigners. These were paralleled by similar Know-Nothing diatribes in the Senate. There Mississippi's Know-Nothing Senator Stephen Adams held forth—as he had the previous year—in typically ignorant long-winded oratory. The Catholic Boston *Pilot* showed its own peculiar brand of Know-Nothingism, by backing its arch-enemy, Whitney, in a proposed law to exclude aliens, because so many of them were German atheists. But few extremist Know-Nothing bills ever got out of committee, and the few that did were allowed to die without a vote.

In the continuing struggle for the speakership, the

Know-Nothings finally split two ways, half going over to the Democrats, the rest to the Republicans, who, having the largest representation, were able to elect Banks. About a hundred of the votes he received were Know-Nothing votes, of whom, Greeley remarked, 20 or 30 "actually believe in the swindle." The failure of the Know-Nothings to stick together was revealed to the nation vividly, also that they were more deeply riven on the slavery issue than the Democrats. It did not help their national prestige.

Before this final outcome, the New York legislature of 120 members, about equally divided among Democrats, Republicans, and Americans, became involved in a similar struggle over the speakership. The Know-Nothing caucus selected Lyman Odell of Livingston, a man of some standing. Here the slavery question was not pivotal, and for two weeks each party clung doggedly to its choice, then, on the forty-ninth ballot, the Republicans and Democrats got together, outvoted the Know-Nothings, and divided all offices among themselves. At least, the Know-Nothings had demonstrated they could act together with some discipline.

The *Know-Nothing Almanac and True American Manual* for 1856—scores of such almanacs were published all over the country—offered as its theme: "Our God, our Bible, the Union and Constitution." It hailed Know-Nothing victories throughout New England, in New York and Delaware, the great progress in the South.

"Why are you poor?" it asked of "American mechanics, working men, women, and sewing girls." Because of the labor market gutted by immigrants ready to work for fifty cents a day, it claimed. A list of "foreigners" employed by the United States Coast Survey was given.

A garbled account of the Louisville election riots said falsely that they were "commenced by foreigners, with a wilful and premeditated determination to destroy indiscriminately the lives of American citizens." The Saint Patricio Irish battalion, it charged, had gone over to the Mexican side in the late war.

Once more it paraded tales of escaped nuns, Theresa

Reed, Miss Bunkley, and Maria Monk, "villified and persecuted" till she "sank under the brutal and unscrupulous attacks and machinations." The *Almanac* advertised a new edition of her *Awful Disclosures* for seventy-five cents, *The Escaped Nun or Confessions of Convent Life* for fifty cents, and anti-Papist books by Gavazzi, Miss Sinclair, and Helen Mulgrave. It presented attacks on Archbishop Hughes, recently republished in *Harper's Magazine,* and quoted Sam Houston, "The design of the American Order is not to put down Catholics, but to prevent Catholics from putting down Protestants." A report was made on Senator Lewis Cass's recent attack on Romanism. The volume was illustrated by engravings of Inquisition tortures, pulleys and burning bodies, and monks' and nuns' indiscretions. This was a curtain raiser for the 1856 campaign now shaping up.

President Bartlett, on request of five state executive committees, called a special national council meeting in Philadelphia on February 18, four days prior to the Washington Birthday convention of the party, in order to consider abolishing secrecy, doing away with the Union oath, and permitting presidential nominations to be made in open session.

In spite of the previous year's controversy, the members were jubilant because of so many victories the previous year all across the country. The only dark spot had been Virginia, and they had no reason to believe that their continued triumphal march would be interrupted. For the old parties, too, were badly divided, North, South, and everywhere, most seriously along sectional lines. A northern Democrat certainly looked at things differently from a southern Democrat. The same went for what was left of the Whigs. The Republican party, exclusively a northern party, conjured up such bitterness that it threatened to wreck the Union. By continuing to soft-pedal the slavery issue, and brightly reiterating "Union, *Union,* UNION," the Know-Nothings hoped to allay animosities.

Again the question of admitting Louisiana delegates came up. They insisted they were in accord with the cry, "Native-born Americans shall rule America," that Catholic members had to swear they did not recognize the temporal power of a Pope. This time, their admission was advocated by ultra-Protestants, including a Presbyterian elder. Even rabid Brownlow of Tennessee turned a somersault by saying that after all, "Gallic" Catholicism in Louisiana was something wholly different from that promoted by Bishop Hughes of New York. The delegation was taken in by a vote of 67 to 50.

Two contending delegations showed up from Pennsylvania. The one opposing Article XII was obviously representative and was seated over the protests of southern members. One delegate, a Tennesseean, left in an angry huff.

In spite of all efforts by the leaders to down any sectional fight, the billy goats of extremism began butting heads again over Article XII. The southerners, who had had the whip hand the previous year, now found they did not have the strength to prevent the elimination of the disputed article. The northerners had succeeded in altering the basis of voting (previously seven votes for each state) to allow each state to vote according to the number of seats held in Congress. Barker moved heaven and earth to keep the New York delegation in line behind Article XII, but it split down the middle.

An entire new platform was adopted, making the party more definitely neutral on the slavery issue. Many northerners, especially from Massachusetts, were incensed. The entire New York delegation and most southern delegates, although a few were outraged, accepted the party stand. However, A. B. Botts of Virginia angrily called the northern Know-Nothings out-and-out Abolitionists and shouted that the time had come for them to part ways. He and others asked for *sine die* adjournment.

The tempest subsided. The new Article VI was put in to replace Article XII; it gave "unqualified recognition" of states rights with no congressional or outside interference. "An attempt to dupe the people," growled delegate J. S. Stockton of Kentucky—"a political trick sacrificing all principle."

The regular convention met on February 22, also in Philadelphia, with 227 delegates present. Two states were missing—South Carolina and Georgia. The five-man Connecticut delegation, strongly Abolitionist, proposed immediate adjournment. Northerners and some southerners contended that the preliminary National Council gathering—although largely composed of the same delegates—had no authority to adopt a platform. They demanded a reopening of the whole controversial slavery issue. Many grumpy anti-slavery motions were presented by northerners, as was a resolution to exclude Louisiana. All were quickly tabled or voted down. The platform was readopted.

Minnesota and Wisconsin withdrew. Connecticut rose, announced withdrawal, and stalked out, followed by the delegates from Massachusetts, Rhode Island, Ohio, and, later, scattered northern delegates, particularly from the Pennsylvania and Iowa groups.

The seceders called for a nominating convention in New York June 12. The Know-Nothing party was broken for good at this point. No longer would it be a force to reckon with. Everything from now on would be anticlimax.

The convention chairman called for nominations. Among southern aspirants were Garrett Davis, John Bell, John J. Crittenden, Kenneth Raynor, and Sam Houston. Houston especially, because of his heroic reputation, had real hopes, and he was actively backed by Andrew J. Donelson of Tennessee, one of the strongest figures the party had attracted, a nephew of President Jackson, who had been a member of Old Hickory's Kitchen Cabinet. Houston had already expressed some of his preferences, should he be chosen. He would like to see the platform dropped entirely, merely the one phrase, "Union and the Constitution." He wanted to be a real "national" candidate. In any event, he would never support his rival Millard Fillmore. "No man who skulks the responsibility and maintains the position of Bat," who can be "Bird or Beast, as victory may incline," was going to get his help. The only southern state Fillmore could carry, he warned, would be Kentucky.

Crittenden said he would never "put forward" any pretensions for the presidency, "But . . . I have a pride of character, which does not permit me to humble myself so far as to shrink from or decline even the presidency itself if offered."

Other possible nominees were Jacob Broom of Pennsylvania, a fine orator and one of the most persistent workers in fertilizing the fields of Nativism; and George Law of New York. Law was determined, even if he lost the nomination himself, to block Fillmore, whom he despised for lack of sufficient nationalistic militancy.

Barker had worked closely with Fillmore against Seward, but he feared that in spite of the former president's vacillations on all issues, he was now too branded with southernism to carry weight in the North—not even in New York State. Even prior to this, Barker had fallen in with George Law's ambitions, and before and during the Philadelphia convention tried to line up the New York delegation behind the shipping magnate.

Though strongly anti-slavery, Law had not aired his views, nor was he likely to go beyond the party's neutral position. He had stated his Know-Nothing ideas firmly, but not fanatically, and Barker was sure he would be the stronger candidate. Besides, Law had plenty of money to put out on the campaign.

But with so many northern delegates withdrawn, the southerners now had the run of the convention, and on the first ballot it was clear that they were strong for Fillmore. Here again the New York delegation split down the middle, half for Fillmore, half for Law. Before the second ballot, deals were made. Andrew Jackson Donelson switched to Fillmore, who then received 179 votes to Law's 24 and Sam Houston's 3. There were scattered votes for Raynor and others. Fillmore was in. Ironically, he was then in Europe celebrating an audience with the Pope. Donelson, running against three others, Raynor, George Law, and R. K. Call, was rewarded with the vice-presidency on the first ballot.

They were campaigning on a catch-all platform cleverly designed to trap voters of every stripe. The harsher doctrines of Know-Nothingism had been toned down. It dealt grandiloquently with many problems, but offered no solutions for any of them. The Know-Nothings, at long last, had turned toward the typical offend-no-one platform, customarily adopted by all parties. What the Know-Nothings did not perceive was that this old-style demagogy—as well as their brief incursion into previous splinter hate-and-fear demagogy—was also discredited in the hour of looming national crisis. Such trickeries serve only for simpler non-controversial times. This, they and the old parties were to discover, partly in this election, most convincingly four years hence.

George Law was unwilling to submit to the party decision, whether he still had ambitions of his own or merely wanted to spike Fillmore's chances. After his loss of the nomination, he assumed an almost open anti-slavery position—looking toward possible nomination by the Know-Nothing northern wing. His tactics split the New York Know-Nothings more deeply and brought him into conflict not only with Fillmore but with Barker. Law sought to bring a strong New York delegation into the splinter camp. In this he was aided by his dutiful Live Oak clubs and by a skillful newspaper manager, Scoville, closely in touch with the seceding faction.

Until Law set to work, the Know-Nothings largely accepted the Fillmore nomination. But Barker control was slipping—in fact, he was thrown out of office by the State Grand Council session on February 26, 1856, while he was still in Philadelphia, and Stephen Sammons of Montgomery was named grand president. Even so, the Council voted to support Fillmore—although there was discontent because the national program meant supine acceptance of the Fugitive Slave Act. The slavery issues were steadily eating into Know-Nothing ranks. One of the first significant defections was Colonel Silas Seymour, the elected Know-Nothing state engineer.

But the inner conflict was muted during the New York spring elections. Nearly everywhere the Know-Nothings won, easily overcoming the as yet poorly organized Republicans with its strident Abolitionism. However, Law continued to abet defection and to spend money and, by March, revolt was well under way. He was a convenient peg at the moment for anti-slavery elements and the "Anti-Fillmore" organization which was started and received an invitation from the Philadelphia bolters to the June 12 New York City convention.

A preliminary state convention, supported by Law and held May 29 at Albany, was organized under the presidency of D. N. Wright of Westchester. Although this independent action violated the secret oaths and tenets, there was no mention of secession from the Know-Nothing order. They were promptly nicknamed the "North Americans" in contrast to the Fillmore "South American" wing. An anti-slavery platform was adopted, and thirty-five delegates were chosen for the June 12 schismatic convention.

Excitement over this overshadowed the regular annual session of the National Council held in New York City on June 3. Bartlett was renamed president and Erastus Brooks became vice-president. The most momentous step was the abolition of secrecy at all National Council sessions. Subordinate councils could follow suit or not, as they chose. The American party, the resolution stated, was no longer an order or a society, but a "broad, comprehensive conservative national party, standing like other political parties, openly before the country."

The Law group felt confident that the June 12 convention would nominate him for president. Actually an inner clique of non-New Yorkers was scheming to ditch him and nominate Republican N. P. Banks of Massachusetts, thus bringing about a union of northern anti-slavery forces in and out of the American party. It was soon obvious that a serious northern rift in the Know-Nothing Party, as significant as the previous North-South national rift, was in the making. This might really wreck all chances for national success. By the second day of the seceders' convention, such an angry mob of regular Know-Nothings gathered outside the hall that the delegates had to call for police protection.

The true drift of the session appeared when a letter was read from the Republican National Committee. By the third day, it was clear that the manipulators planned to lead the anti-Fillmore elements straight into the Republican party. Bitter debate followed. The Law group was pushed aside, and Republican Banks, strongly supported by the six-man Connecticut delegation, and John C. Fremont of California were placed in nomination. The New Jersey delegation bolted, together with scattered other delegates.

The remaining delegates then nominated Banks and William F. Johnson as presidential and vice-presidential candidates. A recess of several days was called in the hopes that the Republicans, in convention in Philadelphia, would make the same selection. This hope faded when Banks declined the nomination, and the Republicans nominated Fremont. The Know-Nothing rump convention thereupon reconvened and also endorsed Fremont. The American party unity was now definitely ruptured. Fillmore could not hope to receive a single anti-slavery vote from his own party. Nor was this the end of the factionalism. The bolters from the bolters, alarmed by the ruin created, swung to an extreme opposition position and nominated southerner Kenneth Raynor, then adopted a contradictory platform that condemned Charles Sumner and denounced repeal of the Missouri Compromise. Raynor promptly declined the honor, if that it could be called, and sought to persuade them to return to the Know-Nothing fold and support Fillmore. Although far from happy himself with the Philadelphia platform, it was necessary, he told them, not to lose sight of larger objectives: "Nationalism should fire the imagination in the administration and the heads of all citizens"; civil and religious freedom had to be maintained "against the encroachment and corrupting tendencies of the Roman Church, allied with the Democratic party"; "national Union" had to "be preserved against all factions."

As for George Law, he was expelled from the SSSB by the vote of the New York Council to which he belonged, and was set adrift from all meaningful political ties. Nobody wanted him to save the Republic. He had nothing left but to dedicate himself to his vast commercial and financial schemes, at which he was most successful.

The Republican Know-Nothing rump candidate, General John C. Fremont, was Georgia born (January 31, 1813) and southern educated, but had gone far beyond that narrow parochial fold. An assistant engineer and second lieutenant of the United States Army Topographical Corps, he explored the plateau between the upper Mississippi and Missouri rivers. As son-in-law of Senator Thomas Hart Benton of Missouri (who furthered his explorations and his rapid preferment), he helped open up the Oregon Trail, investigated the Great Basin between the Rockies and the Sierra Madre and, later, the route to the Sierra Madre via the headwaters of the Arkansas, Rio Grande, and Colorado rivers. These excursions into the dark, unknown wilderness had won him the sobriquet of "The Pathfinder."

He reached California during the Mexican War in time to help seize that province. A shocking execution by him of prominent Mexican prisoners, without trial, and a quarrel with General Stephen F. Kearny, resulted in a court-martial. He was found guilty of mutiny and insubordination, but President Polk, largely at the behest of father-in-law Benton, remitted the sentence. Fremont resigned and returned to California as a private citizen, where he became a state senator. During the winter of 1853–54, he explored and surveyed a southern rail route to the Pacific. Thus the Republicans had a glamorous, accomplished, but highly controversial candidate.

Democratic nominee James Buchanan was a diplomat whose pompous manner belied his large talents. Born in Mercersburg, Pennsylvania, April 13, 1791, he graduated from Dickman College and practiced law in Lancaster, became state legislator, congressman, minister to England and Russia (where he negotiated a trade treaty), senator, secretary of state in Polk's cabinet. He settled the Oregon dispute, feuded with Scott, tried to buy Cuba from Spain, and helped draw up the braggadocio Ostend Manifesto. He wanted a constitutional amendment legalizing slavery and the Fugitive

Slave Act, and so was a dream candidate for the southerners, but was expected to be able to carry enough northern states to be elected. His running mate, John C. Breckinridge, was a southern pro-slavery man from border Kentucky, chosen in the hopes of overturning Know-Nothing strength there.

The Democrats' platform emphasized free government, no discrimination because of birth or religion. "A political crusade in the nineteenth century in the United States of America against Catholics and foreigners is neither justified by the past history nor the future prospects of the country." It also attacked the outright Abolitionists as meddlers in the domestic institutions of the several states, "the safe and proper judges of everything pertaining to their own affairs."

The platform and the two candidates caused anti-slavery Democrats to split off. A convention of Radical Democrats meeting in Syracuse in July endorsed Fremont. The remnants of the Whig party gathered in Baltimore September 17, 1856, and endorsed Fillmore and Donelson. Although 500 delegates were present from twenty-five states, it represented little strength. Many disillusioned Know-Nothings attended, seeing the handwriting on the wall for their own party. Now that the Democratic and Republican parties were almost wholly sectional, they hoped that a national conservative party, via the Whigs would stage a comeback in 1860. As with most conservatives in time of rapid change, their awareness of the pace of events was badly off.

The New York situation grew more confused as the various groups dickered, or tried to consolidate their forces. Conventions and meetings flew around like animated ping-pong balls.

To block further defections to the Republicans, at least to maintain a façade of seeming unity, the New York Know-Nothing Grand Council met August 26 in Syracuse. Solidarity was established by the simple expedient of rejecting the credentials of all delegates known to be anti-slavery or against Fillmore. This bright stupidity by rule-or-ruin people is not uncommon in politics. Even with these precautions, when Fillmore's nomination was ratified twenty-one delegates walked out.

The next day these and the angry outsiders met as the Grand Council of the state, repudiating the other crowd. "Its unconstitutional and illegal section . . . freed Americans from all obligations and allegiance to its decrees." They threw Fillmore aside, endorsed Fremont, and called for a state convention at Syracuse, September 17, to meet simultaneously with the state Republican convention.

At this reunion Fremont and his running mate William L. Dayton were endorsed, but a bitter debate soon developed over whether to remain an independent organization or merge outright with the Republicans. When the latter move gained ground, a minority of the minority bolted and called for a separate convention in Rochester, September 23, this to coincide with the regular Know-Nothing convention.

The Know-Nothing reunion had a familiar face on the platform: Barker was acting as president. Here the 121 bolters, confessing error, were welcomed back into the fold. Nominations for state offices were made—this would be a test of Know-Nothing strength prior to the November presidential elections. Erastus Brooks was put up for governor, and Daniel Ullman headed the electoral college ticket.

The trend of the times showed in the voting. The Republicans carried the state by the largest majority in New York's history. The Know-Nothings dropped to third place, 130,000 votes, only 22 per cent of the total, and elected only two congressmen. Only in Ulster County did they reach 40 per cent, and in Tioga County they dropped to 8 per cent.

The attitude of the Connecticut delegation in endorsing Fremont at the New York schismatic convention in June indicated that most Know-Nothings in the state would not get behind Fillmore. But on July 18, at a stormy session in Hartford, surprisingly the regulars won out, and Fremont was denounced as a "Catholic and Free-Soiler." The resolution declared, "We are the National American party of America." It petitioned that the charter of the "treasonable"

New Haven chapter, led by the state president, N. D. Sperry, be revoked.

Two days later, Sperry presided over the meeting of the State Council in Odd Fellows Hall in Hartford. There the Fillmore supporters were in the minority. A regular who repeated the charge that Fremont was a Catholic was hissed and booed. He persisted and read a letter from President Bartlett advocating the dissolution of the Connecticut organization. This was drowned out by boisterous laughter, and Fremont was endorsed as candidate of the Connecticut Know-Nothing American party.

On August 6, a meeting was held in Hartford of all "opposed to Buchanan." Afterward the Americans adjourned to the Republican Fremont Hall on Asylum Street and an identical "Union" ticket of electors was named by both parties.

The national defeat that followed put the Americans in an ugly mood, but they met early to consider the coming elections for governor. Four hundred delegates showed up for the state convention in Hartford January 10. In a punitive mood, they threw their state comptroller off the new ticket because he had refused to fire an Irish keeper of the State House. Governor Minor was rolled over the barrel of criticism so badly that he barely won renomination.

The Whigs declined to nominate him, but he was hopeful of winning the Republican nomination. Their convention was meeting at Gilmore's saloon, and he managed to swing them to his support. But so much opposition developed, this was reversed, and they put up Gideon Welles, a strong Abolitionist, instead.

Loss of the Whig nomination also lost Minor the support of the powerful *Courant* of Hartford, which branded "Sam" and "Sambo" as identical. It predicted that the hated Democrats, representing "Rum, Romanism, and Slavery," would whip Republicans, Whigs, and Americans soundly. At the same time, the paper continued to attack the Irish ferociously as led "by priests only one degree advanced beyond them in civilization. . . ." The Democratic *Times* branded both Republicans and Know-Nothings as "Irish-haters and Negro worshipers"—a "trap of Hindoo abolitionism."

Minor was beaten badly in every county, but since no candidate had a majority, the matter went to the legislature, which, having a Know-Nothing majority, flouted the popular will and installed Minor in office for another term. In his inaugural address he attacked foreigners with more bigotry than before. But it was clear to all that the Know-Nothings were declining, that the ascendant force was the Republican party.

In the 1856 national elections there were Know-Nothing splits all through the North and Midwest, some secessions in the South also, but there the trend was to the Democrats. In Mississippi and Alabama it was almost a landslide. Everywhere in the South prominent Know-Nothing leaders especially slipped over to the Democratic party, sensing that Fillmore had no chance and fearing that if Buchanan were defeated it would be treachery to the South and to the slavocracy.

The struggle in Pennsylvania was particularly violent, for in addition to 112 votes in the solid South, Buchanan had to cut into the North enough to win 47 more, and so Pennsylvania was crucial. The Know-Nothings were caught in the middle between the Democrats and the Republicans. In the preliminary state elections the Democrats won by a small margin, so the Republicans were glad for an offer of coalition from the Know-Nothings, who accepted all Republican nominations except for president and vice-president. The electors were pledged to vote percentage-wise according to the number of votes cast respectively by the American and Republican party, the tickets being identical except for party name. The deal was cooked up mostly by North Carolina leader Raynor, who had been invited to stump the state in October for "Union and Fillmore." The Democrats snorted that it really meant "Fusion and Fillmore." The trick, Raynor believed, was to block Buchanan enough so that nobody could get a majority in the electoral college and throw the choice into the House of Representatives, where the Know-Nothings, holding the balance of power, could force a compromise —and that compromise could be Fillmore. This deal with the Republicans resulted in Raynor's being called a traitor and worse in North Carolina, and he barely escaped bodily injury at the hands of a mob in Raleigh.

For similar reasons, President Bartlett urged the Indiana Grand Council, since the Know-Nothings had no chance there and Buchanan was strong, to withdraw their candidate and support Fremont. This was also done in Tennessee, but Buchanan carried that state anyway.

On landing in New York to begin his campaign, Fillmore said he wanted domination by neither North nor South. "For my own part, I know only my own country, my whole country, and nothing but my country." Admirable sentiments, which involved no solution of anything. The Democrats culled over his past words for "black anti-slavery sentiments" pockmarking this "polished apple of Union." The Atlanta *Intelligencer* charged that Fillmore had "never ceased to hate and persecute the South until the South . . . bought him off with the presidency." However, desperate efforts were made by the southern Know-Nothing supporters of Fillmore, who now realized that local victories now depended on national success, previously not the case. The *Southern Sun* (Mississippi) printed a repulsive caricature of Fillmore uttering an imaginary soliloquy:

"These secret Know-Nothing signs . . . will elevate me once more to the presidential chair, and then these vile Democrats may censure me as much as they desire for instructing the authorizing of Cuba to murder Crittenden and his men" (Colonel William Crittenden of Kentucky had led fifty southern volunteers on a filibuster expedition to free the island, all of whom were seized and executed in August, 1851. Fillmore was roundly damned for not insisting they be released and instead giving the Cuban authorities the go-ahead signal, which, of course, was the only proper procedure, since they had violated the laws of both countries.)

As the year grew older, the slavery issue deepened.

There was shocking violence in Kansas, where blood flowed and buildings went up in flames. Northern rancor was tremendous when President Pierce condemned the free Topeka government and backed the Missouri pro-slavery gangs roaming the state in blatant defiance of law and decency. Massacres, burning of farmhouses and town dwellings, public buildings and newspaper offices by the pro-slavery crowd and the recognized slavery government were unimpeded by federal forces. The missionary shipments of "Beecher's Bibles" —Sharps rifles—were stepped up. Soon John Brown, his four sons, and three companions matched the opposition's tactics, and pro-slavery settlers were seized, shot, and strung up, and flames rose high across the state as more farmhouses, barns, and corncribs were put to the torch.

The bitter speech by Charles Sumner against the "slave oligarchy" and its "rape of Kansas" resulted in his being beaten almost to death by a southern congressman, an act of savagery that further inflamed sectionalism.

To the degree that this North-South fanaticism increased, the Know-Nothing cry of "Union" lost its strength —at least until it became the northern slogan in the Civil War and was no longer a Know-Nothing catchword, but life and death. The Republican party with its pathethic descriptions of "Bleeding Kansas" was on the ascendancy everywhere in the North. The Democrats ruled the South, but were loosing ground in the North. The Know-Nothings hoped to cut into both followings and more than ever believed that the election would be settled by Congress, that Fillmore would, in the final toss, become president. They kept on throwing up smoke screens: Fremont was a Catholic who would be under Papal influence—utterly false, of course. Both Republicans and Democrats gibed at Fillmore for his fake anti-Catholic position.

The campaign was bitter. The Hartford *Courant,* not noted for its own loftiness or mellifluous restraint, observed, October 21, 1856, "Since the days of Ananias and Sapphira, there has not been so much lying. . . . Newspapers groan with falsehoods." Pamphlets were packed "with brutal lies," all sense of honor was lost. "Never were men more unscrupulous."

In that same Connecticut, the Republicans brought in Andrew H. Reeder, former governor of Kansas, to tell of the arson and murder committed there by pro-slavery marauders from Missouri. The Know-Nothings thumped the Bible, attacked the Church, Pope Gregory XVI, and Archbishop Hughes scathingly. Although the Know-Nothing-Republican fusionists carried the state by a large majority, Fillmore got only 3,000 votes.

When the wild furor was over, Buchanan had 1,838,169 votes, representing 174 electoral votes from 14 slave and five free states. Fremont had 1,335,264 votes, with 114 electoral votes from 11 free states. Fillmore carried only Maryland with its eight electoral votes. Percentagewise, the popular vote was Buchanan 45 per cent, Fremont 30 per cent, and Fillmore 25 per cent. On the basis of the actual vote, the matter would have been thrown to Congress for decision—the Americans had not been so far off in their calculations—but in the electoral college—which always distorts, sometimes flouts, the popular will—the percentages were 59, 39, and 2, giving Buchanan a majority.

Actually Fillmore had a big vote all through the South; he carried nearly all the larger counties and in most states lost out by only a few thousand votes. But the final scoreboard told the story. As a ruling force, Know-Nothingism had been wiped out, except for local counties and cities, in all but one state.

The Democrats had won, but bitter sectionalism was in the saddle; it was merely a brief breathing spell before final disaster, which the Democrats did not and could not avert.

Neither the Know-Nothings' hate program nor their false conciliation program had stemmed the blind torrent rushing to the cataract of national tragedy. In fact, there was no longer any *raison d'être* for the Know-Nothing party. There never had been, from any rational standpoint. Now there was none from any standpoint. It had been born of an hour of political confusion; unusual circumstances had permitted this spawn of darkness, this gargoyle of pomposity and force, to be born. Those circumstances had vanished, not that political confusion was less, but the tide of organized wrath was rising irresistibly. Now, none of the Know-Nothing program had even the slightest bearing on the realities of the national scene.

Down in Murfreesboro, Tennessee, the victorious Democrats, unaware that their turn was next, that they, too, were lost, held a joyous big funeral rite for the Know-Nothings:

HIC YACET

*Samuel, Infamous Son of Abolitionism . . .*
*wounded by Henry A. Wise of Virginia in 1855,*
*died of public opinion in the north 1856.*

*Here lies Sam*
*As great a sham*
*As ever gulled a nation. . . .*

## CHAPTER XIII

# LAST RITES FOR SAM

"SAM" really was not dead yet. True, he was dying—but piecemeal. Massachusetts got rid of the convent snoopers. New Hampshire and Vermont became Republican strongholds. Rhode Island quickly recovered. In Pennsylvania, Know-Nothingism persisted a little longer through coalitions with the Republicans, which did not endear it to southerners. By the end of 1856 the Illinois body was sharply divided between the "Sams" and the "Jonathans"; the latter opposed antagonizing Catholics and came out on top. A hasty conclusion might be that reason and light were belatedly penetrating into the darkness of Know-Nothing minds. An optimistic conclusion—no great political or religious truths or ideals were involved: it was merely impractical, a bit ridiculous, to keep shouting wolf, and ridiculous sheep can have no great success either as rebels or politicians. Neither the Catholic religion nor the Catholic hierarchy was a menace; anyway not in Illinois in the mid-nineteenth century. Protestantism, as a religion and as a force, was menaced more by the new industrialism and materialism. The Know-Nothing effort to re-create the theocratic absolutism of colonial times no longer appealed to the bulk of Protestants misled by Beecher, Morse, Breckinridge, *et al.*

Also, hate of foreigners was abating. All were Americans in the making, and the vast majority were industrious, valuable citizens, not ignorant or unable to understand American ideals "in thrice twenty-one years." Quickly they had learned the incredible roseate myths that enveloped the American dream, plus the practical organized life that made it function. Political success could no longer be built on a bugbear of foreign menace because of fancied differences in origin and customs.

The third Know-Nothing credo, "Union," was also a complete fraud, an appeal to emotionalism by false use of cherished symbols. Their "constitution" was fiction, not basic governmental institutions or constructive laws or the bill of rights. It had become daily more apparent that the Know-Nothings stood for disunion: the disunion of North and South by evasion; and disunion everywhere as to religion, race, and class.

In its final moments, Know-Nothingism still served the dwindling hopes and limited mentality of the slaveowners, of New Haven carriage makers, and of the clockmakers of Plymouth and Bristol, and was still a brief refuge for all badly frightened people, but the elements for an over-all fascist-type putsch in mid-century America were too sectional and dispersed. The opportunities of a new continent were enormous, the pace of national growth too intense. All classes —except the slaveowners and Negroes—enjoyed expanding opportunity. Maladjustments and dislocations were frequent, sometimes sizable, but too shifting and ephemeral to provide the sinews for blind discontent or for a national fascist party —not with such an expanding economy and such burgeoning hope, plus the chance to escape to the West. The closing circle of war-brought ruin and economic and human disaster that later wracked Italy and Germany when fascism appeared simply did not exist in the United States, in spite of recurrences of depression and hard times. The big issue was the broadening of human freedom, not its contraction. The public was no longer willing to stand for secrecy in politics.

The Know-Nothing order had to bow to this universal sentiment, yet without secrecy it was doomed. No system of violence can be directed without secrecy. Absurd mythology cannot be maintained without the discipline of secret ritual. When in 1857 the New York SSSB Grand Council abolished secrecy, the local councils lost half their members; many folded entirely. Some members perhaps were ashamed to be discovered as having skulked in anonymous darkness. The timid, the sneaks, the paranoids were the first to scamper. Promoters of violence also ran for cover. The security and the ego status provided by the gang were lost at once. More intelligent members realized they had been bemused by hocus-pocus and weird hallucinations. Practical politicians perceived that Know-Nothingism was a dead end. Some took refuge, hopeful of continued job holding, in the Republican party. Most had to hunt for some other band wagon. Some were lost and knew it. And so the party was left with only a hard core of sincere fanatics and weak-minded folk, plus a few sleazy small-time politicians who still might squeeze out some juice of self-advantage.

Neither for its practical ends nor as a piece of myth making was Know-Nothingism, even though it came so close to power, really effective. Reason caught up with the Nativists much sooner than in most abnormal political movements; and reason, although never a potent factor in political or inner institutional life, was one thing the Order could not withstand. Light was flooding out the dark-lantern methods, and that meant failure and disintegration.

The OUA chapters suffered the same quick decline. Harper's organization, which had done so much harm to the country, had always been more reasonable, at least in its methods, than the militant SSSB, Wide Awakes, and American Protestant Association, and it lingered on anemically until shortly after the Civil War, a sort of elderly old-slipper brotherhood, not able to attract younger blood. Nearly all the minor secret patriotic organizations disappeared between 1856 and the Civil War.

The American Protestant Association had dwindled even earlier. As anti-Catholic feeling turned to political channels, it was less able to attract attention, and even less so when all eyes turned toward the fate of the Negro and the country itself. By 1857 most militant Protestant anti-Catholic societies had dropped the crusade or had vanished from the scene along with their scurrilous and shameful publications.

And so organized Nativism, which had reached a long, hairy arm out of the dark of unreason and fear to clutch for humanity's troubled soul and extinguish the light of a free society, had pulled back—for the third time. It had almost lifted the hairy carcass of its racism and religious intolerance out of its nightmare pit to the platform of power, but now it was slipping back into the darkness whence it came. This was only partly a triumph of enlightened behavior on the part of the American democracy. Those Know-Nothing talons, clutching at the edge of the platform of command, had been stamped on by the sharp heel of other passions, by devotees of other violences.

But the Abolitionists, however blind to consequences, however empty of imaginative solutions, at least wished to strike the chains from less fortunate human beings, to crush false privilege to earth. There was, at least, nobility in their madness, if also war and death. War and death that were to leave a lasting blight on the nation.

The last American National Council met in Louisville, Kentucky, in June, 1857, and adjourned *sine die,* never to meet again. Activities continued only on local and state levels.

In New York eighty assembly districts failed to send delegates to the SSSB convention in Syracuse, September 15, 1857. Had the Order been based on vital aims and truths, it hardly would have collapsed so quickly after one serious setback. The Know-Nothings, hoping for power, had aroused mob passions; now they were taught their own lesson: that the mob hungers only for success, not truth or enlightenment.

But there was no doubting the dedication of most of those left in the inner circles. These lean die-hards at Syracuse doggedly went through the motions of naming a state ticket. Old-time names were listed. Former State Senator

James O. Putnam of Erie, a vindictive anti-Catholic, was put up for secretary of state; Lyman Odell of Livingston for treasurer; Reverend Hiram Ketchum, anti-Catholic Bible thumper, for the American Bible Society, for Court of Appeals judge.

A watered-down platform, a piddling affair, with little of the old bigotry, sought painfully for new issues. Some were Socialistic. To be sure, there were the old phrases in great gilt scrolls: "good citizens and patriots," "watchful oversight of our free institutions," "this glorious Union, bequeathed by heroes and martyrs," which was "forever" to remain "an altar of liberty . . . an asylum to the oppressed." But these humorless souls also insisted once more that the United States was to be run only by "native-born citizens . . . prepared to swear upon the altar of liberty eternal hostility to every form of oppression."

From this mealy-mouthed prologue the platform rambled on to demand legislation to prevent "foreign influence controlled by unscrupulous politicians," but not a word was said about more severe immigration and naturalization laws. The Bible must be kept as a textbook to inculcate, of all things, "the sentiment of religious freedom in the youthful mind."

Then came a new note. The platform demanded proper railroad and monopoly taxation, the end of free railroad passes to politicians (a Grange and Populist demand thirty years later); continued public ownership and improvement of the Erie Canal; an end of "unwise, unjust, and infamous legislation for the benefit of monied monopolies—evil laws put across by the unscrupulous Republican party lobby and the corrupt Democrats . . . truckling to the powers of Popery and foreigners."

Here were germs of the Anti-Monopoly and Greenback parties of more than a generation later, of the Farmers' Alliance and the Populist party, all of which were to show flickers of Know-Nothingism in their occasional antagonisms toward foreigners, Irish saloonkeepers, Germans, Jews, Mexicans, and the Catholic Church. Indeed, one of their most brilliant southern leaders, Tom Watson of Georgia, twice candidate for president of the United States, became the worst Negro, Jew, and Catholic baiter in the country's history.

Not issues, but organizations were at stake in the 1857 campaign. There was even apathy about slavery, which hurt the Republican vote. The Democrats at long last had managed to reunite themselves, But violent shifts of voter allegiance occurred. Disillusioned Know-Nothings went into the Republican party. Republicans drifted back into the Democratic party. Here and there, as in New York and Kings counties, Republican-Know-Nothing fusions were arranged.

At least a hundred thousand voters stayed away from the polls. The Democrats won 195,000 votes. The Republican total was one third its howling success of the previous year, shrinking to 178,000. The Know-Nothings dropped off from their peak performance of 1855 by almost a third, and to half their shrunken total of the previous year—only 66,000 votes, 15 percent of the total.

In New York City, knowing it was failing, the American party turned hopefully toward fusion with the Republicans in the elections of county officials. After many meetings, separate and joint, a ticket was finally agreed on, four places for each party. But the Democrats walked away with the election. The Republicans polled only 13,560 votes, the Know-Nothings only 8,480, a fourth of the Democratic vote.

By the new 1857 charter, the election of municipal authorities was put off until December. For mayor, the Know-Nothings put up James Cooley, but the Republicans refused to endorse him, instead supporting an independent movement headed by Daniel F. Tiemann, a one-time leader of the earlier Nativist movement of the 'forties, a backer of James Harper. Cooley withdrew, and the Know-Nothings supported the independent ticket, which won by an insignificant plurality. They got few plums out of it.

The American party debacle continued through 1858. At the annual Grand Council meeting in Albany August 24 fifty-seven counties were represented. Henry B. Northrup of Washington County was elected president. A nominating convention was set for Syracuse on September 8 to coincide with the Republican convention in the same city. In the resultant acrimonious debate, the conservative wing, led by Erastus Brooks, was dead opposed to alliance with the anti-slavery party. But the final decision favoring fusion stood 183 to 63.

In Syracuse, the first business of the convention, presided over by Daniel Ullman, was to receive a commission from the Republican convention, asking for a conference to settle upon a common platform and ticket. An anti-slavery platform, somewhat softened to please the Know-Nothings and with a few hints of Nativism, was worked out. It was promptly adopted by the Americans, but was dunked by the Republicans who came up with a strong anti-slavery document with no Nativistic trimmings. The altered version brought howls of indignation in the American convention. Trickery! Treachery! Double-dealing!

All chance of fusion went out the window, and the Americans put up their own ticket: five Republicans, four Democrats, none of whom had ever favored Nativism. The candidate for governor, Lorenzo Burrows of Orleans, was considered a strong man, although given no chance for success. A German by birth was picked for treasurer. This was like throwing a rock through one's own bedroom window, and it brought a wounded howl from the OUA.

In defending the ticket, the executive committee put forth five curious reasons: (1) to recover the old status of balance of powers between the greater parties; (2) good men in office; (3) punishment of the Republicans for weakening the Canal Board (the Republican administration had thrown out American party members); (4) to allay anti-slavery agitation; (5) to break the confidence of the other parties by proving that the Americans had not become a nonentity.

The November elections put the Republicans out in front with a quarter million votes; the Democrats were strong also, with 240,000 votes, but the Nativists polled only 62,000, less than the previous year, less than 12 per cent of the total.

Fusion again was easily carried through in New York

City, however. Although the combined vote was larger, the Know-Nothing contribution was smaller. As before, the Democrats won. Most Know-Nothing ward organizations thereafter ceased to function. No city Grand Council reunion was ever called again. The next year's fusion ticket came out of back-door negotiations with the American party executive committee, which by now was little more than a name. Both Republican and Know-Nothing votes declined sharply, the latter being only a little more than four thousand. That was the last gasp of political Know-Nothingism in New York City. The SSSB became no more than a curious combination of letters.

In the 1859 state elections, the Republicans were again ahead of the field, and the Know-Nothings received only 23,800 votes. Curiously, at this hour of breakup, they held an exact balance of power—not that they had the cunning or initiative left to make use of it.

The presidential election maneuvers of 1860 found the Know-Nothings dispersed everywhere, with no hint of a national convention. A patched-up Constitutional Union party nominated Know-Nothing John Bell of Tennessee and former Senator Edward Everett of Massachusetts. Bell, secretary of the treasury under Whig President William Henry Harrison, in 1841, was a bitter Nativist. At the time of the dreadful Know-Nothing election massacre of Germans in Louisville in 1855, he had said in a Knoxville speech: "It is better that a little blood shall sprinkle the pavements and sidewalks of our cities now, than that their streets should be drenched by blood hereafter; or that the highways and open fields of our country should drink up the blood of citizens, slain in deadly conflict, between armed bands—it may be between disciplined legions—Native Americans on one side, and foreigners, supported by native factions, on the other."

The new party condemned sectionalism and vowed to uphold "the Constitution of the Country, the Union of the States, and the enforcement of the laws." A Constitutional Union convention was held in Utica, New York, in July. Prominent Know-Nothings participated: Brooks, Burrows,

Prescott, also Gustavus Scroggs, president of the SSSB, no doubt mainly as a spectator for he was pro-Republican. The American party had no choice left but to support Unionist Bell or Republican Lincoln.

At the August 26 Schenectady assemblage of the SSSB Grand Council, with Scroggs in the chair, the pro-Republicans controlled the entire official machinery. On the floor, the two factions watched each other like jealous tomcats, fearing a quick coup. When Scroggs named a credentials committee 100 per cent pro-Republican, he was howled down, almost mobbed.

He yielded the gavel to U. P. Prescott, a pro-Bell man, and walked out with all anti-slavery followers. The crowd favoring Bell endorsed the Constitutional Unionists. The Scroggs faction, forming a rival Grand Council, released its members to vote as they desired.

Neither group ever held another meeting. It was a frazzled end, a bitter, futile end to the great Know-Nothing power in New York State. Elsewhere the decay of Know-Nothingism was even more rapid. In Connecticut some of its adherents appeared in fusion with the Republicans as the Union party. In fact such Union parties sprang up nearly everywhere; in the North, usually in combination with Whigs or Republicans; in the South, with Whigs or Democrats. The Connecticut Siamese twins began calling each other names early in the campaign, to the glee of the Democrats. The Know-Nothings, betraying their fusion agreement, issued a separate platform, "repellent to most Republicans," against Catholics and foreigners.

The Union party won by only 564 votes. The administration was rent by continuous feuding, somewhat over Union versus Abolition, but more over patronage and contracts. The Know-Nothings were slowly being squeezed out. "Sam has become a mere skeleton," remarked the *Times*. Beware, warned the *Courant,* without Know-Nothing strength, you "Republicans could hold . . . (your) heads no higher than the old tribe of Abolitionists."

The cat-and-dog fight went on at the January 4, 1859,

Union party convention in the American Hall in Hartford. They did agree on a compromise candidate, William A. Buckingham of Norwich, but fought about the platform. To the Republican plank denouncing electoral corruption the Know-Nothing delegates wished to add a phrase blaming it on foreigners, and, being denied this, shouted that the Republicans wished "to sacrifice the 10,000 votes of American mechanics for 100 ignorant Irishmen." Why drive the foreign vote to the Democrats? retorted the Republicans. Not only that, they voted to change the name of the party to "Republican."

The Know-Nothings licked their wounds eleven days later in the same hall in a hastily called convention of 160 delegates. Former Governor Minor attacked the betrayal. "The Republican broth is distasteful. . . . It is our mission not to follow but to lead." A candidate for governor—not Minor—was named. He declined, and the Know-Nothing executive committee was obliged to re-endorse Buckingham. Otherwise, all bonds with "Black Republicanism" were broken off. Even so, the Know-Nothing votes probably enabled the Republicans to squeeze through to victory. The following year, a Republican landslide blotted out the few local Know-Nothing candidates. The dark lantern was buried forever in Connecticut.

All through the South, except in Maryland, Kentucky, and New Orleans, the collapse was even more rapid. Know-Nothingism was done for in Virginia before the end of 1857. There was no chance of overthrowing northern Locofocoism, the Lynchburg *Virginian* observed early that year, and the Know-Nothings had little weight in purely local affairs.

In North Carolina they continued to fight the Democrats a trifle longer, but public apathy was too great for much smoke to show. A Raleigh paper called them "Know-Nothing-American-Whig-Black-Republican-Sam-Federal-Plug-Ugly-Rip-Rap-Shoulder-Hitter-Dark-Lantern-Culvert Party."

The entire executive committee went over to the Democrats, and no 1857 state convention was called. A few local candidates ran, a few were elected, and, curiously enough, the Know-Nothing majority in the Senate was maintained and three extra seats were won in the lower chamber. One congressman was elected, but promptly declared he was a Democrat, not a Know-Nothing. By 1859 not a trace of Kenneth Raynor's party could be found. Raynor himself slipped away and joined up with the North in the war, an act of "treason" that made it impossible for him ever to live in the state again.

In Georgia, Atlanta was captured again. A few county conventions were held, and fifty-five counties sent delegates to the state convention, which advocated "Unionism with coequal states, obedience to the Constitution and Laws," religious freedom, separation of church and state, honest elections. It condemned "foreign paupers" and the western free land policy; "Squatter sovereignty" was "a Republican scheme." It denounced the exclusion of slavery from the territories. Opposition was expressed to the building of the Pacific railroad because it gave government funds to private owners.

Benjamin Hill, a brilliant debater (later to become a wealthy lawyer, Democratic governor, and senator) headed the Know-Nothing ticket, running against Joe E. Brown, a Baptist temperance fanatic, a former plowboy whose postwar deals with the carpetbaggers and northern corporations, often at the expense of Georgia's treasury, made him a multimillionaire, a perennial senator, and the worst-hated man in the state.

Hill concentrated his attacks on the looting of the state-owned railroad and upon the Democratic betrayal of Free-Soilers in Kansas. But Brown won handily, although 32 Americans (against 86 Democrats) were elected to the Senate, 50 Americans and 105 Democrats to the House. Two American congressmen were successful. After that the party went into *rigor mortis.*

In Tennessee the Know-Nothing forces were still enthusiastic. Their platform, only faintly tinged with Nativism, concentrated on "Union." According to candidate Robert Hatton, Tennessee was entitled to $30,000,000 as its share of the value of federal lands given away to railroads. This should be demanded and used for schools. "The sons of the Hessians who fought against liberty are getting remuneration in Iowa, while true Americans get nothing." He stressed the danger of officeholding by Catholics bound by temporal obedience to the Pope, and actually used his fists on his Democratic opponent, Isham G. Haws, for stating the "infamous" doctrine that foreigners should be allowed to vote in the territories. Andrew Johnson called the Know-Nothings Abolitionists, yet many big slaveholders were still backing the American party.

Haws was elected by a comfortable majority. The score in the Senate stood American 7, Democrats 18; in the House, 13 to 45. This was the last Know-Nothing appearance in Tennessee. Its members joined the "Independent Opposition," mostly Whig, which the Democrats branded as "Know-Nothing."

In Kentucky the usual anger over Free-Soilism in Kansas was displayed, along with worry about foreign criminals in New York. An escaped pathological nun—Mary E. B. Miller—was paraded. The elections gave the Know-Nothings continued control of the state, but on a reduced scale. Only two Know-Nothing congressmen were elected.

The state convention of 1858—only local elections were at stake—gathered in Louisville, June 27, with 300 delegates. An innocuous platform was adopted, with the usual anti-foreign slogans and the alleged evils of foreigners voting in territories. The following year, even in Kentucky, all was over. The American party evaporated into thin air, leaving scarcely a trace, except for the blood on the stones—until the Ku-Klux Klan came along.

In the 1857 Missouri elections, the Know-Nothings dropped far below the Free State group and the Democrats. Two congressmen were elected the following year, but membership had largely drifted off into other parties. A telling Missouri cartoon—at least for Missourians—was that of Harriet Beecher Stowe fattening up a baby for Know-Nothing sacrifice.

Down in Texas, the Know-Nothing hold was broken in Austin and San Antonio, but the dark-lantern crowd had a strong candidate for governor in Sam Houston. He conducted an active campaign. The Democrats roused Mexican citizens—they would suffer intimidation if Houston were elected. Too late to do them any good, the Know-Nothings pushed an hysterical story that inflamed the whole state, about an American Protestant girl studying at a convent school who had been reported dead, whereas actually priests had spirited her to France. The girl's body was disinterred and identified, and the furor pished out like stale air. In any case, Houston was snowed under, and both houses of the legislature became overwhelmingly Democratic.

This election marked the complete collapse of Texas Know-Nothingism. Even Houston himself hastened to denounce Know-Nothingism and "any other ISM" which made just as much sense, he said, as damning matrimony or horsemanship. But he ran as a Democrat in 1859 and was elected.

The year 1857 also marked the death of Know-Nothingism in Arkansas, Mississippi, Alabama, and Florida. In Alabama in 1857 it became "The Whig and American party," which the Democrats redubbed the "Plug-Ugly party." No gubernatorial candidate was put up. A number of Know-Nothing legislators were elected, but no congressmen, and the party folded completely the following year.

The SSSB was doornail dead forever. Civil war soon made all minor party alignments meaningless. Only the OUA continued to give a few last asthmatic gasps.

After the Civil War Barker set up the secret American Shield, soon renamed the Order of the American Union, which spread to sixteen states but was too feeble to exercise political influence, and soon disappeared. Well before its end Barker had gone back into the dry-goods business in Pittsburgh. The OUA was briefly revived in 1877, when another wave of religious bigotry swept the country, and the Maria Monk story was revived.

After the war, for a long time the nation's fabric was too badly torn for any national movement to get started. It would take half a century for the pattern to be somewhat rewoven and not even in the next century would a successful bona-fide national party arise. The Republicans and Democrats were the frazzled ends of insistent sectionalism and war hatreds. Like a red thread, these divisions still run through the two major parties, preventing a proper consideration of national problems and human rights. It has perpetuated a one-party system in a good part of the South and in numbers of New England and Midwestern states. Thus, aside from sectionalism, we are saddled with only a pseudo two-party system, a system of shadowboxing. Its great merit—although a questionable one—is that thus far it has worked.

When uneasy peace returned, the Union slogan could get nowhere. The Republican party claimed a monopoly on "Union," and the bayonets to enforce the claim. In the South the Ku-Klux Klan adopted it, speaking much about constitutionalism and law. But obviously they were speaking out of the sides of their mouths; this was merely protective coloring in order to regain white supremacy by unlawful terrorism. Actually they were bitter in defeat, still hating the Union. Thus the old Know-Nothing doctrines flourished again, but only in the conquered South.

The Negroes, homeless and hungry after the war, a liberated horde thrown upon society without forethought in the brutal process of war, were in many places as badly off as modern European refugees. The Army of Occupation organized them into the secret Union or Liberty League in order to further mixed regimes. They had the help of such farsighted "spat-on" citizens as Joe Brown of Georgia and Cotton of Louisiana, who joined the carpetbaggers in grabbing the remaining visible wealth and promoting the dominance of northern industrialists and financiers.

The reaction against any democracy that included Negro citizens was the Ku-Klux Klan—with its Grand Wizards, Dragons, Genii, Hydras, Titans, Goblins—names in themselves indicating the childish, twisted mentality of the founders and those who could accept such gibberish. The Klan was organized in Pulaski, Tennessee (controlled by the

Know-Nothings as early as 1854), chiefly by students and discharged "reb" veterans and was headed by a Confederate war general. There and in Kentucky the local SSSB councils had been called clans or klans. The Ku-Kluxers spread fast across the South, with their white hoods, galloping horses, torches, whips, ropes, and guns, committing cowardly nighttime tortures, thefts, and murders. In Louisiana and elsewhere the Klan was paralleled by the knights of the White Camellia and elsewhere by other secret terrorist societies with odd or sweet-smelling names, plus citizens' secret White Councils.

The methods, many slogans, a few of the actors, some of the mumbo-jumbo ritual, were the same as in Know-Nothingism. Besides their Know-Nothing talk of Union and the Constitution, with the accent on patriotism and white supremacy, they demanded the disenfranchisement of all non-Caucasian voters, and they chastised and murdered Negroes, non-Baptists, Jews, Catholics, and foreigners. It "degenerated into a mob of rioters and marauders who plundered and abused friend and foe alike, sparing neither party nor sex." It was the Terror.

In Louisiana in the space of two years, the White Camellias murdered or maltreated 2,000 people of both sexes. In Bossier Parish 120 Negroes were taken to the Red River and slaughtered en masse. In Mississippi, Georgia, Florida, Alabama, the Carolinas, Virginia, the night murders ran into thousands. In Texas in 1870, the secretary of state told the Senate that there had been 905 terrorist murders in the previous two years. Everywhere Negro teachers were the victims of torture and death. In 1870, in Maryville, Missouri, a crowd of 4,000 watched twenty-seven-year-old Raymond Gunn, chained to the ridgepole of his home, being burned alive. What was left of his piano was torn to pieces for souvenirs.

Thus, the usual result of prolonged military occupation was brought into being throughout the South. In the end, it saw established in power a one-party totalitarian white system in the hands of previous enemies of the Union, its power based on lynching and corruption. The new terrorist white supremacy governments of the South turned out to be even more venal, more willing to barter away local resources to northern financial power than the previous mixed carpet-bag regimes, and they were far more murderous. Thus Know-Nothingism, ruling by secret terror societies, lynching, and disenfranchisement of black citizens, maintained itself over the years by illiteracy, ignorance, race hate, mob law, and police brutalities.

After the war, a new sectionalism emerged in the country, the struggle of the embattled farmers of the West, in the Grange, Anti-Monopoly, and Greenback parties, the Farmers' Alliance and the Populist party, against the financial East. This fight originated among cattlemen and other growers in Texas and Arkansas, spread North, soon took in the share-croppers and tenants, white and black of the South—the new "free" slaves and human debris resulting from the Civil War, the Ku-Klux Klan governments, and northern financial exploitation. Populism, although Jefferson was its god, had some Know-Nothing aspects. It was largely Protestant, temperance-dominated, hating Irish and Germans for their alcoholic and super-conservative proclivities, hating Mexicans in the Southwest, often distrusting Catholics, and railing about "The Jew Shylocks of Wall Street."

These ideas were strong among the Videttes, the secret clique, to this day never exposed, which ruled the Populist party behind the scenes. They had secret rituals, oaths, passwords, grips, signs (some derived directly from the Know-Nothings), and officers bearing military titles (many were Civil War veterans), and they acted in concert to impose their slates on the open conventions of the party.

Populism's greatest southern leader was Tom Watson of Georgia—twice in the declining days of the Populist party, in 1904 and 1908, its presidential candidate. As early as 1904, Watson, who earlier had defended the right of Negroes to speak on his platform, had turned into a Negro baiter of the worst ilk, who gloated on writing about the features, pigmentation, and viciousness of Negroes in the most stomach-sickening fashion. "In the South, we have to lynch him [the

Negro]," he wrote January 1, 1917, in his *Jefferson Weekly,* "and flog him, now and then, to keep him from blaspheming the Almighty by his conduct on account of his smell and color." In caps he wrote: HIDEOUS OMINOUS MENACE OF NEGRO DOMINATION. He attacked Woodrow Wilson as a "Nigger lover." Wilson, he said, had "sent Booker T. Washington a message of condolence and confidence when the Coon was caught at a White Woman's bedroom door and was deservedly beaten for it."

By his 1908 campaign Watson added Catholic baiting and "preservation of Protestant rule" to his Negro baiting. He revived all the lurid convent tales of murdered bastard babies and priestly orgies with nuns. He gave credence to the whole Maria Monk nonsense and the tales of lechery at the Hôtel Mon Dieu Convent in Montreal. One article was entitled, "One of the priests who raped a Catholic woman in a Catholic Church." "Shad-bellies . . . foot-kissers . . . chemise-wearing bachelors" were some of the epithets he dreamed up. He called the Pope "Jimmy Cheesey . . . a fat old dago" who "lived with voluptuous women." Catholic priests who happened to have large noses or thick lips he described in detail, denouncing them as sensualists and rapists.

"Look at that nose," he said of one Catholic prelate. "Such a proboscis always marks the sensual man." Designating one priest by name, he wrote, "How does he keep from it —when so many of the fair sex are held behind the bars of convent dungeons—at the mercy of priests?" He advertised a pamphlet for twenty-five cents that enumerated the filthy questions the perverts asked in confessionals. He wrote in the *Jeffersonian:* "Through his questions, the priest learns which of his fair penitents are tempted to indulge in sexual inclinations. Remember, the priest is often a powerful sexed man, who lives on rich food, drinks red wine, and does no manual labor. He is alone with a beautiful, well-shaped young woman who tells him she is tormented by carnal desire. She will never tell what he says or does. . . . *He* can forgive her sin. She has been taught that in obeying *him,* she is serving God."

His interpretation of history was remarkable—Columbus was "a rapacious and human monster, seeking to add another hemisphere to the dominion of the Pope."

Claiming that Roman attempts against his life were being planned, he hired bodyguards. The only physical molestation was perpetrated by him when he recognized a Knights of Columbus member, who was "like a red rag to a bull" for him. "I am fighting 236 Knights of Columbus singlehanded." He asked 300 American Protestants to send him $100 each for the struggle. He could do a lot, and did, with that $30,000.

He was not fighting the dragons singlehanded. In 1911 he organized the "Guardians of Liberty" to save the country from Catholics and foreigners. It was made up of "American Americans," Civil and Indian War veterans, Congressman Charles D. Haines, and Joe Brown's son, Joseph H., Charles B. Skinner, and General Nelson A. Miles, former head of the United States Army. It grew to national proportions and speakers toured the country, especially General Miles, whose spread-eagle talk was entitled "The American Danger."

"I stand for the ideals of the Old South," babbled Watson; "the men behind the guns must be American-born; for the time is surely coming when he who is in command must issue the order, 'Put none but Americans on guard tonight.' " He pulled all the old Know-Nothing slogans out of the closet, and they made him a wealthy man and a United States senator.

The opportunity to add Jew baiting to his arsenal came in 1915. The young Jewish employer, Leo Frank, was convicted of rape (although certainly innocent) in a courtroom menaced by a howling mob, against which no judge and no jury dared act independently—the same sort of thing that happened in Alabama's Scottsboro case. The cries of the mob apparently also terrorized the Supreme Court of the land, except for dissenting Justice Holmes.

Fearing the governor would commute Frank's sentence to life imprisonment, which he did, Watson raised up an armed mob against the governor's mansion, and the governor, on leaving office, had to flee from the state, taking refuge first in California, then in Hawaii.

Watson called for a Vigilante committee—"Rise! People of Georgia!" "When 'mobs' are no longer possible, Liberty will be dead." On August 12, he wrote, "THE NEXT JEW WHO DOES WHAT FRANK DID, IS GOING TO GET EXACTLY THE SAME THING THAT WE GIVE TO NEGRO RAPISTS."

Four days later, Frank was taken from the state prison and hanged, a heel was driven into his dead face, his clothing and the hanging rope were torn into pieces as souvenirs for the mob, and all day "Fiddling John Corcoran" played a ballad about the raping on the Marietta Court House steps to 15,000 people.

"Let Jew libertines take notice," exulted Watson. "THE VOICE OF THE PEOPLE IS THE VOICE OF GOD . . . Millions of good people, not doped by Jew money and lies . . . enthusiastically greeted the triumph of law in Georgia. *Womanhood is made safer everywhere.*" In issue after issue, he dwelt upon the noses, the sensuous lips, lustful eyes, and other physical features, to prove that Jews were all sexual perverts.

Yet the people of Georgia elected this lyncher, this sex-haunted creature to the United States Senate. In fairness to him, it should be noted that he died in Washington of a tumor on the brain. His coffin was overshadowed by an eight-foot cross of roses sent by the Ku-Klux Klan.

About the time of the Frank lynching, on the Bald Top of Stone Mountain, ten miles from Atlanta (long a stronghold of Georgia Know-Nothingism) a great fiery cross lit up the countryside, and rites were carried out for the rebirth of the Wizards and Dragons. The Ku-Klux Klan was ready to ride again. Limited to "White Protestants," it rode all across the South in an orgy of tortures, floggings, and lynchings of Negroes, Catholics, Jews, and "Reds." It rode north across the Mason and Dixon's line into the Midwest, on into Connecticut and New England, where the sadisms of the Know-Nothings and of colonial days were re-enacted. It started in fear; it was building up popular emotions before World War I. It grew even stronger as a typical postwar expression of fear and intolerance. By 1922 it had 5,000,000 members in all parts of the country. Some years later, its head was convicted of murder. It was postwar juvenile delinquency —and quite as murderous—carried on by supposed adults.

Know-Nothingism also rode high, wide, and handsome in the cabinet of the United States. In 1919 Attorney General A. Mitchell Palmer used the FBI to arrest some two thousand people under the wartime Espionage and Sedition Acts. Men and women were torn from their homes in the dead of night, separated from their families, and 249 foreign-born, including naturalized citizens, were thrust aboard the United States transport *Buford* and, without due process of law, were shipped out of the country. Backed by the Know-Nothing-Klan shouts of "Ship 'em or shoot 'em," Palmer tried to obtain even more arbitrary powers from Congress.

There have been numerous other manifestations of Know-Nothing hate and fear and violence—too many to enumerate—some local, others of larger scope. Another strong anti-Catholic American party existed briefly in California in the mid-1880's led by Frank Pixley, editor of the *Argonaut.* On its heels, the White Caucasian League of the West Coast, plus the Native Sons and labor forces, brought on the dreadful anti-Chinese riots of San Francisco and Seattle, in which Chinese were murdered, burned alive, their properties put to the torch—days of crime and Barbary Coast orgies worse than those of the earlier Sidney Ducks.

In 1889, John Jay and Reverend James M. King founded the anti-Catholic National League for the Protection of American Institutions. It had backers in high quarters. Ironically, its efforts to prevent Vermont tax funds from being given to religious institutions were blocked by the Protestant church, which received the bulk of such monies. It failed to prevent the establishment of a Catholic chapel at West Point. The League, close to President Benjamin Harrison, was able to have his Indian Bureau cut off all appropriations to Catholic Indian schools, but not those to Protestant Indian schools. Thereafter, little Indians were to have no choice except to become Baptists, Methodists, etc. For some years the League also managed to block the New York Freedom of Worship Bill which sought to extend religious liberty to reformatories and penal institutions.

Know-Nothingism is far from dead, although the average citizen may not be directly aware of the flood of anti-foreign, anti-Negro, anti-Semitic, anti-Catholic literature that goes out to devotees all over the land, some of it financed by Texas oil tycoons. Whatever we may be required to oppose and to fight, hate and fear alone cannot build a nation, cannot keep it alive, cannot prevent its degeneration. Such blind emotions permit corruption to hide behind secrecy and purported national safety and the flag; they hasten disintegration and destruction.

For a century and a half these revivalistic upsurges of superstition, ignorance, and blind herd emotion have occurred regularly every ten to fifteen years. They manage regularly to create national disturbance. Over somewhat longer periods, they have come within reach of national power. The day may still come when country-wide panic builds up to a tragic end of our democratic system and institutions and the headlong decline of our strength by such false flexing of muscles. It would all be done in the name of freedom and democracy, of course.

This rhythmic process, which few trouble to examine, perhaps cannot be altered by anthropological or psychological research, not by any rational approaches. Such knowledge, if assembled, could even become the tool of a government determined to keep the public uninformed or falsely informed.

All this must be partly due to the inadequacy of our education. Pupils are not taught the struggles of history, the meaning of history, the forces of history. Teachers often dare not discuss such things or their contemporary meaning; they are the slaves of the most ignorant Know-Nothing parents in each community. History then becomes a Mohammedan repetition of names and dates, which students know enough to hate from then on out.

Know-Nothingism must also be partly due to the ever-widening gulf between our vast accumulation of scientific and technical knowledge and the man on the street. The crowd, which at times worships (and always fears), but more often destroys, what it does not understand, has shown an ever-greater tendency to sneer at intellectuals, philosophers, poets, artists; and all over the world today the masses are in a mood to rise up and strike down the very knowledge by which they live so comfortably so they can vegetate with their primitive emotions and the magna charta of barbarism. Can they be blamed when many intellectuals have been caught in the vicious circle of status seeking or have let themselves be silenced, when the pseudo-intellectuals and optimistic time servers are, with exceptions, the leaders of radio, television, and our mass publications?

The artists cannot produce great art unless there is a general esthetic understanding and love for art in the population; but we have little of this, less than the Mexican Indians or Italians or the dark peoples of Africa. Nor can the thinker lift himself by his bootstraps. He is dragged along in the disintegration of social values, the raising up of false gods. He cannot swim far out of the stream and survive.

The shortcomings of the social sciences must also be partly at the root of Know-Nothingism. The politicians who spring from the masses, but with secret support from privileged self-seeking groups, for the most part are shockingly ignorant of social forces and economics. They have not begun yet to comprehend the meaning, the cultural effects of the machine age, now more than a century old, let alone anticipate the tremendous revolution in society and ideas being ushered in by the dawning electronic age. This they promise to foul up even more disastrously.

Perhaps another root cause is the rapid expansion of our material benefits without any corresponding expansion of intellectual, spiritual, or esthetic capacities. Instead, we get a steady growth of obedient conformity, a suspicion of all ideas, a steady leveling of all national effort and ideals to the lowest common denominator. Democracy still has to prove that it can find a way to refine itself and provide opportunities for superior talents outside the business, mechanical, and sports fields. Our only gods seem to be materialism, the quick dollar, and speed. This reverence for material gadgets and high-tailed chrome leads us into an elastic prison, without spiritual light or air. Out of the inner emptiness emerge subconscious monsters. Juvenile delinquency, the root causes of which we dare not examine, is merely one of the minor apes. Faster and faster busybodyness cannot bring escape from inner boredom and frustration.

If Know-Nothing manifestations are again abroad in the land, the answer certainly does not lie in the extension of coercive control. No other country on earth has as great a police and military apparatus as the United States, yet no country has so much crime. Even Congress, once dedicated to discussing great issues, in good part has become a third-rate police bureau, investigating minor idiocies such as quiz shows and payola, but few major problems. McCarthy did it better. The Robespierre methods have not changed much since the great Massachusetts Know-Nothing smelling committee. Most of our patriotism today is on the Know-Nothing level: a curious combination of fear, big profits, self-comfort, power, and privilege, and so our wisdom and our reputation continue to decline in a troubled world. At least the Know-Nothingism of the 1850s was militant and alive; Know-Nothingism today is an apathetic thing, induced by the steady corrosion wrought by fear and unprincipled power.

# *ABRIDGED BIBLIOGRAPHY*


Adams, William Francis. Ireland and Irish Immigration to the New World from 1815 to the Famine. New Haven, 1932

An American. The Sons and Sires. A History of the Rise, Progress and Destiny of the American Party. Philadelphia, 1855

Asbury, Herbert. The French Quarter. New York, 1936

——— Barbary Coast. New York, 1933

——— The Gangs of New York. New York, 1927

Beecher, Lyman. Autobiography. 2v. New York, 1864

——— Plea for the West. Cincinnati, 1835

——— Works. 3v. Boston, 1852

Billington, Ray Allen. The Protestant Crusade, 1800–1860

Blanshard, Paul. The Irish and Catholic Power. Boston, 1853

Brand, C. The History of the Know-Nothing Party in Indiana

Brownson, Orestes. Native Americanism. Brownson's Quarterly Review, II 3d ser. 1855

Bucholz, H. E. Governors of Maryland. Baltimore, 1908

Busey, Samuel C. Immigration, Its Evils and Consequences. New York, 1856

Carroll, Anna Ella. The Great American Battle; or the Contest between Christianity and Political Romanism. New York, 1856

Chamberlain, Ivory. Biography of Millard Fillmore. Buffalo, 1856

Cross, Andrew B. Private Prisons for Women. Baltimore, 1854

Cross, Ira. Origin, Principles and History of the Know-Nothing Party, Iowa State. Iowa State Historical and Political Review, IV:526–59. 1906

Cole, Arthur Charles. Nativism in the Lower Mississippi. Mississippi Valley Historical Proceedings, VI:258–75. 1913

Cullen, James Bernard. The Story of the Irish in Boston. Boston, 1889

Desmond, Humphrey J. The Know-Nothing Party. A sketch. Washington, 1904

Essary, Frederick J. Maryland in National Politics. Baltimore, 1915

Hambleton, James P. A Biographical Sketch of Henry A. Wise, with a History of the Political Campaign in Virginia in 1855. Richmond, 1856

Handlin, Oscar. Immigration as a Factor in American History. Englewood Cliffs, New Jersey, 1959

Hansen, Marcus Lee. The Immigrant in American History. Cambridge, 1940

Hamilton, Charles Granville. Lincoln and the Know-Nothing Movement. Washington, 1954
Harper, Joseph Henry. The House of Harper: A Century of Publishing in Franklin Square. New York, 1912
——— I Remember. New York, 1834
Harper, Mrs. L. St. John. Maria Monk's Daughter. An Autobiography. New York, 1855
Haynes, George H. The Causes of the Know-Nothing Success in Massachusetts. American Historical Review, III: 67–82. Washington, October, 1897
——— A Chapter from the Local History of Know-Nothingism. *New England Magazine*. September, 1896
——— A Know-Nothing Legislature. American Historical Association Annual, 1926. I, 175–87. Washington, 1897
Hughes, John. Complete Works. 2v. New York, 1866
Hutchinson, E. Young Sam or Native Americans' Own Book. New York, 1855
Jenning, J. P. The Know-Nothing Movement in Illinois, 1854–6. Illinois State Historical Journal, VII, 7–33
Julian, George W. Political Recollections, 1840–1872. Chicago, 1884
Lee, John H. The Origins and Progress of the American Party in Politics. Philadelphia, 1855
Longstreet, Augustus B. Know-Nothingism Unveiled. Washington, 1855
McConnville, Mary St. Patrick. Political Nativism in the State of Maryland (1830–60). Washington, 1928
McGann, Agness Geraldine. Nativism in Kentucky. Washington, 1944
McGee, Thomas D'Arcy. A History of Irish Settlers in North America from the Earliest Period to the Census of 1850. Boston, 1855
McGrath, Sister Paul of the Cross. Political Nativism in Texas (1825–60). Washington, D.C., 1936
McGuire, John Francis. The Irish in America. London, 1868. New York, 1873
Mechlin, John Moffat. The Ku Klux Klan: A Study of the American Mind. New York, 1924
Morse, Samuel F. B. ("Brutus") Foreign Conspiracy Against the Liberties of the United States. (Reprint from the New York *Observer*). New York, 1835
——— The Proscribed German Student, Being a Sketch of Some Interesting Incidents in the Life and Melancholy Death of the Late Lewis Clausing. New York, 1836
——— Letters and Journals. 2v. New York, 1914
Noonan, Carrol John. Nativism in Connecticut, 1829–60. Washington, 1938
One of the Expelled. A Complete Exposé of the Order of "Know-Nothings." Philadelphia, 1854
Overdyke, W. D. History of the American Party in Louisiana. Louisiana Historical Quarterly, XV–XVI. Baton Rouge

——— The Know-Nothing Party in the South. Louisiana State University, Baton Rouge, 1950
Peyton, Hurt. The Rise and Fall of the Know-Nothings" in California. Quarterly of the California Historical Society. IX;i–2. March–June, 1930
Samuels, Charles and Louise. Night Fell on Georgia. New York, 1956
Scaggs, William H. The Southern Oligarchy. New York, 1924
Schmeckebier, Lawrence Frederic. History of the Know-Nothing Party in Maryland. Baltimore, 1899
Scisco, Louis Dow. Political Nativism in New York State. New York, 1901
Senning, John P. The Know-Nothing Movement in Illinois. State Historical Society Journal VII. 1914–15
Shea, John G. A History of the Catholic Church in the United States. 4v. New York, 1892
Sherf, J. Thomas. The Chronicles of Baltimore, Baltimore, 1874
——— History of Baltimore, City and County. Philadelphia, 1881
——— History of Maryland. 3v. Baltimore, 1879
——— History of Western Maryland. 2v. Philadelphia, 1882
Smith, M. H. Sunshine and Shadow in New York. New York, 1868
Smith, Joseph T. Eighty Years, Embracing the History of Presbyterianism in Baltimore. Philadelphia, 1899
Sterner, B. C. Citizenship and Suffrage in Maryland. Baltimore, 1895
Stickney, Charles. Know-Nothingism in Rhode Island. History Seminar of Brown University. Providence, 1894
Stone, W. L. The Elder Maria Monk and the Nunnery of the Hôtel Dieu. Newcastle on Tyne, 1837
Thomas, M. Evangeline. Nativism in the Old Northwest, 1850–1860. Washington, 1936
Tuska, Benjamin. Know-Nothingism, 1854–60. New York [1930?]
Vann Woodward, C. Thomas Watson. Agrarian Rebel. New York, 1838
Whitney, Thomas R. A Defence of the American Policy as Opposed to the Encroachments of Foreign Influence and Especially to the Influence of the Papacy in Political Interests and Affairs of the United States. New York, 1856
Wise, Henry A. Life and Death of Sam in Virginia. Richmond, 1856
Withe, Carl Frederick. The Irish in America. Baton Rouge, 1856

Many personal memoirs, volumes of addresses and writings contain rich material, information, the feeling of the times, and often contain references to the Dark Lantern Conspiracy, such as those of Seward, Sumner, Bryant, Horace Greeley, Channing, Garrison, Emerson, Theodore Parker, Margaret Fuller, Thurlow Weed, Webster, Frederick Law Olmstead, Ignatius Donnelly, Wendell Philips, George William Curtis, Tom Watson, Benjamin H. Hill, Henry Clay, John C. Calhoun, Fremont, Phineas T. Barnum, Samuel Griswold Goodrich, Chester Harding, Hariet Kezia Hunt, John Neal, Thomas Low Nichols, Josiah Quincey, etc.

# *INDEX*